The Culture of Yellow

For Robert, Max, and Adrian

The Culture of Yellow

or, The Visual Politics of Late Modernity

Sabine Doran

B L O O M S B U R Y

NEW YORK • LONDON • NEW DELHI • SYDNEY

Bloomsbury Academic

An imprint of Bloomsbury Publishing Plc

1385 Broadway	50 Bedford Square
New York	London
NY 10018	WC1B 3DP
USA	UK

www.bloomsbury.com

Bloomsbury is a registered trade mark of Bloomsbury Publishing Plc

First published 2013

© Sabine Doran, 2013

Library of Congress Cataloging-in-Publication Data
A catalog record for this title is available from the Library of Congress.

ISBN: PB: 978-1-4411-8587-7
HB: 978-1-4411-8444-3
ePub: 978-1-4411-9690-3
ePDF: 978-1-4411-6949-5

Typeset by Fakenham Prepress Solutions, Fakenham, Norfolk NR21 8NN
Printed and bound in the United States of America

Contents

Contents

Acknowledgments

The "yellow book," as it was called for many years, was first conceived in the office of the late Gert Mattenklott (1942–2009), when he was teaching at the University of Marburg. He had invited me to his office to show me a copy of Richard Le Gallienne's prose fancy "The Boom in Yellow," but his real purpose was to suggest that the color yellow might be a suitable topic for a dissertation. I had, in fact, noticed from my seminars with Mattenklott on modernism and the *fin de siècle* that yellow appeared to have a special status for authors of this period. Thus, with no inkling of the arduous and sometimes tortuous journey that lay ahead, I began to explore the possibility of a "yellow book." Mattenklott accompanied this project for many years, and his tutelage culminated in a Ph.D. dissertation at the Free University of Berlin under his supervision. I deeply regret that he did not live to see the fruit of this project (although it turned out to be quite a different work than the dissertation). A comparatist at heart, a philosopher of the senses, of the marginalized and the exiled, and a brilliant essayist, Mattenklott inspired me to become the academic I am, and the spirit of his multifaceted thought hovers over every page of this book.

I am deeply grateful for the provocative thought and advice of Karl Heinz Bohrer, whose theory of the moment or suddenness (*Plötzlichkeit*) and of aesthetic negativity shaped the project from the very beginning. But it was through our many personal discussions, in Paris and at Stanford University (where I was a visiting researcher), that I came to better understand how his insights were crucial to the analysis of yellow in modernist texts. I should also like to thank Hayden White for his generous advice. His theory of tropological figures, which inspired my concept of "multivalent figuration," allowed me to resist the notion of color symbolism that has plagued the study of color. My conception of stigmatization and victimization owes a great deal to the cultural theory and religious anthropology of René Girard, whose warm encouragement I deeply appreciate.

Another valued interlocutor for this project was John Burt Foster, Jr. As the editor of *The Comparatist*, he published an article of mine that would become the basis for Chapter 5, and, as a reader of the final manuscript, he dispensed timely and sagacious advice. I am thankful to Gail Finney, who, both as a reader of the manuscript and as the author of an excellent study of *Salome*, has been a source of inspiration and expert guidance. A lengthy conversation with Werner Busch on Proust and Vermeer at a conference in Berlin on color was invaluable for Chapter 4, as was an email interview with Helmut Federle, concerning his painting *Asian Sign* (discussed in Chapter 5).

I would like to acknowledge the following sources, where early versions of parts of this work first appeared. A short section of Chapter 5 draws on "Im Kulminieren zerschellen: Ein Gegenentwurf zum Gesamtkunstwerk in Hans Henny Jahnns *Perrudja*" (*Es ist seit Rahel und erlaubt, Gedanken zu haben*," ed. Steven R. Huff and Dorothea Kaufmann [Würzburg: Koenigshausen & Neumann, 2012]: 207–29). Parts of Chapter 1 are based on "Writing van Gogh through Francis Bacon: Mayröcker's Non-Human Aesthetics" (*Gegenwartsliteratur* 10 [2011]: 116–38). Some of the ideas in the Introduction and in Chapter 5 were first worked out in "Synaesthesia in European Film Theory" (*European Film Theory*, ed. Temenuga Trifonova [New York: Routledge, 2009]: 240–54). Sections of Chapters 4 and 5 draw on my article "Chronos/Chroma: Yellow Figures in Proust's *La Prisonnière* and Bely's *Petersburg*" (*The Comparatist* 28 [2004]: 53–75). And finally, "The Temporality of Short Fiction and the Yellow Nineties" (*Currents in Short Fiction: Tale, Novella, Short Story*, ed. Holger Klein and Wolfgang Görtschacher [Tübingen: Stauffenberg, Studies in English and Comparative Literature, Vol. 20 2004]: 81–9) represents an early version of some of the arguments found in Chapter 3.

I would like to express my gratitude to the following institutions: to the Gallery Beyerle for permission to reproduce the work of Federle; to the Jewish Museum, Berlin, for the photo of the *Roll of Cloth with Yellow Stars* and for the permission to reproduce it; to the Bacon Estate for permission to reproduce Francis Bacon's *Study for a Portrait of van Gogh I*; to the Van Gogh Museum in Amsterdam, for permission to reproduce several of Van Gogh's works; and to the Mendel Grossman foundation for permission to reproduce two of Grossman's most compelling photographs. I am also grateful to the University of California, Riverside for a subvention that allowed me to obtain the permissions for the images that appear in this volume.

I would like to thank my colleagues in the UC Riverside Department of Comparative Literature, who have been supportive at every step of the way. Many thanks to each of you, and especially to our graduate students.

The manuscript could not have found a better editor than Haaris Naqvi, whose encouragement, careful attention to detail, and belief in the project went beyond what any author has a right to expect.

I would like to thank my parents, Ingetraud and Heinz Wolters, for their unconditional and lifelong support and encouragement.

Finally, I do not know how to thank my husband, Robert Doran, without whose continuous support this project would have never seen the light of day. I am deeply indebted to his relentless criticism, copious suggestions, and thorough editing at every stage. The noise of our twin boys, Max and Adrian, formed a musical accompaniment to my writing, and their seemingly superhuman efforts to crawl, then walk, then speak, have inspired me to persevere and overcome. It is thus to Robert, Max and Adrian, that this book is dedicated.

Illustrations

Black-and-White Figures

Color Plates

Introduction

The decade was running its course, but it was only in 1894 that it acquired the designation of "yellow." [...] The color had been further popularized by an increasing interest in the works of French novelists, whose books, because of the tone of the book covers, were commonly known as "yellow backs." There was something vivid and daring about that color, something of the times. [...] Yellow and fin de siècle began to have connotations that were open to many meanings: but all leading to a definable sense of modernity, challenge, emancipation.[1]

From the earliest cave drawings to our contemporary image-obsessed culture, colors have exercised an irresistible fascination. Whether associated with particular moods or mental states ("red with anger," "pale white"), with political ideologies (Communist red, the environmentalist Greens) or with particular races (black for African Americans, white for Caucasians, red for Native Americans, yellow for Asians), color has always been seen as an index of meaning. Yet the broad cultural significance of specific colors has rarely been addressed. Reduced to its symbolic—that is, highly conventionalized—function, color is typically understood as a fixed system of reference that is easily decoded. However, this approach to color obscures its dynamic nature, its culturally conditioned ambiguities and dualities. What is needed is a new perspective that recognizes the complex nature of color and its inscription in a network of meaning.

Color has become an increasingly popular topic in the humanities and sciences, in particular the color blue. Because of its importance for German Romanticism (with its central image of the "blue flower"), blue has attracted a good deal of interest from literary scholars and art historians. Two recent examples are Michel Pastoureau's *Blue: The History of a Color* (2001) and Angelika Overath's *Das andere Blau, Zur Poetik einer Farbe im modernen Gedicht* (The Other Blue: Poetics of a Color in Modern Poetry) (1987). However, the vast majority of work on color is concerned with color in general, as in John Gage's *Color and Culture: Practice and Meaning*

---

[1] Frances Winwar, *Oscar Wilde and the Yellow Nineties* (New York: Harper & Brothers, 1940), 239.

from Antiquity to Abstraction (1999) and *Color and Meaning: Art, Science and Symbolism* (2000), or the anthropologically inflected study by Michael Taussig, *What Color Is the Sacred?* (2009).[2]

Yellow, on the other hand, is one of the least discussed colors in scholarly writing. And yet, as I seek to show in the pages that follow, yellow becomes, during the *fin-de-siècle* and early twentieth-century period, the modern color *par excellence*: avant-garde artists and writers saw in yellow a way of expressing the ambiguities of their time; the rise of certain cultural phenomena were subsumed under its banner (e.g. yellow journalism, the "yellow peril"); and, reprising its role as the marker of marginal groups, it became the ultimate stigmatic color in the "yellow star" Jews were forced to wear in Nazi Germany. The reasons for this sudden and profound interest in yellow are multifaceted, involving numerous, interrelated factors.

Yellow books and the color of scandal

The iconic starting point for this study is the decade that came to be known the Yellow Nineties.[3] As Holbrook Jackson writes in his book *The Eighteen Nineties*, yellow was the "color of the hour, the color of a time-spirit."[4] To understand how this yellow *Zeitgeist* came to define the last decade of the nineteenth century, the role of late nineteenth-century aestheticism and, in particular, of the decadent movement, becomes important.

During the second half of the nineteenth century, avant-garde French novels as well as sensational fiction, adventure stories and cheap biographies were published with yellow covers and were marketed especially at railway stations in Britain. Already in 1846, Edgar Allen Poe noted the connection between yellow and sensationalist writing when he dismissed the "eternal insignificance of yellow-backed pamphleteering,"[5] thereby emphasizing the cheapness of the novels and the low esteem in which they were held in the British publishing industry.

In the French context, on the other hand, yellow covers were also used as a distinctive marker, but they served to emphasize the innovative style and artistic value of avant-garde writing. These somewhat scandalous

---

[2] One could also mention in this context the burgeoning area of word-image studies, which has taken an interest in color. See Jacques Le Rider's *Farben and Woerter* (Color and Words), 2000.

[3] Frances Winwar was one of the first scholars to use the term. See ibid., 239.

[4] Holbrook Jackson, *The Eighteen Nineties* (London: J. Cape, 1927), 46.

[5] Joseph Twadell Shipley, *Origins of English Words: A Discursive Dictionary of Indo-European Roots* (Baltimore: Johns Hopkins University Press, 2001), 167.

avant-garde novels marked in yellow soon became a *topos* in literature and painting. Russian writer Anton Chekhov (1860–1904) has one of his protagonists refer to the "French books in yellow covers": "it is not unusual to find in them the chief element of artistic creation—the feeling of personal freedom which is lacking in the Russian authors."[6] Vincent van Gogh (1853–1890) thematizes the yellow covers of French novels in his *Still Life with Bible* (1885), which features his favorite modern novel, Emile Zola's *Joy of Life* (*La joie de vivre*, 1884), and, even more explicitly, in his *Parisian Novels* (1887), which shows a stack of yellow-backed books. Van Gogh's thematization of yellow becomes more pronounced during his so-called "yellow period" (1886–90), during which he famously sojourns in the South of France, ostensibly to establish a community of artists under the roof of the Yellow House. Van Gogh's short-lived collaboration with fellow painter Paul Gauguin in the Yellow House intensifies the engagement with the literary *topos* of yellow, bringing out stigmatic resonances that would later reappear in posthumous dialogues with Van Gogh, particularly in the work of Antonin Artaud, Francis Bacon, and the contemporary Viennese writer Friederike Mayröcker (see Chapter 1).

Along with Zola's naturalist novels, one of the main inspirations of the French avant-garde was Joris-Karl Huysmans's seminal novel *Against Nature* (*A rebours*, 1884), which describes the retreat of antihero Des Esseintes into the excesses of an artificial world of his own creation. Although the ideals advocated in the novel represent a continuation of the Romantic idea of *l'art pour l'art*, they also indicate a rejection of the Romantic valorization of nature and the natural. Instead, the decadent movement celebrated artifice, even the superficial, particularly as a form of self-fashioning. The seemingly amoral or immoral quality of Huysmans's novel (a quality it also shared with naturalism) lent it and the movement it inspired an aura of scandal. But for a young generation of writers the novel was a watershed. Oscar Wilde (1854–1900) proclaimed: "this last book of Huysmans's is one of the best I have ever seen."[7]

Huysmans's intoxicating ideal of aesthetic self-fashioning helped define the figure of the dandy. Characterized by a relentless concern with style and outer appearance, "[the dandy] must live and sleep before a mirror,"[8] observed Charles Baudelaire. But the dandy also represents, during a time of

---

[6] Anton Chekhov, "A Dreary Story," in *The Steppe and Other Stories*, trans. Ronald Wilks (London, New York: Penguin Books, 2001), 216.

[7] Quoted in Joseph Pearce, *Literary Converts: Spiritual Inspiration in an Age of Unbelief* (New York: HarperCollins, 1999), 5.

[8] Baudelaire, *The Painter of Modern Life and other Essays*, trans. John Mayne (London: Phaidon Press, 1995), 28.

rapid industrialization, an "aesthetic opposition"[9] to a society dominated by the capitalistic forces of mass production and the mass culture it engendered. The highly individual, aestheticized lifestyle of the dandy thus becomes a form of political protest. From the perspective of a conservative bourgeoisie, the dandy necessarily appeared as a scandalous and threatening figure of dubious morality. The controversial personal life of Oscar Wilde, the era's most celebrated dandy, epitomized this culture of scandal; and it was his association with the color yellow—namely with yellow-backed books that connoted an insidious confluence of homosexuality and a morally depraved avant-garde—that solidified yellow as the color of stigma and scandal during this era, an association it would retain throughout the earlier part of the twentieth century, culminating in the use of the "yellow star" by the Nazis to stigmatize and ghettoize the Jewish population.

Interestingly, Wilde also refers to the phenomenon of the yellow book in his novel *The Picture of Dorian Gray* (1890). As the protagonist (who is, to a certain degree, Wilde's alter ego) gazes at a "yellow book," he has the sense that "the sins of the world were passing in a dumb show before him."[10] This was an extraordinary act of prescience, for it was only three years after *Dorian Gray* that Aubrey Beardsley, together with Harland and John Lane, published the famous quarterly entitled *The Yellow Book*, which, more than any other phenomenon, helped give the Yellow Nineties its name. How *The Yellow Book* captured the "quintessential elements"[11] of the *fin-de-siècle* spirit is the subject of the second chapter of this book.

For modernists such as Marcel Proust (1871–1922) and James Joyce (1882–1941), Wilde's arrest and tragic fall remain a touchstone of what one could call their "visual politics." Joyce's deconstruction of the "Wilde phenomenon" in his mock-epic *Ulysses* is subversively linked to yellow imagery (Chapter 2), while Proust intertwines, in what is considered the longest sentence of *In Search of Lost Time* (over two and half pages long), Wilde's scandal with the arrest and trial of the Jewish officer Dreyfus for anti-Semitic motives (in the famous Dreyfus Affair [1894]). But the most emblematic inscription of yellow in Proust's novel is the repeated reference to a detail of a Vermeer painting (*View of Delft*): the "little patch of yellow wall," on which the writer Bergotte focuses obsessively in his hour of death

[9] Gert Mattenklott develops the notion of "aesthetic opposition" in Mattenklott, *Bilderdienst: Ästhetische Opposition bei Beardsley and George* (Frankfurt am Main: Syndikat, 1985).

[10] Oscar Wilde, *The Picture of Dorian Gray*, in *The Complete Works of Oscar Wilde, Volume 3*, ed. Joseph Bristow (Oxford: Oxford University Press, 2005), 274.

[11] Dennis Denisoff, "Decadence and aestheticism," in *The Cambridge Companion to the Fin de Siècle*, ed. Gail Marshall (Cambridge: Cambridge University Press, 2007), 31.

(Chapter 4). Through the "little patch of yellow wall" Proust unfolds a topography of yellow in multiple perspectives. But the "patch" also reveals an inter-textual connection with Honoré de Balzac's use of a similar phrase ("little patch of wall") in his 1833 novel *Eugénie Grandet*, which itself activates a system of yellow figuration, namely in figures of gold (value) and greed (liked to Jews). Chapter 4 thus shows how inscriptions and reinscriptions of yellow became significant in a non-visual medium such as the novel.

Yellow stigma and yellow polarity

Yellow stigmatization has a long and convoluted history going back to the European Middle Ages, when Jews and prostitutes were forced to wear yellow signs or clothes to separate them from the general population and to emphasize their marginal status.[12] This legacy of yellow stigmatism persists into late modernity. Thus yellow dominates the modern imagination of prostitutes' clothing, as in Edouard Touraine's *Le Rire* (1901), a famous caricature of prostitutes entirely dressed in yellow, with their clients. The yellow dresses of the singer and dancer "Jane Avril" in Henri de Toulouse-Lautrec's posters (1893) became iconic for the late-modern perception of prostitution.[13]

Of course the most spectacular and insidious example of yellow stigmatism is the "yellow star" used as an instrument to persecute Jews in Germany during the Second World War. In his *The Yellow Badge in History*, Guido Kisch locates the origin of yellow stigmatism:

> On November eleventh 1215 a most brilliant assembly of 412 bishops, 800 abbots and priors, numerous representations of prelates and cathedral chapters, and deputies of almost all Christian princes convened in Rome in the Church San Giovanni in Laterano. Pope Innocent III (1198–1216) presided over this illustrious gathering, the Fourth Lateran Council, one of the most important ecumenical councils and of lasting

[12] See also Andrea-Maria Reichel's discussion of "Gelb als Farbe der Verachteten" (Yellow as color of the Stigmatized), in which she emphasizes that different shades of yellow are, from the fifteenth century onward, used as a negative color. See Andrea-Maria Reichel, *Die Kleider der Passion. Für eine Ikonographie des Kostüms* (Dissertation, Humboldt-Universität Berlin, 1998), http://edoc.hu-berlin.de/dissertationen/kunstgeschichte/reichel-andrea/PDF/Reichel.pdf [accessed January 14, 2013].

[13] Melissa Hope Ditmore observes: "Black and white and yellow are the colors of choice for clothing requirements for prostitutes in Europe. A yellow scarf or headdress was required in Vienna, Seville, and Venice" (*Encyclopedia of Prostitution and Sex Work: A–N, Volume 1*, ed. Melissa Hope Ditmore [Westport, CT: Greenwood Publishing Group, 2006], 108).

influence on Christian faith and life all over the world. In canon 68 the conciliar decrees ordained that "Jews and saracens of both sexes in every Christian province and at all times shall be marked in the eyes of the public from other peoples through the character of their dress."[14]

Kisch clarifies that, although the Fourth Lateran Council did not itself impose the yellow badge on Jews, the "doctrine of the Jews' responsibility for the crucifixion of Christ, predominant during the Middle Ages," enabled the marking of Jews with a yellow sign in the same way as other offenders: "among the distinguishing marks it was chiefly the yellow badge that caused the degradation of the Jews legally as well as socially."[15]

The fact that the stigmatizing force of yellow returns most emphatically—and tragically—in the "yellow star" that Jews were forced to wear in Nazi Germany shows that this history still had an influence (despite the fact that the yellow badge had been officially abolished in Prussia in 1812): "the German badge-law of 1941 imposed on all Jews over six years of age the permanent wearing of the six-pointed star, outlined in black on yellow cloth with the black superscription 'Jew.'"[16] But we must take note of an intervening event between the abolition of the yellow badge in 1812 and its reinstatement in 1941: the Star of David (which is not necessarily yellow) had been chosen in 1896 as an emblem of Zionism; thus, through the historically specific connotations of the color yellow, the Nazis effectively convert what had become a positive emblem of a religious community into a negative sign of exclusion—an ambivalence made possible by the polarizing nature of yellow itself.

Historically, in Western culture, yellow is the color of light, illumination, enlightenment, and gold (absolute value), but it is also the color of death, decay, and excrement (a figure of negativity). Thus, unlike the dialectical colors of black and white, yellow contains opposition within itself—a point made by Johann von Goethe in his famous *Theory of Colors* (*Zur Farbenlehre*, 1810), which, along with Newton's *Opticks* (1704), is one of the fundamental statements on the nature of color. Whereas Newton's objective approach, namely his "optical spectrum," laid the groundwork for the scientific study of color, Goethe's subjective emphasis on human color perception was influential on artists and writers. Goethe's polemical critique of Newton's theory of color is based on his holistic worldview. Arguing against Newton's assertion that color is a phenomenon of light (though most physicists today agree with Newton's position), that all colors are contained in white light,

---

[14] Guido Kisch, *The Yellow Badge in History* (New York: Historia Judaica, 1942), 13.

[15] Ibid., 25.

[16] Ibid., 31.

which can be split by a prism into a spectrum of all the colors,[17] Goethe asserts that color is a fusion of light and darkness, according to the principle of "polarity" (the synthesis of opposites).

In the historical part of *Theory of Colors* (Part VI), entitled "Effect of Color with Reference to Moral Associations," Goethe focuses on the (cultural) *meaning* of color. We find the following commentary on yellow, which notes its dialectical ambivalence:

765. This is the color nearest to the light.

766. In its highest purity it always carries with it the nature of brightness, and has a serene, gay, softly exciting character.

770. If, however, this color in its pure and bright state is agreeable and gladdening, and in its utmost power is serene and noble, it is, on the other hand, extremely liable to contamination, and produces a very disagreeable effect if it is sullied, or in some degree tends to the *minus* side. Thus, the colour of sulphur, which inclines to green, has something unpleasant in it.

771. When a yellow color is communicated to dull and coarse surfaces, such as common cloth, felt, or the like, on which it does not appear with full energy, the disagreeable effect alluded to is apparent. By a slight and scarcely perceptible change, the beautiful impression of fire and gold is transformed into one not undeserving the epithet foul; and the color of honor and joy reversed to that of ignominy and aversion. To this impression the yellow hats of bankrupts and the yellow circles on the mantles of Jews, may have owed their origin.[18]

Goethe here alludes to the stigmatizing force of yellow as an effect of yellow's polarities.[19] However, while the principle of polarity is guided by the assumption of an underlying unity, the opposing values contained

[17] Goethe compared Newton's classic experiment in the *camera obscura* to "prismatic torture." See John R. Williams, *The Life of Goethe: A Critical Biography* (Oxford: Wiley-Blackwell, 2001), 206. As Williams points out, Goethe's aversion to the instruments Newton uses in the laboratory "didn't stop him from using those very instruments of torture in his attempts to combat scientific theory" (ibid.).

[18] Johann Wolfgang von Goethe, *Goethe's Theory of Colour*, trans. Charles Lock Eastlake (London: John Murray, 1840), 307–8. (German original: Johann Wolfgang von Goethe, "Sinnlich-sittliche Wirkung der Farbe," in *Naturwissenschaftliche Schriften I, Werke, Kommentare, Register, Volume 13* [Munich: Verlag C. H. Beck, 1989], 496).

[19] Although, generally speaking, Goethe's color theory is dominated by the optical sense, celebrating the God-like organ of the eye, it already announces in its introductory part forms of communication with other senses, the "lower" senses (such as touch and smell). This announcement is then nowhere more distinctly realized than in his reflection on yellow's materiality, which determines its perception.

in yellow deconstruct the idea of an integral whole; for there is neither resolution nor redemption from yellow's stigmatizing force. When yellow is found on material, when it is materialized, a "scarcely perceptible change" occurs—with irreversible consequences: the materiality of yellow introduces an irrevocable rupture with yellow's purity as the color closest to the light. Yellow's negativity stems from its materiality. Thus yellow is often seen as a figure of materiality itself, of the earthly or the creaturely as contrasted with the spiritual. To speak about the yellowness of light (a figure of reason or spirituality) or of gold (a figure of value) is to reduce it to its material dimension, thereby effecting a de-spiritualization. Yellow thus emphasizes and exposes a materiality in a way that is distinct from other colors. This logic of an irreversible turn towards the negative thus becomes a model of explanation for the use of yellow as a stigmatizing color. Goethe's analysis of the shift from yellow as a phenomenon of light to a consideration of its materiality prefigures the nineteenth- and twentieth-century exploitation of the ambivalence of yellow as well as its stigmatizing potential.

The link Goethe establishes between yellow's materiality (the shift from the color of light to the color of decay and excrements) and its ethical dimension (the shift between highest and lowest moral values) also points to the potential violence inherent in yellow's turn from the most positive to the most negative values. Goethe hauntingly anticipates the revival of yellow to stigmatize Jews; indeed, it is chilling to read paragraph 771 from the perspective of a post-Holocaust world.

However, the Holocaust stretches the polarity of yellow to its breaking point. The "culture of yellow" culminates, as it were, in apocalyptic scenarios, while the unrepresentability of the "yellow star" (as a Nazi-creation) is thematized by artists as diverse as Paul Celan, Thomas Pynchon, Jiři Weil, Daniel Libeskind and Frank Stella (see Chapter 6).

Romanticism and the apotheosis of blue

In Goethe's color theory, yellow is the lightest and blue the darkest color in the spectrum; yellow and blue thus form dialectical poles, creating tensions. According to Goethe, color is the resolution of the tension between darkness and light. Light dimmed by darkness creates the lighter colors: yellow, orange, red. The dialectical relationship between polar opposites thus creates forms of intensification (brightness or darkness of color), which is part of what Goethe also called an "upward movement" that he saw both as a result of the principle of polarity as the driving force of nature, and as part of the functioning of the color circle (a symmetrical arrangement of diametrically opposed colors such as blue and yellow, colors that "reciprocally evoke each other in the eye").[20]

First established in his botanical work, the idea of "growing upwards" became one of Goethe's leading principles. As he famously states in his epic poem *Faust*: "The eternal Feminine leads us upward" (Das Ewig-Weibliche zieht uns hinan). Similarly, in his novel *Wilhelm Meister's Apprenticeship* (1795–96), considered the first *Bildungsroman*, the upward movement through education is the driving force, in dialectical relation to the lateral movement of error.

The German Romantic writer Novalis (1772–1801) criticized Goethe's *Bildungsroman* as inartistic; in particular, Novalis was disdainful of Goethe's assumption of a guiding rational principle and its fulfillment.[21] Interestingly, Novalis expressed his criticism through his use of color. In his posthumously published novel, *Heinrich von Ofterdingen* (1802), which can be read as a response to Goethe's *Wilhelm Meister*, sound and blue melt into each other in an erotic fantasy Novalis sees embodied in the blossoming of what he calls the "blue flower"—an image that would become one of the leading symbols of German Romanticism. Defusing the dialectical relationships characteristic of Goethe's color theory as well as of *Wilhelm Meister*, Novalis creates in his anti-*Bildungsroman* a dreamlike atmosphere pervaded by fragmentary meta-reflections that interrupt the narrative flow. The form of the fragment, understood as a splinter of the whole, signifies a break with all rationalizing principles; through an emphasis on anti-totalizing forms, the inspiration of the individual is thus liberated (in fantasies and dreams), giving access to utopian visions.

The emphasis on *u-topia* (literally no-place, associated in Novalis with the immaterial quality of the color blue, the color of the sky, of the ocean, of fluidity) had a special significance at the beginning of the Industrial Revolution, when the dominance of rational concepts and the loss of individuality were feared. The *topos* of blue thus remained an important point of reference for writers and artists throughout the nineteenth and twentieth centuries.[22] From the Expressionist group of artists called The Blue Rider (Der Blaue Reiter), established in 1911 by Wassily Kandinsky, Franz Marc and Gabriele Münter, to Bertolt Brecht's ironic use of the motif of the

---

[20] Goethe, *Goethe's Theory of Colour*, section 50.
[21] See Hendrik Birus, *"Größte Tendenz des Zeitalters* oder *ein Candide gegen die Poesie gerichtet*? Friedrich Schlegels und Novalis Kritik des *Wilhelm Meister*," in *Goethes Kritiker*, ed. Karl Eibl and Bernd Scheffler (Paderborn: Mentis Verlag, 2001), 27–44.
[22] See Angelika Overath, *Das andere Blau: Zur Poetik einer Farbe im modernen Gedicht* (Stuttgart: Metzler, 1987).

"blue-moon" in his poem "Memory of Marie A" (1927), blue continued to signify utopian moments.

Thus for *fin-de-siècle* and avant-garde writers yellow becomes an important foil to blue. These modernist writers saw the ambivalence of yellow both as a counterpoint to a utopian Romanticism and as a more appropriate figure for the political, social, and aesthetic ambivalence of their time.

Yellow and mass phenomena

At a time when the idea of "crowd phenomena" was being explored by social psychologists such as Gustave Le Bon (in his seminal 1895 study *The Crowd: A Study of the Popular Mind*) and Sigmund Freud (in *Group Psychology and the Analysis of the Ego*, 1922), yellow allowed avant-garde writers and artists to connect various mass cultural phenomena, such as the rise of mass media (yellow journalism), mass immigration from Asia ("yellow peril"), and mass stigmatization (the yellow star that Jews were forced to wear under National Socialism). These writers and visual artists seized on the dual nature of yellow as a key to understanding its stigmatizing and scandalizing potential.

In 1905, a decade before the outbreak of the Russo-Japanese war, the term "yellow peril" was used to warn of an "Asian invasion" into the West; it referred primarily to two phenomena: the emigration of Chinese laborers into Western countries at the end of the nineteenth century, and the Japanese military expansion of the twentieth century. The "yellow peril" thus refers to a mass phenomenon that is both usurping and out of control. German emperor Wilhelm II is generally credited with coining the term in his speeches. A lithograph attributed to him depicting the "yellow peril" features the Archangel Michael leading Western (Christian) civilization against the threatening appearance of a golden Buddha, which appears in dragon-like clouds of smoke. The imagery of a non-human, yellow race invading en masse, in animal-like hordes, became a frequent motif in American fiction: in Sax Rohmer's *The Insidious Dr. Fu Manchu* (1913, which explicitly refers to the "yellow peril")[23] and Jack London's 1910 story "The Unparalleled Invasion" (which talks about "the chattering yellow populace"),[24] as well as in the Russian Symbolist poet Vladimir Soloviev. (These works are analyzed in Chapter 5).

---

[23] "Imagine that awful being, and you have a mental picture of Dr. Fu Manchu, the yellow peril incarnate in one man" (Sax Rohmer, "The Insidious Dr. Fu-Manchu," in *The Fu-Manchu Omnibus* [Lexington, KY: CreateSpace, 2011], 17).

[24] Jack London, "The Unparalleled Invasion," http://london.sonoma.edu/Writings/ StrengthStrong/invasion.html [accessed July 12, 2011].

The threat of the "yellow peril" was also frequently used in newspaper tycoon William Randolph Hearst's newspapers, which were themselves associated during this time with what came to be called "yellow journalism." The term "yellow journalism" derives from a comic strip by Richard Outcault entitled *The Yellow Kid* (the title was changed from the original title *Hogan's Alley*, because the previously minor character of the Yellow Kid develops into the protagonist of the series). The Yellow Kid is a bald boy dressed in a yellow shirt, who lives in a ghetto. His yellow shirt functions as a kind of billboard for commentaries written in ghetto slang. Outcault's comic strip first appeared in the weekend editions of Joseph Pulitzer's *New York World* newspaper. In the battle between Pulitzer and the upstart Hearst, the migration of the *Yellow Kid* to Hearst's daily *New York Press* in 1897 (seen as a real coup at the time) gave rise to the term "yellow kid journalism," which evolved into the pejorative expression "yellow journalism." (However, in its original formulation, "yellow kid journalism" had a positive connotation; it suggested an enthusiasm for the new medium of the mass circulation newspaper). The *Yellow Kid* became a symbol of the struggle for dominance between Hearst and Pulitzer, culminating in the sensational (and controversial) coverage of the Spanish-American War (1898).

Just a few years before the appearance of the *Yellow Kid*, American sociologist and writer Charlotte Perkins Gilman (1860–1935) published the seminal short story "The Yellow Wallpaper" (1890), which, though often read as a feminist manifesto, is one of the most emblematic works of the "culture of yellow." Gilman's story evokes the yellow imagery of an irritating wallpaper pattern, which already points to the themes of sensationalist journalism and racism, before the terms "yellow press" and "yellow peril" are coined. A comparison with Virginia Woolf's "The Mark on the Wall" emphasizes Gilman's and Woolf's ecstatic form of writing, which is rooted in the experience of the *moment*—a potentially redemptive moment marked in yellow, an aesthetic temporality vehemently set against the background of sensationalist and warmongering journalism (see Chapter 3).

The terms "yellow peril" and "yellow press" integrate visual and textual practices. They evoke what visual theorist W. J. T. Mitchell calls "imagetexts": interplays between words and images that augment, supplement, and mutually reinforce each other. Mitchell distinguishes "imagetexts" from "image-texts" (with a hyphen); the latter term designates "*relations* of the visual and the verbal," marking "a problematic gap, cleavage, or rupture in representation."[25] Imagetexts, on the other hand, define an indissociability

---

[25] W. J. T. Mitchell, *Iconology: Image, Text, Ideology* (Chicago: University of Chicago Press, 1986), 89.

of text and image, as is the case in the figures of "yellow peril," where the graphic and verbal elements of signification are intertwined to such a degree that it is difficult to discern where one stops and the other starts. According to Mitchell's concept of the imagetext, then, yellow figures show both how to read and how to see: "yellow" is inscribed; it becomes legible on (skin or canvas); and yet, at the same time, it is irreducibly visual. Mitchell's concept thus helps us to see that it is a matter of an *inscription* of yellow that exceeds both the merely visual and the merely verbal dimensions. Saying, for example, that Asians have "yellow" skin is an inscription of yellow, for Asians are no more "yellow" than Native Americans are "red" or Caucasians are "white."

This process of inscription applies of course to all colors. What is distinctive about yellow is its positive-negative polarity, which, as was discussed above in relation to Goethe's color theory, tends to resolve towards the negative side (stigmatism). This polarity is at work, for example, in the "yellow peril"—for in Asia yellow is a sacred color, the color of the Emperor and his clothes, even as it is a marker of exclusion in the Western imaginary. Thus although color is often based on certain immutable physical characteristics (red blood, yellow sun, etc)., the value system implied in a color is always culturally conditioned.

Synaesthesia and the multivalent figuration of yellow

In any discussion of color, the question of *synaesthesia* (the simultaneous stimulation of two or more senses) almost invariably comes to the fore. This study sees synaesthesia, or more precisely, "synaesthetic networks," as the key to understanding the signifying potential of yellow outside of traditional color symbolism (the inadequacy of which I noted at the outset). Although the term "synaesthesia" was coined only late in the nineteenth century, the concept has a prehistory. Eighteenth-century philosopher Johann Gottfried Herder (1744–1803) was the first to theorize it, under the notion of what he called *Doppel-Empfindung* (double-sensation).[26] Together with fellow philosopher Moses Mendelssohn, Herder criticized Louis Bertrand Castel's development of the ocular harpsichord (*Clavecin pour les yeux*, 1725)—a keyboard instrument that projects different colors as it is played—arguing that Castel's invention was flawed because it did not allow enough time for eye and ear to experience their synaesthetic potential (Castel also authored

---

[26] See Heinz Paetzold, "Synästhesie," in *Ästhetische Grundbegriffe: Historisches Wörterbuch*, vol. 5, ed. Karlheinz Barck (Stuttgart and Weimar: Metzler Verlag, 2002), 841.

a well-regarded treatise, *Optique des couleurs*, in 1740). Rapid sequences of colored images forced the eye to simply "stare" at them, without its being able to truly "see."[27]

Herder's criticism already points to the split between two competing visions of synaesthesia: the one describing it as a phenomenon that is universally experienced once the proper stimuli are provided (as in the example of the ocular harpsichord); the other (following Herder) emphasizing the exceptionality of synaesthetic phenomena. Herder's insistence on the specificity and singularity of synaesthetic experience implies a contemplative dimension, an intellectual intervention into an otherwise sensual experience. For Herder, the imagination (*Einbildungskraft*) is, as Katherine Arens points out, the "staging area in the mind for stimuli from our senses, together with what is preserved by memory in us."[28]

Herder's anthropological definition of "double-sensation" was taken up by Romantic poets such as Friedrich Schlegel, for whom this idea will form a central part of a "universal poetics." Based either on religious spirituality (Wilhelm Heinrich Wackenroder), the lyrics of nature (Joseph Eichendorff), or a new mythology (Novalis), the Romantic poetics of synaesthesia is based on a principle of *mediation*, which not only involves various senses (sound, form, color), but also the encounter with temporal forms of immediacy that strive to overcome the medium of representation itself through direct sensory connections, in a unification. (These direct sensory connections, which originate in the Romantic notion of immediacy, are seen in modern times as realized through moments of shock, in the temporal mode of "suddenness," or in what Virginia Woolf will call "moments of being.")[29]

With the advent of reproductive media—quintessentially film—the temporal notion of immediacy gains a renewed significance, thus requiring a rethinking of the concept of synaesthesia. Avant-garde writers and painters incorporated cinematic techniques into their work, creating synaesthetic effects through relationships between different media. For early twentieth-century theorists such as Walter Benjamin, the cinematic medium was often seen in terms of its potential fulfillment of the Romantics' and the Symbolists' notion of synaesthesia. As Rebecca Coma observes, Benjamin saw the artistic agenda of Romanticism realized in film:

[27] See Johann Gottfried Herder, *Kritische Wälder oder Betrachtungen über die Wissenschaft und Kunst des Schönen. Viertes Wäldchen*, vol. 1, ed. M. Bollacher (Frankfurt am Main: Deutscher Klassiker Verlag, 1992), 322.

[28] Katherine Arens, "Kant, Herder, and Psychology," in *Herder Today: Contributions from the International Herder Conference*, ed. Kurt Mueller-Vollmer (Berlin: De Gruyter, 1987), 194.

[29] See Karl Heinz Bohrer, *Suddenness: On the Aesthetic Moment of Appearance* (New York: Columbia University Press, 1994).

By presenting the intrinsic interpenetration of the various mediums, film, for Benjamin, reveals art as such to be a differentiated collectivity that is both an allegory and an instance of a redeemed social world. Film is the ghostly medium which promises and threatens to accomplish— threatens to unravel precisely by accomplishing—what for Romanticism remained an unthinkable and impossible ideal.[30]

Benjamin recognized that the dominant function of film was a form of distraction rather than revelation.[31] Film can be "threatening" in the sense that its proximity to reality can allow it to substitute itself for the real social world. Nevertheless, following his Romantic impulse, Benjamin theorized film's potential to redeem itself as a medium of human self-representation.

However, it is in the film theory of Russian director Sergei Eisenstein that the visual politics of synaesthesia, in particular as it relates to yellow, truly comes into its own. Eisenstein's opposition to the harmonizing and unifying notions of synaesthesia—emblematized in Richard Wagner's notion of the "total work of art" (*Gesamtkunstwerk*) and in Wassily Kandinsky's stage composition *The Yellow Sound* (1909)—overturns the conventional, Romantic view of synaesthesia as a unification of the senses. Thus Eisenstein's anti-symbolic conception of color, developed through his guiding idea of a synaesthetic "system of imagery," provides the key to understanding the use of yellow in late modernity.

Eisenstein's ideas about synaesthesia were first developed in an encounter with Japanese Kabuki Theater, whose performances he had attended in Moscow in the 1920s. In these performances, Eisenstein observed a way of acting that simultaneously appeals to multiple levels of cognition and affect.[32] In *Film Sense*, Eisenstein defines synaesthesia as the "production from one sense-impression of one kind of an associated mental image of a sense-impression of another kind."[33] As an example, Eisenstein cites the "ability *to*

[30] Rebecca Comay, "Benjamin and the Ambiguities of Romanticism," in *The Cambridge Companion to Walter Benjamin*, ed. David D. Ferris (Cambridge: Cambridge University Press, 2004), 149.

[31] In her article "Between Contemplation and Distraction: Configurations of Attention in Walter Benjamin," Carolin Duttlinger explores Benjamin's notion of *distraction* as "an umbrella term for a range of perceptual responses," which differs from Siegfried Kracauer's notion of *distraction* as a modern form of escapism. However, Duttlinger emphasizes that this complex notion of distraction is absent from the essay "The Work of Art in the Age of Mechanical Reproduction." See Carolin Duttlinger, "Between Contemplation and Distraction: Configurations of Attention in Walter Benjamin," *German Studies Review* 30, no. 1 (2007): 42.

[32] Steve Odin, "The Influence of Traditional Japanese Aesthetics on the Film Theory of Sergei Eisenstein," *Journal of Aesthetic Education* 23, no. 2 (1989): 70.

[33] Sergei M. Eisenstein, *The Film Sense*, trans. Jay Leyda (New York: Harcourt Brace & Company, 1969), 149.

see sounds in terms of color and to hear color as sounds."[34] The emphasis on synaesthesia as a form of imaging differs radically from the spiritual notion of synaesthesia propagated by artists such as Kandinsky and Scriabin, who claimed that the artist's synaesthetic sensations enable experiences that are otherwise inaccessible. On the contrary, Eisenstein's notion of synaesthesia involves an interface between creator (the director), medium (the film) and receiver (the spectator).

In a section of his *Film Sense* (1942) entitled "Color and Meaning," Eisenstein prefaces his observations by remarking "let us compose our own 'rhapsody in yellow'"—an oblique reference to Kandinsky's *The Yellow Sound*, which he seeks to criticize. (It is significant that Eisenstein develops his notion of synaesthesia through a reflection on yellow—as if the color yellow were especially apt to produce synaesthetic effects). Eisenstein thus constructs his theory of synaesthesia in opposition to *The Yellow Sound*, a work that, along with Alexander Scriabin's *Prometheus: The Poem of Fire* (1910, for orchestra and "color organ") is often considered the archetype of consciously conceived synaesthetic art. Discussing *The Yellow Sound*, Eisenstein observes: "first the whole stage suddenly grows blurred in dull red light. Secondly complete darkness alternates with harsh white light. Thirdly, everything suddenly turns a faded gray (all colors disappear!). Only the yellow flower shines ever brighter."[35] Kandinsky's synaesthetic spectacle is based on the principle of simultaneous contrast through which complementary colors intensify each other: blue intensifies yellow, and vice versa. (In 1839, Michel Chevreul developed the principle of the simultaneous contrast for modern painting, *De la Loi du Contraste Simultané des Couleurs* [*The Principles of Harmony and Contrast of Colours*]). Eisenstein describes Kandinsky's use of complementary colors (mainly blue, black, and yellow) as a form of religious revelation: detached from all external reference, it is driven by a will to abstraction resulting in the spiritualization of color. Eisenstein's critique highlights the mysticism of Kandinsky's insistence on absolute abstract relationships between colors, sounds, and shapes, claiming that Kandinsky's complete refusal of realism—his reductive formalism— leaves his art open to political manipulation. Eisenstein writes:

> The method employed here is clear—to abstract "inner tonalities" from all "external" matter. Such a method consciously attempts to divorce all formal elements from all content elements; everything touching theme or subject is dismissed, leaving only those extreme formal elements that in normal creative work play only a partial role. [...] We cannot deny

---

[34] Ibid., original emphasis.
[35] Ibid., 116.

that compositions of this kind evoke obscurely disturbing sensations—
but no more than this.[36]

To be more precise, Eisenstein's criticism is directed against a particular
form of abstraction, one that insists on purely physiological relations—what
Kandinsky calls, in his theoretical tract *Concerning the Spiritual in Art*
(1914), the "principle of inner need."[37] By limiting external elements, the
inner elements (that is, as Kandinsky says, "the emotion in the soul of the
artist") come to the fore, thereby giving access to the "nonmaterial."[38]

Together with theosophists such as Madame Blavatsky and Rudolf
Steiner, Kandinsky predicted the advent of what he called an "Epoch of Great
Spirituality,"[39] a time in which the artist would be at the center of a process of
transformation, revealing "inner states of being," such as those manifested in
synaesthetic relations between sounds and colors.[40] However, for Eisenstein,
synaesthesia is not based on a teleological model (whether cosmological
or spiritual), but on a dynamic process resulting in the crystallization and
exposure of what he calls the "system of imagery"[41] that synthesizes the
concept of a film:

> In art it is not the *absolute* relationships that are decisive, but those
> *arbitrary* relationships within a system of images dictated by the
> particular work of art. The problem is not, nor ever will be, solved by
> a fixed catalog of color-symbols, *but the emotional intelligibility and
> function of color will rise from the natural order of establishing the color
> imagery of the work, coincidental with the process of shaping the living
> movement of the whole work.* Even within the limitation of a color-range
> of black and white, in which most films are still produced, one of these
> tones not only evades being given a single "value" as an *absolute* image,
> but can even assume absolutely *contradictory* meanings, *dependent only
> upon the general system of imagery that has been decided upon for the
> particular film.*[42]

[36] Ibid., 117. Eisenstein's criticism of Kandinsky's lack of a political orientation becomes
more pressing during the period when he was writing his theory of cinema *The Film
Sense*, with the specter of fascism haunting Europe.

[37] Wassily Kandinsky, *Concerning the Spiritual in Art*, trans. and intro. M. T. H. Sadler
(New York: Dover Publications, 1977), 26.

[38] Kandinsky, *Concerning the Spiritual in Art*, 349.

[39] Quoted in Kevin T. Dann, *Bright Colors Falsely Seen: Synaesthesia and the Search for
Transcendental Knowledge* (New Haven, CT: Yale University Press, 1998), 54.

[40] As Kevin Dann shows in *Bright Colors Falsely Seen* (59), the myth that Kandinsky
himself was synaesthete and therefore expressed himself in synaesthetic art was perpet-
uated by art historians such as Sixten Ringbom.

[41] Eisenstein, *The Film Sense*, 151.

[42] Ibid., 150–1, italics in the original.

Eisenstein thus replaces the idea of color symbolism with a dynamic process of signification that emerges organically from the work itself, by which seemingly arbitrary relationships become meaningful. Of course these meanings are not divorced from color associations deriving from outside the work; Eisenstein is simply arguing that these meanings necessarily undergo a transformation, which he identifies with the vocation of art itself.[43]

In practice, each "system of imagery" is tied to the specific historical and social context out of which it emerges and is therefore strictly opposed to any form of absolute meaning; it is radically embedded in the world of political and social signification. Eisenstein thus critiques Kandinsky's divorce of form from content because of its implicit denial of the social world. However, Eisenstein is not against formalism as such. Eisenstein's own color cinematography is famously based on formalistic patterns of red, black, and white, with clearly defined meanings (e.g. the motif of the swan changing from white at the beginning of *Ivan the Terrible* to black at the end). His notions of synaesthesia and color in general are based on forms of collective rather than subjective perception; and for that very reason his insistence on political and social embeddedness understands itself as being constructed on the basis of what Susan Buck-Morss has called "synaesthetic systems."[44] According to Eisenstein, synaesthetic networks organize worldviews by coordinating emotional and intellectual forms of perceiving and understanding (as in montage), whereas in Kandinsky the world is bracketed, as it were, to harmonize inner feelings with spiritual and cosmological orders.

In a rhetorical move, Eisenstein relates Kandinsky's unidimensional and spiritual use of yellow to the Nazis' use of yellow stigmata by evoking Goethe's comments, quoted above, on the historical and ethical dimension of yellow. (We must remember that Eisenstein's *Film Sense* was written in 1942 at the

---

[43] Eisenstein himself started out with ties to constructivism—an artistic movement that emphasized abstraction and organization—eventually breaking with the movement after becoming critical of their attempts to establish fixed catalogs of color and sound relations based on "purely physical relationships."

[44] Susan Buck-Morss describes in her article "Aesthetics and Anaesthetics" the operation of a "synaesthetic system" with regard to potential correspondences on a historical scale, thereby relating the personal to the collective forms of the imagination: "The field of the sensory circuit thus corresponds to that of 'experience,' in the classical philosophical sense of mediation between subject and object, and yet its very composition makes the so-called split between subject and object (which was the constant plague of classical philosophy) simply irrelevant. In order to differentiate our description from the more limited, traditional conception of the human nervous system which isolates human biology from its environment, we will call this aesthetic system of sense-consciousness, decentered from the classical subject, wherein external sense-perceptions come together with internal images of memory and anticipation, the 'synaesthetic system'" (Buck-Morss, "Aesthetics and Anaesthetics: Walter Benjamin's Artwork Essay Reconsidered," *October* 62 [1992]: 12–13).

height of World War II, just a year after Hitler had invaded Russia, breaking the non-aggression pact of 1939). After quoting from Goethe's *Color Theory*, Eisenstein comments: "Before proceeding further on our "yellow path" (which seems to have landed us among Nazi revivals of medieval darkness!), let us note some facts about the color green…"[45] By invoking Goethe's theory, Eisenstein demonstrates his concern for the historical and ethical dimension of color signification. The oblique reference to the stigma of the "yellow star" as a recurring technique of stigmatization situates and frames Eisenstein's use of color in terms of synaesthetic networks.

***

I should note that this study does not purport to be a history of yellow, even if it can be considered a contribution to the cultural history of late modernity. The book is thus organized thematically, with each chapter treating a different yellow figure (e.g. yellow books, "yellow peril," "yellow star"), each of which represents an important aspect of the "culture of yellow" that emerged in late modernity. While this study is heavily weighted towards the period 1890–1940, its scope is not limited by these dates. Instead, I have endeavored to develop a concept of "cultural time" through the color yellow and its multifarious uses.

Rather than an exhaustive or comprehensive examination of the color yellow, I have instead focused on its major motifs and figures. Nevertheless, what I am calling yellow's "visual politics"—the nexus between the aesthetic and the ethico-political—is not a rare or isolated phenomenon found only in select works. It rather means that certain works reveal through yellow a general cultural mood that is inextricable from ethical and social concerns. Thus beyond the mere duality of the color yellow—its "polarity"—is what I call its "multivalent figuration": the idea that yellow connects divergent conceptual and affective realms, such as art, politics, religion, physiology, and ethics, in time-bound matrices—a concept adapted from Eisenstein's notion of synaesthesia, as described above (also discussed in Chapter 5), but also from Mikhail Bakhtin's concept of the "chronotope" (see the Conclusion). In short, I contend that when the color yellow is highlighted in a significant context, a much larger and more encompassing meaning is invariably activated. The aim of this study is to unpack these latent cultural meanings and to reveal the processes of their production—their structure or "system,"[46] as it were.

[45] Ibid., 136.
[46] See the Conclusion to this study.

Van Gogh's Yellow

From that day my Van Gogh made astonishing progress; he seemed to divine all that he had in him, and the result was that whole series of sun-effects over sun-effects in full sunlight. Have you seen the portrait of the poet? The face and hair are chrome yellow. The clothes are chrome yellow. The necktie is chrome yellow with an emerald scarf pin, on a background of chrome yellow. That is what an Italian painter said to me, and he added: "Merde! merde! Everything is yellow! I don't know what painting is any longer!"

—Paul Gauguin

In *Wings of Desire* (1987), German director Wim Wenders's cinematic collage about post-war Berlin, Peter Falk, who plays one of the ex-angels in the film, asks himself: "Why was the Jewish star yellow?" He then answers his own question: "Van Gogh painted yellow sunflowers, and he killed himself." What seems, at first glance, to be a perplexing answer (for Van Gogh was neither Jewish nor was he persecuted), highlights at the same time an important tendency in the reception of Van Gogh's work as it relates to the stigmatic use of the color yellow in the twentieth century.

In 1910, the magazine *Die Kunst* declared Van Gogh to be "the father of us all," because his "problems are the problems of our time."[1] However, from the perspective of this study, he becomes more concretely the father figure of yellow as a *metacolor*—i.e. color as a critical function. This approach is thus distinguished from those that see Van Gogh's use of yellow as primarily a personal obsession or as reflecting the psychological or physiological condition of his genius.[2] However, Van Gogh's paintings from his so-called

---

[1] At the beginning of his chapter "Van Gogh's Impact on Literary Expressionism," Patrick Bridgewater summarizes in *Van Gogh and Expressionism* (ed. Jill Lloyd and Michael Peppiatt [New York: Hatje Cantz, 2007], 75) the impact that the reception of Van Gogh's work had on pre-World War I literature and the visual arts, quoting Max Pechstein naming Van Gogh "the father of us all."

[2] Van Gogh's obsessive use of yellow has been the object of numerous commentaries; these typically explore the relationship between physiology and Van Gogh's psychological

"yellow period" (1888–90) do not simply use yellow; they also *thematize* it—that is, the yellow color is meant to signify something on its own (even if it is not in any way "autonomous"), apart from its specific aesthetic function in the painting. This use of yellow was inspired by the French literary avant-garde, which not only published its books with so-called yellow backs, but also explored the negative (stigmatic, scandalous) potential of yellow in such figures as Emile Zola's prostitute Nana in his eponymous novel (1880) and Victor Hugo's ex-convict Jean Valjean in *Les Misérables* (1862). Van Gogh similarly makes reference to yellow as a color of stigmatization, as the color of the wretched victims of society.

Van Gogh: From yellow books to *The Yellow House*

Towards the end of his life, hospitalized in Saint-Rémy, Van Gogh dreamed of painting "une librairie jaune" (a yellow bookshop),[3] reflecting that: "I don't know, though, not always being a pessimist—I keep telling myself that I still have it in my heart to paint a bookshop one day with the shop window yellow-pink, in the evening, and the passers-by black—it's such an essentially modern subject."[4] Van Gogh's association of yellow with modernity demonstrates the highly self-conscious way he inscribes himself in the

condition. Van Gogh is used as an example in Michel Foucault's *History of Madness* (1962). In *Chroma: A Book on Color* (Minneapolis: University of Minnesota Press, 2010), Derek Jarman asks: "Was Van Gogh's illness xanthosis?" (90), pointing to an abnormal condition in which there are deposits of yellowish fatty material in the skin and the internal organs that cause a yellow appearance. In *Vincent van Gogh: Chemicals, Crises, and Creativity* (Boston, Basel, and Berlin: Birkhaeuser, 1992), Wilfred N. Arnold offers an extensive examination of the relationship between the significance of yellow in Van Gogh's work, his use of chemicals and drugs, and his psychological disposition, concluding that the influence of illness and external effects on Van Gogh's color perception cannot be dismissed, but that his "artistic preference remains the best working hypothesis to explain the yellow dominance" of his color palette (238).

[3] Carl Nordenfalk has analyzed Van Gogh's relationship to literature in detail. See Carl Nordenfalk, "Van Gogh and Literature," *Journal of the Warburg and Courtauld Institutes* 10 (1947): 132–47. While Nordenfalk also points to the significance of yellow books in Van Gogh's early works, Wouter van der Veen, in a recent study entitled *Van Gogh: A Literary Mind* (Amsterdam: Waanders Publishers, 2009), emphasizes in more detail Van Gogh's exploration of modern French works, such as Maupassant's *Bel Ami*, as a form of entertainment: "Among the books he consulted and enjoyed, there was one thing that was fundamental to his subsequent reading program, which brightened up his intellectual horizons: he discovered that more than anything he needed to laugh, to be entertained" (187).

[4] Vincent van Gogh, Letter 823, To Theo van Gogh, Saint-Rémy-de-Provence, Tuesday, 26 November 1889, http://vangoghletters.org/vg/letters/let823/letter.html [accessed December 12, 2012].

contemporary and twentieth-century artistic movements he helped shape: from Van Gogh's short-lived collaboration with Paul Gauguin, from which he envisioned the establishment of a community in the South of France (at what Van Gogh called the Yellow House), to the posthumous dialogue in such figures as Francis Bacon, Friederike Mayröcker, Antonin Artaud and Akira Kurosawa, Van Gogh's work becomes central to the "culture of yellow" that emerged in late modernity. In this sense one can speak of Van Gogh's yellow in terms of what Erin Manning calls a "relational matrix,"[5] which would not merely refer to the specific imagery of Van Gogh's work, but also to Van Gogh's yellow imagery as part of a cultural process in which Van Gogh was himself an essential part.

The signature paintings of Van Gogh's "yellow period" are his series of *Sunflowers* (1888); these paintings epitomize Van Gogh's idea of a co-presence of life and death, an idea that recurs repeatedly in his works from this point forward. The sunflower paintings were intended as a kind of decoration for collaborator Paul Gauguin's room in the Yellow House, which was the subject of an eponymous painting in 1888. Van Gogh's vision of the Yellow House as a place for artists to intermingle and work together was, however, short-lived; his collaboration with Gauguin quickly ended in scandal.[6]

Van Gogh's painting *The Yellow House* (Color Plate 1) offers what could be called a blueprint for his yellow period. Melissa McQuillan describes its "yellow essence":

> Though dwarfed by the building behind, its simple cubic form is more sharply delineated, its dark green trimmed windows and doors strongly contrasting with lighter-value yellow. Like the sequence of viaducts, though through different means, they invite penetration. The "Yellow House" is the most brilliant yellow in the painting. It sets a kind of yellow essence to which the ochres, oranges and greenish yellows seem to aspire. [...] Space, color and environmental details specify and

---

5 In *Politics of Touch: Sense Movement, Sovereignty* (Minneapolis: University of Minnesota Press, 2007), Erin Manning foregrounds the processual body as one that makes "relational matrices" possible—creating new relations between "terms, subjects, and ideas" (xiii).

6 Van Gogh's interest in collaborative work was also very much influenced by his strong attraction to Japanese aesthetic culture, which he idealized as a "collectivity of religion of nature" (Debora Silverman, *Van Gogh and Gauguin: The Search for Sacred Art* [New York: Farrar, Straus and Giroux, 2000], 43). After his arrival in Arles, Van Gogh writes in a letter to his brother: "But, my dear brother—you know, I feel I'm in Japan" (Vincent van Gogh, Letter 585, To Theo van Gogh, Arles, on or about Friday, 16 March 1888, http://vangoghletters.org/vg/letters/let585/letter.html [accessed December 12, 2012].

position the "Yellow House." Around its central place in the composition the rest of the world seems to coalesce, revolve and spill away.[7]

The idea of a "yellow essence" that makes other colors pale in comparison would come to define much of Van Gogh's work. Van Gogh's yellow is a radiant or luminous yellow, as Van Gogh himself called it, a triumphant yellow, anticipating the decade (the 1890s) in which the color yellow becomes emblematic. The spatial construction of the Yellow House as the focal point of the painting not only serves to emphasize the subject matter, but also to activate the viewer, who is invited to be a co-creator. The viewer is drawn into the figure of the house, which symbolizes Van Gogh's notion of collaboration and collective work. The change of title from its earlier versions, from "The House and its Environment" and "The Street" to "The Yellow House," reveals Van Gogh's explicit stylization of the house around the color yellow, connoting a kind of artistic Enlightenment.

Van Gogh thus transforms a rather common house, which he had rented with the help of his brother Theo, into a center for spiritual renewal in its illumination and inviting openness. In a letter describing *The Yellow House* to Theo, Van Gogh observes:

> Likewise croquis of a square no. 30 canvas showing the house and its surroundings under a sulphur sun, under a pure cobalt sky. That's a really difficult subject! But I want to conquer it for that very reason. Because it's tremendous, these yellow houses in the sunlight and then the incomparable freshness of the blue. All the ground's yellow, too. [...] Milliet finds it horrible, but I don't need to tell you that when he says he can't understand that someone can enjoy doing such an ordinary grocer's shop, and such stiff, square houses with no charm at all, I reflect that Zola did a certain boulevard at the beginning of *L'assommoir* and Flaubert a corner of quai de la Villette in the summer heat, at the beginning of *Bouvard et Pecuchet*, that aren't half bad. And it does me good to do what's *difficult*. That doesn't stop me having a tremendous need for, shall I say the word—for religion—so I go outside at night to paint the stars, and I always dream a painting like that, with a group of lively figures of the pals.[8]

The motif of the Yellow House, of a house in the sun, on an ordinary street, is conceived in the context of an imaginary artistic dialogue with the literary tradition of French naturalism, i.e. with Zola and Flaubert. Their works had

---

[7]   Melissa McQuillan, *Van Gogh* (London: Thames and Hudson, 1989), 171–2.

[8]   Vincent van Gogh, Letter 691, To Theo van Gogh, 29 September, 1888 in Arles, http://www.vangoghletters.org/vg/letters/let691/letter.html [accessed November 8, 2011].

already established a model of how to depict ordinary life on the basis of an aesthetic negativity, which was often coded specifically in yellow.

Prior to Van Gogh's "yellow period" he painted yellow books, a gesture that reveals more explicitly his debt to French naturalism. Thus *Still Life with Bible* (1885) is painted in somber dark tones against a black background (this was characteristic of his Dutch period); the canvas shows an open bible with an extinguished candle next to it, juxtaposed with an edition of Zola's novel *Joy of Life* in yellow in the foreground. As Van Gogh himself commented on the work, it was painted with "a little lemon yellow." Both the title of Zola's novel and its vibrant yellow cover create an aesthetic and cognitive dissonance with the ideology of the seventeenth-century still-life genre he appears to conjure, namely the idea of spiritual value based on the Christian faith. Van Gogh's resolutely secular outlook is enhanced through the duality of yellow, which, through its spiritual (illumination) and material polarities, emphasizes a dichotomy between divergent sources of value (the Bible and avant-garde art). Throughout his career, Van Gogh sought to avoid religious representation. Thus Van Gogh's use of the color yellow is not, like that of his sometime collaborator Paul Gauguin, immersed in the spiritual meaning of yellow, but emerges out of an already established literary tradition in France.

Invoking the literary tradition of the French modernists, Van Gogh anticipates the emerging culture of yellow in *Piles of French Novels* (Color Plate 2)—a study for the slightly larger still life *Parisian Novels* (a work realized towards the end of his stay in Paris in 1887). Here yellow-backed books are not contrasted with the somber palette of his Dutch period, with the Christian faith and symbols of mortality; having no extrinsic reference point, they appear to be self-contained. The yellow-backed books are exposed as a body of work on a pink tablecloth in front of a yellow background. The yellow-backs merge into the background, emphasizing the yellow theme.

Piles of French Novels is thus a study for *Parisian Novels*, in which yellow books appear in a similar manner; however, the tablecloth and the wallpaper in the background are now organized in vertical and horizontal lines, in detailed patterns that draw attention to the material of the fabric. What becomes obvious in the transition from the study *Piles of French Novels* to the painting *Parisian Novels* is Van Gogh's focus on the materiality of texture itself, which, in its "fluid interplay of drawings, prints and painting," shows itself as a "variant of Japonism."[9] While *Piles of French Novels* exposes yellow as a literary *topos*, *Parisian Novels* intertwines the literary tradition

9 Silverman, *Van Gogh and Gauguin*, 218–19.

stylistically with a reference to the Japanese prints that influenced painters and writers in the late nineteenth and early twentieth centuries.[10] The emphasis in *Parisian Novels* on a continuity between the mostly yellow-backed books and the texture of tablecloth and tapestry makes the whole painting appear like a book to be read. An early example of experimentation with broken brushstrokes that would later come to define the Van Gogh style, the transition from *Piles of French Novels* to *Parisian Novels* is important historically for its emphasis on style in relationship to a specific themati-zation of "yellow books" (a motif I explore in detail in Chapter 2, namely in the relation between the yellow-backed books associated with French avant-garde fiction and the emerging culture of scandal, coded in yellow).

Van Gogh's English friend, Archibald S. Hartrick, called *Parisian Novels* "the first of a series of yellow pictures."[11] Despite the fact that it is in Van Gogh's later still lifes that yellow is striking as the dominant color, Hartrick emphasizes, both conceptually and thematically, the prominence of yellow as rooted in the literary tradition; he thus sees the focus on "yellow books" as marking the emergence of Van Gogh's "yellow period."[12] Moreover, as a "programmatic statement," Van Gogh's still lifes of yellow books can be read in the context of contemporary debates about the genre of the artistic biography. As Douglas W. Druick and Peter K. Zegers point out, Van Gogh contextualizes his work and states its references and intentions in the form of "a manifesto picture."[13]

While *Parisian Novels* emphasizes mostly diagonal and vertical lines, *Lemons, Pears, Apples, Grapes, and Orange*, 1887 (Color Plate 3), activates the dynamic of a circular brushstroke, drawing the viewer into the painting. In this work, Van Gogh is "unifying his palette around a dominant yellow," even carrying the "yellow harmony onto the surrounding frame, in criss-cross markings that resemble Japanese calligraphy."[14] The painting was

---

[10] Silverman specifies Van Gogh's focus on Japanese prints and emphasizes that one of his patterns of interest "was fabric, evident in the many prints in his collection that depicted the process of textile production" (ibid., 215).

[11] Archibald S. Hartrick, *A Painter's Pilgrimage through Fifty Years* (Cambridge: Cambridge University Press, 1939), 46.

[12] Jan Hulsker corrects Hartrick and instead points to Van Gogh's still lifes: "Perhaps the still life with apples [*Basket with Apples*] is one of the canvases he had in mind, for here at least there is a strong yellow in the apples. In any event, the important still life [*White Grapes, Apples, Pears, Lemons, and Orange*] does match his description. It depicts yellow pears (quince pears as Vincent himself called them), lemons, white grapes, and a solitary orange, and it also has a yellow background" (Jan Hulsker, *The Complete van Gogh. Paintings, Drawings, Sketches* [New York: Harry N. Abrams, Inc. Publishers, 1980], 296).

[13] Douglas W. Druick and Peter K. Zegers, *Van Gogh and Gauguin: The Studio of the South*, (New York: Thames & Hudson, 2001), 90.

[14] Belinda Thomson, *Van Gogh. The Art Institute of Chicago* (New York: Harry N. Abrams Inc., 2011), 48.

also featured in an impromptu exhibition Van Gogh organized with artist friends such as Toulouse-Lautrec and Bernard.[15] It is thus just at the moment when Van Gogh appears to define his artistic self-understanding as part of a collective movement that his use of yellow attains the iconic quality for which he is known today. Commenting on *Lemons, Pears, Apples, Grapes, and Orange*, McQuillan remarks:

> This extraordinary painting appears to be nearly monochromatic, and thus the texture gives restless vibrancy to the surface and searches out the contours of the seething mass of fruit. [...] In Arles and Saint-Remy van Gogh sometimes painted suns into his landscape skies. Here, ripened fruit seems to stand for the sun's energy, as later would the similarly monochromatic *Sunflowers*, although their brilliance does not prompt the same sensation of bedazzlement.[16]

Unlike the sunflower paintings, where Van Gogh unfolds the ambivalence of yellow in a two-way dynamic, dramatizing blossoming (life) next to death (wilting, and decay), *Lemons, Pears, Apples, Grapes, and Orange* draws the viewer into the luminous center while also radiating outward. Both paintings, however, initiate Van Gogh's thematization of a yellow that is bursting with "the energies of spermatic painting."[17]

Julius Meier-Graefe, an influential art historian and publicist of the early twentieth century who "transformed van Gogh into one of the most celebrated artists of the modern movement,"[18] comments on the irony of calling "these amazingly vital masses of fruit" *still life*: "The apples glow, they seem to be at the point of bursting; the whole essence of their species seems to be concentrated in them; a piece of furious vitality has fallen by chance into this basket."[19] Meier-Graefe's emphasis on the "furious vitality" ("he did not paint with hands, but with naked senses") creates the image of

---

[15] Belinda Thomson elaborates on the exhibition that Van Gogh organized in November–December 1887: "Unfortunately, this ambitious undertaking, in which Van Gogh hung about one hundred canvases, was forced to close early because of a misunderstanding with the restaurant's management and thus passed unnoticed by the press. But it was the result of Van Gogh's energetic networking in Paris, and achieved, albeit briefly, his dream of seeing the artists of the 'petit boulevard' [...] in mutual cooperation and reaching out to the public" (Thomson, *Van Gogh Paintings: The Masterpieces* [New York: Thames & Hudson, 2007], 48).

[16] McQuillan, *Van Gogh*, 161.

[17] See Silverman, *Van Gogh and Gauguin*, 244, with respect to Van Gogh's "sexualized practice of art."

[18] Stefan Koldehoff, "When Myth Seems Stronger than Scholarship: Van Gogh and the Problem of Authenticity," in *Van Gogh Museum Journal 2002* (Amsterdam: Van Gogh Museum, 2002), 9.

[19] Julius Meier-Graefe, *Modern Art: Being a Contribution to a New System of Aesthetics, Volume 1* (New York: G. P. Putnam's Sons, 1908), 205.

an energy that is bursting out of the painter, whom he also describes as a volcano, splashing with color as if it were blood. Van Gogh's use of color is not presented as being mediated, but is rather seen as a "material function of his body,"[20] like his relation to nature ("he did not go to Nature; she dragged him to her").[21]

In his impressionistic biography *Vincent van Gogh*, subtitled in its later editions *Roman eines Gottsuchers* (*Novel of a God-Seeker*), Meier-Graefe's evocative description of Van Gogh's funeral brings together the leitmotifs of Van Gogh's "yellow period"—sunflowers, wheat, and sun:

> When they had all come to pay tribute a fanfare sounded, and Yellow, his black-eyed mistress, entered in her Chinese robe of state. Ten women came with her, the fairest of the Empire, garbed in gentler tones of the same yellow, and stood at her side bearing sunflowers. His beloved made a deep obeisance before the catafalque, and the ten women did likewise. And as they bowed, all the sheaves of wheat in the field, all the flowers and the fruit bowed down likewise, and the sun shed his rays on the cottage in Auvers.[22]

Van Gogh's funeral is transformed by Meier-Graefe into a scene of animation. The death of the artist is overcome, as it were, by the animation of the motifs of his paintings (sun, sunflowers, wheat), which are brought to life through the posthumous power of Van Gogh's work. In the widespread glorification of Van Gogh's work (to which Elias Canetti referred as the "van Gogh religion"),[23] Van Gogh's yellow is transformed into the sacrificial symbol of Christ's blood ("colors were splashed about like blood," as Meier-Graefe states).[24]

Emblematized by the sunflowers and their emphasis on the ambivalence of yellow (some are dying, while others are in blossom), Van Gogh's work of the "yellow period" is closely intertwined with biographical details such as the painter's excessive exposure to the sun. In the 1930s, Georges Bataille refers to the relationship that Van Gogh establishes between the sun, self-destruction and aesthetic creativity as a "vision of excess" that culminates in

---

[20] Ibid.

[21] Ibid., 202.

[22] Meier-Graefe, *Vincent Van Gogh: A Biographical Study* (London: Medici Society, 1922), 107.

[23] Elias Canetti reports about the rise of the "van Gogh religion" in his boarding school, when his teacher remarked "that she had only understood what Christ was all about since coming to know the life of van Gogh" (Elias Canetti, quoted in Nathalie Heinich, *The Glory of van Gogh: An Anthropology of Admiration* [Princeton, NJ: Princeton University Press, 1996], 45).

[24] Meier-Graefe, *Modern Art*, 205.

the heroic gesture of a self-sacrifice.[25] Quoting Van Gogh and his apocalyptic comments on the solar system ("and the sun is sick, he said twice"),[26] Bataille establishes Van Gogh himself as a larger-than-life figure, interpreting the Dutch painter as the liberator who sacrifices himself in order to become Prometheus: he "tore from within himself nothing less than the sun."[27] Bataille thus interweaves Van Gogh's biography (suicide and self-mutilation) with his sunflower paintings (in their emphasis on the brevity of life), thereby absorbing the ambivalence of yellow into a heroic structure of sacrifice.[28]

However, as Rosalind Krauss emphasizes in her essay "Anti-Vision," Bataille points through the sacrificial act to "a reflexive modality of vision,"[29] by which she means the activation of different senses towards which Van Gogh himself gestures when he describes the first versions of sunflowers as "symphonies in blue and yellow" (combining the Impressionist technique of using complementary colors, blue and yellow, with a rhythmic brushstroke).

In later versions of the sunflower series, Van Gogh uses a yellow-on-yellow tonality (thicker layers of paint and exclusively yellow chromatics), while at the same time schematizing each blossom more distinctly: "he regularized the petal-like forms with greater clarity so that they align rhythmically with one another and contrast with the double-flowers' systematic impasto."[30] The intense yellow impression, especially of the last sunflower paintings, is thus due to an exposure of a yellow chromatics shaped through dynamic structures and formations, thereby giving the impression of a rhythmic, living performance.

Van Gogh himself reflects upon his sunflowers as animated and animating, a motif he acknowledges as his own.[31] In the format of a triptych, common to altarpieces, Van Gogh's last sunflower paintings are supposed to frame the

---

[25] See Martin Jay, *Downcast Eyes: The Denigration of Vision in Twentieth Century French Thought* (Berkeley: University of California Press, 1994), 224.

[26] "The sun in its glory is doubtless opposed to the faded sunflower, but no matter how dead it may be this sunflower is also the sun, and the sun is in some way deleterious and sick: it is sulfur colored [*il a la couleur du soufre*], the painter writes himself twice in French" (Georges Bataille, "Sacrificial Mutilation and the Severed Ear of Vincent van Gogh," in *Visions Of Excess: Selected Writings, 1927–1939* [Minneapolis: University of Minnesota Press, 1985], 66).

[27] Ibid., 63.

[28] See Eric Michaud, "Van Gogh, or The Insufficiency of Sacrifice," *October* 48 (1989): 39.

[29] Rosalind Krauss, "Antivision," *October* 36 (Spring 1986): 147.

[30] Druick and Zegers, *Van Gogh and Gauguin: The Studio of the South*, 271.

[31] In a letter to Gauguin, Van Gogh writes: "You talk to me in your letter about a canvas of mine, the sunflowers with a yellow background—to say that it would give you some pleasure to receive it. I don't think that you've made a bad choice—if Jeannin has the peony, Quost the hollyhock, I indeed, before others, have taken the sunflower" (Vincent van Gogh, Letter 739, To Paul Gauguin, Arles, Monday, 21 January 1889, http://vangoghletters.org/vg/letters/let739/letter.html [accessed December 12, 2012].

portrait of *La Berceuse* as "torches or candelabra," which enhance the yellow tones of the Berceuse's head: "And then the yellow and orange tones of the head take on more brilliance through the proximity of the yellow shutters."[32] Drawing attention to the yellow of *La Berceuse*'s forehead through the yellow of *The Sunflowers*, the sensation of enhancement itself is performed in high-key notes of yellow, in a movement between opposites: for *La Berceuse* (or "'our lullaby,' the woman by the cradle,"[33] as Van Gogh explains the meaning of the title) is the embodiment of a maternal image (beginnings) and yet, at the same time, is clearly marked by the signs of hard labor (her hands, her forehead) and exhaustion (endings).

The Yellow Christ: Van Gogh and Gauguin

The dozen sunflower canvases that Van Gogh envisioned reflect on the ideal of a "Pre-Raphaelite Brotherhood,"[34] which he saw in terms of a joint project with Gauguin.[35] Relating his work to the emblematic power of sunflowers (as exhibited in the art of the Pre-Raphaelites), Van Gogh bases his yellow imaginary, as it unfolds under the roof of the Yellow House, on contemporary movements. In Van Gogh's work, yellow is conceptualized as both a color *in movement* and as the color *of a movement* in his signature paintings of sunflowers—paintings that also framed the relationship to his collaborator Gauguin.

Although Gauguin's claim that he is the father of Van Gogh's monochrome-yellow scenarios cannot be considered accurate (for Van Gogh's yellow imagery goes back, as we have seen, to the *topoi* of yellow books and sunflowers), his comments on Van Gogh's yellow contributed to establishing yellow, as we said above, as Van Gogh's *metacolor*. Towards the end of his life, Gauguin comments on Van Gogh in his *Intimate Journals* (written on one of the Marquesas Islands) as follows:

> With all these yellow and violets, all this work in complementary colours, a disordered work on his part, he accomplished nothing but the mildest of incomplete and monotonous harmonies. The sound of

[32] Vincent van Gogh, Letter 776, To Theo van Gogh, Saint-Rémy-de-Provence, on or about Thursday, 23 May 1889, http://vangoghletters.org/vg/letters/let776/letter.html [accessed December 12, 2012].

[33] Vincent van Gogh, Letter 740, To Arnold Koning, Arles, on or about Tuesday, 22 January 1889, http://vangoghletters.org/vg/letters/let740/letter.html [accessed December 12, 2012].

[34] See Druick and Zegers, *Van Gogh and Gauguin*, 139.

[35] Ibid.

the trumpet was missing in them. I undertook the task of enlightening him—an easy matter, for I found a rich and fertile soil. […] From that day my Van Gogh made astonishing progress; he seemed to divine all that he had in him, and the result was that whole series of sun-effects over sun-effects in full sunlight.

Have you seen the portrait of the poet? The face and hair are chrome yellow (1). The clothes are chrome yellow (2). The necktie is chrome yellow (3) with an emerald scarf pin, on a background of chrome yellow (4). That is what an Italian painter said to me, and he added: "*Merde! merde!* Everything is yellow! I don't know what painting is any longer!"[36]

Despite Gauguin's condescending tone ("*my* Van Gogh made astonishing progress"),[37] the passage suggests an intertwinement of the memory of the painter-figure Van Gogh (whom Gauguin sees, as Artaud will, as a poet) with Gauguin's series of reflections on yellow figures in his paintings, most notably *The Yellow Christ*, 1889 (Color Plate 5), which he painted shortly after his collaboration with Van Gogh (from October to December 1888, in the southern French city of Arles). Gauguin refers here posthumously to Van Gogh's monochromatic use of yellow, which obviously also dominates *The Yellow Christ*; however, it is the title itself—its naming function—that actualizes the stigmatizing force of yellow. Naming a color and using a color are not equivalent gestures. The conjunction of "yellow" and "Christ" produces a singular meaning-effect that exceeds that of the mere perceptual fact of seeing a Christ-figure painted in yellow. The emphasis is rather on the emblematic dimension of the color yellow as the very theme of the painting.

In *The Yellow Christ*, Paul Gauguin thus revives the stigmata of the Jew, his entire body painted in yellow, on the cross. It represents the culminating point of the yellow iconography Gauguin had developed while working with Van Gogh in Arles. But despite their collaboration, Van Gogh's and Gauguin's techniques differed radically. Van Gogh uses thick layers of

[36] Paul Gauguin, *Gauguin's Intimate Journals*, trans. Van Wyck Brooks (Mineola, NY: Dover Publications, 1996), 10.

[37] Druick and Zegers point to Gauguin's condescending tone in this remark; moreover, Gauguin is painting *The Painter of Sunflowers* (1988) already towards their period of collaboration in the Yellow House and touches upon the question of creation and imitation. In *The Painter of Sunflowers* (1988), Gauguin presents Van Gogh painting five sunflowers in such a way that the painter seems to apply paint directly to the sunflowers in front of him, as Druick and Zegers argue (in *Van Gogh and Gauguin: The Studio of the South*, 240). Shown from a high angle, expressing the painter's (Gauguin's) superiority, and showing Van Gogh himself with distorted features, Gauguin formulates in *The Painter of Sunflowers* his critique of Van Gogh's realism. However, even in this rather sinister and critical portrait of Van Gogh, which also indicates the brewing tensions between the painters, Gauguin emphasizes the iconic status of Van Gogh's sunflowers.

chrome yellow to materialize the ambivalent forces of yellow: forces of life and light (seeds, sunflowers in blossom) as well as of decay (sunflowers dying, harvest). Gauguin, on the other hand, seeks to dematerialize the canvas by using thin layers of colors, levelling out the surface. Art historian Debora Silverman observes that

> the treatment of Christ's body is the most attenuated area of Gauguin's brushing on the canvas. The yellow color saturates the support and appears matted down, lacking texture and modeling, and almost fuses with the canvas as if a single unitary surface. [...] These technical strategies of suppressed surfaces had aimed to obliterate the distance between physical reality and the "non-corporeal" realm of the divine. [...] In *The Yellow Christ* form and content were [...] joined for the goal of visual and spiritual transcendence of the confines of physical materiality.[38]

Thus in *The Yellow Christ* Gauguin seeks to transcend physical reality by reconnecting with the luminous clarity of medieval and primitive paintings depicting visionary scenarios. Gauguin's emphasis on the non-corporeal allows for the intrusion of vision into the visual, that is, the creation of a single visual field with intense compression of near and far as well as acutely heightened color choices; sulfur yellow and orange convey the release from "worldly anchorage"[39] through the lack of texture and modelling, which, by dematerializing the canvas, releases the depicted figures to a realm of "metaphysical purity" (attained through suffering).

The three Bretonnes, cut off at the front of the painting, are mesmerized by the tragedy of the Crucifixion. Behind the stigmatized Jew on the cross, a man climbs over a wall, signifying the transition between the spiritual realm of the Crucifixion and the real world. The dividing line between both scenes is connected through the fiery red appearance of the trees, symbolically saturated with Christ's blood. The raw-boned Christ-figure, seen from a low angle against the sky, overshadows both realms. Christ, the spectacle towards which the three Bretonnes turn and to whom the fleeing man turns his back, is the medium, the interface, as Jacques Rancière argues, that "transfers the images into the text and the text into the images."[40] Rancière's emphasis on the words that install visibility is crucial to the understanding of Gauguin's painting, for it is the title "Yellow Christ"—the inscription—that is brought to life. Christ, a Jew, does not merely wear a yellow sign or a yellow cap; his

---

[38] Silverman: *Van Gogh and Gauguin*, 282–3.
[39] Ibid., 433.
[40] Jacques Rancière, *The Future of the Image*, trans. Gregory Elliott (London: Verso, 2007), 89.

whole body is painted in stigmatizing yellow. He is a stigma through and through.

The ambiguity of the transcendent and the real that structures the painting is the ambiguity of yellow itself as a victimary sign, which is both named and made visible as what W. J. T. Mitchell calls an *imagetext*. We can thus read this painting as exploiting the dual nature of yellow to figure the dual nature of the victim: the stigmatized aspect signifies disorder (the end of the Master's work and the dispersal of the disciples) and the divinized aspect signifies a shining new order (salvation). Through the color yellow, through its fundamental ambivalence as both stigmatism and enlightenment, Gauguin is able to figure the ambivalence of Christ as the victim-savior, the religious agitator who is also the founder of Christianity.

We might here invoke René Girard's concepts of scapegoating and sacrifice. According to Girard, the sacrificial victim has a dual nature: on the one hand, the marginalized figure set apart from the community and blamed for its ills (the scapegoat), and, on the other, the unifying force of this figure's sacrifice that makes possible a return to peace and order. According to Girard, this process is the product of collective misrecognition; the marginal figure is divinized: "the scapegoaters do not understand their own scapegoat mechanism, and they project upon their victim both their dissensions and their reconciliation. This is the double transference of the sacred which appears as both a source of disorder and a source of order. Its mythical embodiments are both malefactors and benefactors."[41] Thus what I am suggesting is that Gauguin, by way of a provocative representation of Christ as yellow, is able to perform, through pictorial representation, the essential ambivalence of the sacrificial victim, thereby rooting Christianity in the scapegoating practices of archaic religion. Therefore one can read Gauguin as showing, like Girard, that Christianity reveals the truth about the scapegoating process, its reliance on stigmatization and mystification. (And let us recall that the religious meaning of "stigma" itself embodies the dual meaning of yellow: the marks that appear on intensely devout individuals in a state of religious ecstasy and that recall the crucifixion wounds of Jesus are both painful and rapturous, a wound and a blessing).

In an earlier self-portrait (1888), Gauguin uses the inscription of the Christ-like figure of Jean Valjean from Victor Hugo's epic novel *Les Misérables* to evoke yellow stigmata. In his novel, Hugo describes Valjean as being forced to bear a "papier jaune," a yellow paper, indicating his ex-convict status. From this early sign of exclusion Valjean will be converted

---

[41] René Girard, *The Girard Reader*, ed. James G. Williams (New York: Crossroad, 1996), 118.

to a new life through the priest's gift of the candlesticks; this conversion from victim to savior is thus effectively figured through yellow, as the color of both light and exclusion. Indeed, Jean Valjean is presented as a Christ-like figure throughout the novel; his trajectory from society's victim to society's redeemer is carefully calibrated. Gauguin saw Valjean as the archetypal modern victim with whom he could identify. Commenting on his *Self-Portrait with Portrait of Bernard* (1888), Gauguin writes:

> It is the face of an outlaw, ill-clad and powerful like Jean Valjean—with an inner nobility and gentleness. The face is flushed, the eyes accented by the surrounding colors of a furnace-fire. This is to represent the volcanic flames that animate the soul of the artist [...] The girlish background, with its childlike flowers is there to attest our artistic purity. As for this Jean Valjean whom society has oppressed—cast out [...] In endowing him with my features I offer you as well as an image of myself a portrait of all the wretched victims of society.[42]

The yellow background of the self-portrait thematizes the victimary sign as the stigmatized/divinized aspect of the artist. Like Valjean, the artist identifies with the outcast, Jean-Valjean, who is both elevated and excluded—who is elevated by his exclusion.

Self-Portrait—Les Misérables integrates three figures: Gauguin himself in the foreground, Emil Bernard as a portrait on the wall (a painting within the painting), and Vincent van Gogh, whose name appears at the bottom in the dedication. The three artists, who collaborated together in the Yellow House in Arles, France, form an artistic threesome. A year later, in *Self-Portrait with Yellow Christ*, 1889 (Color Plate 6), Gauguin also evokes a kind of "Trinity" or cross-imagery, showing himself in the middle, framed by the citation of *The Yellow Christ* on the left side and a depiction of a mug with primitive art on the right, pointing to himself as an artist torn between the savage, the primitive, and the divine. Gauguin's self-portrait is placed at the center of the painting, over a split background: on the left side, a detail of *The Yellow Christ*; on the right, a red mug that harks back to his painting *Les Misérables*, in which his face also appears in red. Gauguin's quotations of different media and realms—the realm of the spiritual in the figure of Christ; the artistic realm in the self-portraits of the artist—create a crescendo effect, in which the Passion of Christ is transformed into the passion of the artist, depicted as a wretched victim. The red trees of *The Yellow Christ* are replaced by the redness of the artist himself.

In his last painting in the series of Christ-paintings, *Christ in the Garden*

---

[42] Gauguin, quoted in Silverman, *Van Gogh and Gauguin*, 32.

of Gethsemane (1889), the Christ-figure carries Gauguin's features:[43] his red beard, red hair, and his nose evoke "Christ's bloody sweat in the garden,"[44] in an abstract red that expresses the "suffering and defeat of the ideal, with the sacred *surnaturelle* as the prefigured blood on the head of the Savior rebuked, a hunched and limp body to be redeemed only by sacrifice."[45] Gauguin sent a sketch of his Gethsemane painting to Van Gogh, in which he also exposes the supernatural red color on the head of the savior/artist, provoking a harsh reaction from Van Gogh, who saw Gauguin's (and Bernard's) return to religious subjects as "decline rather than progress," affirming that "with me there is no question of doing anything from the Bible."[46] Instead, Van Gogh's counter-imagery to Gauguin's supernaturalism (inspired by Provençal Catholic culture) is found in a series of female portraits such as *La Berceuse* "to which he attributed a specifically consolational and spiritual function."[47]

What Gauguin is figuring in the religious imagery of his Pont-Aven paintings such as *The Yellow Christ* is a moment of detachment, which he visualizes through the flatness and clear-cut background of the figures, making them appear motionless. Commenting on Gauguin's *The Vision after the Sermon*, Rancière sees the textual dimension of Gauguin's religious allegories as primary: "forms do not proceed without the words that install them in visibility."[48] Gauguin's visual and linguistic figures of the "Yellow Christ" and "Jean Valjean" reveal a form of spiritualism in abstraction,[49] in contrast to the "metamorphoses of matter," or "matterism,"[50] that

---

[43] Druick and Zegers interpret the red hair as a reference to Van Gogh, arguing that Van Gogh portrayed himself "as a member of the van Gogh family of redheads in the context of a subject that Vincent had twice failed to realize"; they continue: "Gauguin scarcely disguised his strategy. He recognized that Vincent's destroyed Gethsemane canvases had been self-portraits—at least allusively, through the artist's personal investment in the Gethsemane theme, if not more literally, as Vincent may well have depicted a Christ who bore some resemblance to himself. Gauguin's *Christ in the Garden of Olives* both unmasks and wrests away this identity, appropriating it along with the spiritualized ideal of a discipleship of painters to which it belonged" (Druick and Zegers, *Van Gogh and Gauguin*, 291).

[44] Silverman, *Van Gogh and Gauguin*, 300.

[45] Ibid.

[46] Vincent van Gogh, Letter 823, To Theo van Gogh, Saint-Rémy-de-Provence, Tuesday, 26 November 1889, http://vangoghletters.org/vg/letters/let823/letter.html [accessed December 12, 2012].

[47] Silverman, *Van Gogh and Gauguin*, 312.

[48] Jacques Rancière, *The Future of the Image*, 88.

[49] Rancière points in this context to Kandinsky's notion of the spiritual in art: "In the space of visibility that his text constructs for it, Gauguin's painting is already a painting of the sort Kandinsky would paint and justify: a surface where lines and colors have become expressive signs obeying the single constraint of 'internal necessity'" (ibid., 87).

[50] The opposition between "idealism" and "matterism," which Rancière tracks back to the "old controversy over drawing and color" (ibid., 86), leads him with respect to Gauguin

characterizes Van Gogh's "kinetic aggressiveness,"[51] which is emphasized through the interplay of color, texture and fabric. Thus in Van Gogh, the clear-cut lines are rather whirling movements, in which every brush-stroke is "sculpting time" (to use Russian film director and theorist Andrei Tarkovsky's term), to gain access to a temporality of the now. Cutting into the thickness of the color yellow, the enactment of this time-pressure through texture creates a fluidity that transgresses the visual aspect of the image. The performance of movement is thus thematized in texture and color, towards a form of inscription, which "circulates across the media of sculpture, painting, and verbal narrative."[52]

In Van Gogh's *The Sower*, the citron-yellow spectacle of the burning sun beats down on the figure of the sower. The seeds materialize in the emanating rays of the sun depicted in a multi-layered chrome yellow, through which Van Gogh saw himself celebrating Christ as an "aesthetic force."[53] Van Gogh writes about Christ as a sower:

> He lived serenely, as a greater artist than all other artists, despising marble and clay as well as color, working in living flesh. That is to say this matchless artist [...] made neither statues, nor pictures, nor books; he loudly proclaimed that he made [...] living men, immortals. [...] Though this real artist—Christ—disdained writing books on ideas (sensations) he surely disdained the spoken word much less—particularly the parable. (What a sower, what a harvest, what a fig tree! etc.).[54]

Van Gogh approaches the divine as embodied, not mediated. Christ's art was, in Van Gogh's view, that of *agir-créer*, "action-creation."[55] Through the idea of Christ, Van Gogh shifts away from the notion of individual bodies. Instead, Van Gogh's figures of the sower, the reaper, the artist on his way to

to the conclusion that a new correspondence between words and images is established, in which words are made into images (ibid., 87). Rancière's emphasis on the primacy of the word is thereby, I would argue, not accidentally shown with respect to Gauguin (and Kandinsky). In opposition, Van Gogh's insistence on the "matterism" of a "living yellow" reinscribes yellow into an imagetext driven by its haptic aspect.

[51] Ibid., 206.
[52] Mitchell, "The Future of the Image: Rancière's Road Not Taken" (*Culture, Theory and Critique* 50, vol. 2–3 [2009]: 140). Mitchell's argument for the primacy of the image, the archaic sign, in opposition to Rancière's emphasis on the primacy of the word, marks two different approaches to the "future of the image." However, as I imply in my analysis of Gauguin's and Van Gogh's late work, Van Gogh's colorism, his matterism, is clearly resisting the form of abstraction (and dependence on the word) that Gauguin performs in his approach to color.
[53] Ibid., 176.
[54] Ibid., 175–6.
[55] Ibid., 176.

work are de-centered subjects; driven by the rhythm of their movement, they are dramatized in yellow as a cyclical process of beginnings and endings.

The movement from the motif of the sower to that of the reaper, from sunflowers to paintings of cypresses, is itself a cyclical movement in Van Gogh's work, shifting the focus towards emblematic motifs of death (the reaper, cypresses), often expressed through a "vertiginous visual movement"[56] of swirling forms. Painted from the perspective of a worker in a field, Van Gogh's W*heatfield with a Reaper*, 1889 (Color Plate 7), refers the figure of the reaper to the larger community of laborers. With a scythe in one hand and a sickle in the other, the reaper is reaping the wheat like a devil, while nevertheless giving the impression of "almost smiling":[57]

> Phew—the reaper is finished, I think it will be one that you'll place in your home—it's an image of death as the great book of nature speaks to us about it—but what I sought is the 'almost smiling.' It's all yellow except for a line of violet hills—a pale, blond yellow. I myself find that funny, that I saw it like that through the iron bars of a cell.[58]

The idea of a celebration of death is suggested by the golden tones of the ripe wheat in high-key notes of yellow. Van Gogh observes of this painting: "It is—if you like—the opposite of that sower I tried before. But there's nothing sad in this death. It goes its way in broad daylight, the sun flooding everything with a light of pure gold."[59] In the first version of *Wheatfield with a Reaper*, Van Gogh "aimed for radiance."[60] Similarly, as in *The Sower*, the figure of the reaper is as yellow as the sun and the wheat itself; the sun is hugging the mountains in the same way as the reaper seems to be embedded in the swirling movement of the wheat. As a "new exercise in yellow," Douglas Druick sees the canvas as evidence of Van Gogh's continued engagement with Gauguin.[61] However, in the replica of the painting, painted shortly after the first version in September 1889, Van Gogh tones down the chromatic scale and in the process the oppositional color schemes as well.[62]

---

[56] Silverman, *Van Gogh and Gauguin*, 413.

[57] Van Gogh quotes Théophile Silvestre's expression of death "almost smiling," which Silvestre coined in his tribute to the life and work of Delacroix: "So died, almost smiling, Ferdinand, Victor, Eugène Delacroix, painter of the first order, who had a sun in his head and a storm in his heart" (quoted in Elsphet Davies, *Portrait of Delacroix* [Edinburgh: Pentland Press, 1994], 193).

[58] Vincent van Gogh, Letter 800, To Theo van Gogh, Saint-Rémy-de-Provence, Thursday, 5 and Friday, 6 September 1889, http://vangoghletters.org/vg/letters/let800/letter.html [accessed December 4, 2012].

[59] Ibid.

[60] Judy Sund, *Van Gogh* (London: Phaidon Press, 2002), 253.

[61] Druick and Zegers, *Van Gogh and Gauguin*, 289.

[62] Sund, *Van Gogh*, 252.

While the figure of the reaper remains, it is his reaping activity that is emphasized. The sensation of chopping is enhanced through the dull contrasts and
the alignment of reaper, tree, and sun in the second version of the painting,
thus exposing yellow as a life-taking force. The reaper is thus the pendant to
the bursting of energy (sunflowers, sower): he is chopping off life, celebrating
death in half-tones of yellow. If Van Gogh's still lifes of yellow books *(Piles of
French Novels, Parisian Novels)* are programmatic for interweaving his work
into a collective notion of a "culture of yellow" in late modernity, *Wheatfield
with a Reaper* programmatically reflects on Van Gogh's path-breaking
confrontation with endings (the wilting of the sunflowers that intensifies the
meaning of the reaper).

The path that the reaper has already chopped out and the mounting
wheat surrounding him open up a future dimension, signified by the
myriad paths and roadways that cut through Van Gogh's series of wheatfield
paintings. However, only in *Wheatfield with a Reaper* is the path part of
the reaper's reaping activity: it announces death in the midst of the golden
wheat that is about to be chopped off. Through the insistence on movements
between bursting and reaping, radiance (blossoming) and withering (dying),
Van Gogh's *metacolor* strikes as a color in relentless movement between
opposites, constantly announcing and thematizing death in the midst of life
(in blossom, ripe).

However, the vitality of Van Gogh's yellow is certainly first and
foremost defined by the heated atmosphere that courses through his
work. The sun at the center of bright circular brushstrokes creates what
Bataille called in 1937 "boiling points" in Van Gogh's work.[63] Van Gogh's
dramatization of a heated atmosphere in his paintings has been reflected
upon as an oscillation between an internal condition (his feverish
temperament) and the explosiveness of an external condition (which Van
Gogh sensed and expressed in settings such as one sees in the painting
Night Cafe [1888]). Already during Van Gogh's lifetime, Van Gogh's
use of color is described by the critic and painter G. Albert Aurier as a
"burning flame," reflecting the "feverish temperament" of the artist: "it is
matter and all of Nature frenetically contorted [...] raised to the heights
of exacerbation; it is form, becoming nightmare; color, becoming flame,

---

[63] "Vincent Van Gogh belongs not to art history, but to the bloody myth of our existence
as humans. He is of that rare company who, in a world spellbound by stability, by sleep,
suddenly reached the terrible 'boiling point' without which all that claims to endure
becomes insipid, intolerable, declines. For this 'boiling point' has meaning not only for
him who attains it, but for all, even though all may not yet perceive that which binds
man's savage destiny to radiance, to explosion, to flame, and only thereby to power"
(Georges Bataille, "Van Gogh as Prometheus," *October* 36 [1986]: 60).

lava, and precious stone; light turning into conflagration; life into burning fever."[64] Especially after the Second World War, Aurier's notion of Van Gogh's transformation of life into heat, into a "burning fever," becomes a *topos* in the reception of Van Gogh's work. This can be seen, in particular, in the work of Francis Bacon.

After the burning: Francis Bacon and Van Gogh

Although widely considered to be the humanistic icon of modern art, Van Gogh has been reinterpreted largely according to the anti- or post-humanist proclivities of twentieth-century writers and artists. In particular, his singular artistic technique—cutting into thick layers of monochrome yellow—has been the subject of much reevaluation. In his six *Studies for a Portrait of van Gogh* (1956–7), Francis Bacon pays homage to Van Gogh's *Painter on his Way to Tarascon* (1888), a painting that was destroyed in a fire in Dresden during World War II. Working from reproductions of the painting, Bacon's homage to Van Gogh drama-tizes the artist's "boiling points," transforming the walking artist into a burnt landscape, accelerating his walk downhill through a scratching technique that refers back to Van Gogh's own technique of cutting into thick layers of color. What is important to know about Bacon's art is its ability to forge a middle path between the extremes of the purely *optical* code of abstract art and the *optical-haptic* code of abstract expressionism, which "dissolve[s] all forms in a fluid and chaotic texture of manual lines and colors."[65]

Conceived during Van Gogh's "yellow period," *The Painter on his Way to Tarascon* anticipates the paintings conceived in Arles, during Van Gogh's collaboration with Paul Gauguin. *The Painter* depicts the artist on his way to work, identifying art with labor and, moreover, with a work in progress, thereby thematizing the idea of the creative process. Furthermore, as an image of Van Gogh himself at work, it particularizes and personalizes what might otherwise be taken as a general or universal idea. However, to the extent that Van Gogh is himself a symbol or icon of humanist art (even if, as we will see, his work suggests a dialectic between the human and non-human), a synecdochal aspect is nonetheless present.

[64] G.-Albert Aurier, "The Isolated Ones: Vincent van Gogh," *Mercure de France* (1890), http://www.vggallery.com/misc/archives/aurier.htm [accessed November 8, 2011].
[65] Daniel W. Smith, introduction to Gilles Deleuze, *Francis Bacon: The Logic of Sensation*, trans. Daniel W. Smith (Minneapolis: University of Minnesota Press, 2003), xiii.

Bacon's homage to Van Gogh in his *Study for a Portrait of van Gogh I* (Color Plate 8) is much darker—literally and figuratively—than its model: the Mediterranean sunlight gives way to a coal-like hue; in fact, the landscape appears to be as burnt as the body of the artist himself. Van Gogh's head, easel, and equipment shine through in yellow; it is Van Gogh's deathly appearance that is stressed, "perhaps even caused, by the bodily landscape, which is not distinct enough to frame it."[66] The heated atmosphere surrounding Van Gogh's work suggests a burning sensation: the figure of the walking painter, his body, and the surrounding landscape appear to have been burnt—a burnt bodyscape.[67] Thus the burning of Van Gogh's *living yellow* in his sunflowers and wheat fields appears, in Bacon's rendition, to be transformed into a *deadly* yellow.

While the subdued colors of the first *Study* are followed by an explosion of color in the subsequent works of the series,[68] the shadow of the artist stands out despite the darkness of this first *Study*, just as it did, rather boldly, in Van Gogh's original, thereby invoking a metaphorical interpretation of the artist as the one who casts shadows (influence) even at night, that is, even without an external source of illumination. In effect, Bacon's *Study* is itself a "shadow" of Van Gogh's *The Painter*, in the double sense of being influenced and being literally "darker" than its model. Throughout Bacon's work, shadows "subvert the classical distribution of light in painting and undermine the mimetic function"; "the shadows in the portraits are not extensions of the subject but a part of its reality."[69] In *Study for a Portrait of van Gogh I*, the shadow is part of the burning reality that affects the painter and his surroundings, so that the body of the painter almost seems to melt into the shadow. Instead of unfolding the life story of Van Gogh the painter, Bacon unfolds the story of his "death-to-come."[70] In imitation of Van Gogh's famous jagged style, Bacon uses scratching and cutting techniques that appear even more violent than those of his model. Broad brushstrokes plow across the canvas; the paint is heaped on thickly in an expressive style that is considered exceptional in Bacon's work.

---

[66] Ernst van Alphen, *Francis Bacon and the Loss of Self* (Cambridge, MA: Harvard University Press, 1993), 144.

[67] The dark colors of the burnt bodyscape reverse Van Gogh's treatment of the body as landscape, characteristic of his self-portraits: "Bacon, in contrast, makes the space that surrounds van Gogh in the van Gogh series into a metaphor of the body" (ibid., 144).

[68] Michael Peppiatt comments on the explosion of color after the first *Study*: "Suddenly Bacon's chill interior world of dark blue drapes and tubular structures spills out into an even more pitiless exterior where the light shares flesh and vegetation black" (in *Francis Bacon: Anatomy of an Enigma* [London: Weidenfeld & Nicolson, 1996], 167).

[69] Hannah Westley, *The Body as Medium and Metaphor* (Amsterdam: Rodophi, 2008), 87.

[70] Ibid.

The process of dehumanizing the body culminates in a dissolution of facial features, a becoming face-less. But this dissolution is then reinfused with a new, non-human content; for the wandering figure's face in Bacon's painting manifests ape-like features—a procedure that recalls Gilles Deleuze's idea of a "Body without Organs."[71] Inspired by a line in Antonin Artaud, this notion is developed extensively in Deleuze's and Guattari's *Mille Plateaux*: *Capitalisme et schizophrénie 2*;[72] it refers to a *virtual* body, that is, a body that transcends the limits of actual bodily being. The "Body without Organs" thus generates alternative notions of becoming, such as becoming animal, becoming woman, becoming molecule, etc., which are made possible by the disorganization of the body. However, becoming animal does not mean becoming "like an animal," but rather signifies the possibility of an exchange of energies between human and animal existences, forming alliances and potentialities. Constructed out of intensities, the "Body without Organs" forms "plateaus" ("productive connections between immanently arrayed material systems without reference to an external governing source").[73]

The body of the artist is such a "Body without Organs": what seems at first to be a facial mask reveals itself as the head of an ape. In effect, Bacon is performing an anthropomorphism in reverse: the human takes on the attributes of the animal—a *devolution*, through which the shadow of the artist hovers between man and animal. The dialectic between the yellow animal and burnt man alternates between structure and chaos, chromatic and achromatic color, or non-color. Deleuze's question concerning the alternation between opposites is a propos: "How to render the nonvisible visible in painting, or the nonsonorous sonorous in music?"[74] Deleuze treats this question from the perspective of the "diagram":

> The diagram is the operative set of traits and color-patches, of lines and zones. Van Gogh's diagram, for example, is the set of straight and curved hatch marks that raise and lower the ground, twist the trees, make the sky palpitate, and which assume a particular intensity from 1888 onward. [...] The diagram is indeed a chaos, a catastrophe, but is

---

[71] See also Inge Arteel, *Gefaltet, Entfaltet. Strategien der Subjektwerdung in Friederike Mayröcker's Prosa 1988–1998* (Bielefeld: Aisthesis Verlag, 2007), 56–65. However, while Arteel uses the work of Deleuze to establish a theory of the subject (*Subjekttheorie*) in Mayröcker's work, I propose to shift the focus away from a subject-oriented approach towards a non-human aesthetics.

[72] Deleuze and Guattari, *Mille Plateaux: Capitalisme et schizophrénie 2* (Paris: Minuit, 1980), 198.

[73] Daniel Smith and John Protevi, "Gilles Deleuze," *The Stanford Encyclopedia of Philosophy* (Spring 2013 Edition), Edward N. Zalta ed., http://plato.stanford.edu/archives/spr2013/entries/deleuze/ [accessed February 9, 2013].

[74] Daniel Smith, Introduction to Deleuze, *Francis Bacon*, xxiii.

also a germ of order and rhythm. [...] As Bacon says, it "unlocks areas of sensation." The diagram ends the preparatory work and begins the act of painting.[75]

Referencing both Van Gogh and Bacon, Deleuze describes the dialectic between chaos and rhythm as a necessary process that prepares the creative act. The rhythmic order that emerges out of catastrophe, out of its chaos, becomes in Van Gogh and Bacon visible in their way of modulating color. Deleuze sees the "coloring sensation" as the essence of Bacon's and Van Gogh's logic of sensation. As a burning sensation, the heated glowing matter of yellow that Van Gogh modulated into a life story (by confronting the vital sensations with the brevity of life) is in Bacon transformed into a story of "a death-to-come." The reversal of Van Gogh's color scheme from monochrome-yellow to the greyness of ashes emblematizes the perception of Van Gogh's work as that of a visionary who foreshadowed the catastrophes of the twentieth century. Thus it is almost as if the burnings of the Holocaust and of Hiroshima were inscribed in Bacon's grey ashes, which in turn were prefigured by Van Gogh's apocalyptic yellow scenarios.

Reading Bacon and Van Gogh with Friederike Mayröcker

In addition to Deleuze, Bacon's transformation of Van Gogh's painter into a faceless, dehumanized figure also becomes the subject of a prose piece by the Viennese writer Friederike Mayröcker, entitled "Vincent van Gogh: 'Painter on his Way to Tarascon'/Francis Bacon: 'Study for a Portrait of van Gogh I.'"[76] In her essay, Mayröcker attempts to create what she calls "parallel texts," in which painterly and writerly approaches to Van Gogh's work come into dialogue with one another. Creating parallels between artists, writers, and philosophers, in an interactive process—that is, one in which a network of references dissolves the subject matter of the text into relationships, structures, recurring motifs, and couplings—allows Mayröcker to dilute works of their "content"[77] and to stage sensations such Van Gogh's yellow.

---

[75] Deleuze, *Foucault*, trans. Sean Hand (Minneapolis: University of Minnesota Press, 1988), 83.

[76] Friederike Maröcker, "Vincent van Gogh: 'Maler auf dem Weg nach Tarascon'/Francis Bacon: 'Studie zu Porträt von van Gogh I'," in *Gesammelte Prosa, Band 5: 1996–2001*, ed. Klaus Reichert (Frankfurt/Main: Suhrkamp, 2007).

[77] These forms of abstraction shatter a narrative approach to art. Instead, Mayröcker adopts a performative approach centered on percepts and affects, placing her own writing in a direct parallel with the art of Francis Bacon, an artist who is mentioned

In constantly changing scenarios, the artist figure on his way to work is described as walking on an increasingly tortuous path illuminated by Van Gogh's cutting technique, which is dramatized as a blinding, monochrome yellow landscape.[78]

Constantly in flux and in movement, Mayröcker uses multiple points of view to bring out different color sensations, tonalities, and modulations through the appearance, shape, and hue of yellow plants. Surrounding the walking figure of the painter, there are the "leaves of corn cobs,"[79] "corn fields,"[80] "glowing microbes (corn cobs),"[81] "corn hassocks"[82] and "corn grass,"[83] often in combination with yellowish "blades of reed."[84] These are characterized by the sharpness and pointiness of their shape and yellow color, thereby creating an alliance between haptic and optical sensations. Moreover, the corn cob (*Maiskolben*) suggests a biographical reference to Van Gogh—since *Kolben* in German also means (owing to its shape) "revolver," alluding to the fact that Van Gogh took his life with a revolver on an open wheatfield, a scenario prefigured in his *Wheat Fields with Reaper at Sunrise* (1889). The leitmotif of "corn cobs," in its reference to the color yellow and the shape of the revolver, creates a nexus between life and work, art and death, as well as image and word.

A grid of vertical lines and elementary contrasts dissolves into the color grey, the color of ash, the dominant color of Bacon's *Study for a Portrait of van Gogh I*. The ash-grey that dominates Bacon's painting is thereby dramatized, towards the end of the prose piece, in the contrasting elements of flames and water that animate the verticality that Mayröcker thematizes in a *scène en abîme* invoking Bacon:

> The upwards-, and downwards-pictures, the YELLOW PICTURES THROAT PICTURES YELLOW THROAT PICTURES, and through the ghost of light, with cloth and rag bloody at foot and ear, what

quite frequently in her works of this period, particularly in her novel *brütt oder Die seufzenden Gärten* (Frankfurt/Main: Suhrkamp, 1998).

[78] Tellingly, in Mayröcker's text, the voice of a woman (who is never named) describes Bacon's *Study for a Portrait of van Gogh I* to a blind man. Towards the end of the text, the figure of the blind man seems to merge into the figure of Joseph, a recurrent interlocutor in Mayröcker's work, who appears in *brütt oder Die seufzenden Gärten* in the role of the absent lover. The color yellow, Van Gogh's signature color, emerges as a common thread, for its presence unifies the "scenarios" that organize Mayröcker's text.

[79] "Maiskolbenblätter" (ibid., 420).

[80] "Maisfelder" (ibid).

[81] "leuchtenden Mikroben (Maiskolben)" (ibid).

[82] "Maisgrasbüschel" (ibid., 423).

[83] "Maisgras" (ibid., 424).

[84] "Schilfgras" (ibid., 421).

do I know, foot and snow, loincloth and hand, scream and song of mourning.[85]

Parallels and verticals cross each other at this intersection, which can be read as a formulaic form of abstraction for the coupling of sensations: "YELLOW PICTURES" plus "THROAT PICTURES" add up to "YELLOW THROAT PICTURES." Mayröcker's abstract formula opens up a third dimension along the vertical lines of the pictures, a formula Mayröcker defines as "upwards- und downwards-pictures." The up- and down-movement leads into the depth of the throat, into the "throat pictures" that are described as shining through specters of light. Accompanied by the sound of screams and whimpering, the immateriality of light is contrasted with the appearance of a bleeding foot and ear.

The scenario of a wounded and screaming body recalls a familiar theme in Bacon's work, which appears most famously in his series of *Screaming Popes*.[86] Implacable downward movements characterize Bacon's images of screaming heads, as in his *Study after Velazquez's Portrait of Pope Innocent X*, in which vertical brushstrokes lead into and through the open mouth, as if pulling the whole body into an abyss. The verticality of the scratches in the contrasting colors of yellow and violet (similar to Bacon's *Study for a Portrait of van Gogh I*, where yellow shines through the vertical lines of grey scratches) lead into the depth of the throat, being all but a scream—which resonates in its verticality with Mayröcker's expression of "upwards- and downwards pictures," further specified as "THROAT PICTURES."

In Bacon's (and Mayröcker's) emphasis on the vertical dimension, the scream that has neither origin nor *telos* is unleashed as a primal force, made visible through the use of vertical lines.[87] Vertical lines thus lead downward

---

[85] Ibid., 422.

[86] The recurrent motif of screaming mouths was inspired by different sources, including medical texts and photographic stills of the nurse in Sergei Eisenstein's film *The Battleship Potemkin* (1925). Bacon first saw the film in 1935, and kept a photographic still of the scene that showed a close-up of the nurse's head in a panic scream with broken spectacles hanging from her blood-stained face. The close-up of the screaming mouth is one of the centerpieces of the montage of up- and downward-movements that Eisenstein used in the famous Odessa steps scene, which depicts with brutal force the army massacring the masses on its way down the steps. Edward Munch's *The Scream* is also an often-mentioned reference. Wieland Schmied comments: "But whereas Munch portrays nature as a giant ear that seems to conserve the sound-waves, the vaults of Bacon's Vatican only reflect the noise of the scream and cannot contain or preserve it" (*Francis Bacon: Commitment and Conflict* [New York: Prestel, 1996], 21).

[87] Bacon stated that he chose the portrait of the Pope because it allowed him to use the color purple (like Velazquez), in contrast to yellow.

in a process of accumulating sensations;[88] however, without elevating the figure (of the Pope, in this case), the accumulation of color and throat in Mayröcker rather pulls everything into the open mouth, into the "black hole" of the scream. The figure of the Pope is driven by an invisible, extrinsic force that affects the body, becoming visible through the tortured, deformed body.

In Mayröcker's formula of "YELLOW THROAT PICTURES," the coloring sensation is modulated through its coupling with the organ of the throat; however, the coagulation of color and throat does not synthesize sound and color. Instead, the color yellow is synthesized with the sound-producing organ, is becoming an organ, the organ of the scream. Whereas the scream itself in Mayröcker's text is deferred, the scream in Bacon's painting is silenced through the surrounding drapes and dark colors. In both cases, we are confronted with a potential screaming power announced by the organ of the scream, which pulls downwards into the verticality of the abyss, the abyss of the YELLOW THROAT.

Conjoining the color yellow with the organ that produces the scream, Mayröcker defers the synthesis of scream (sound) and color, thereby also deferring the synthesis of sound and vision. Instead, Mayröcker's "musical score," as she announces her piece in the opening, offers us a "haptic sight" of the throat and its screaming potential—or what could be described as *haptic sound*, following the logic of the "haptic sense of sight."[89]

The double coupling of vision/touch and sound/touch in Mayröcker reveals the haptic dimension to be a reductive process: reducing, as it were, the modern myths of the artist (Van Gogh) and of humanistic art forms to a non-human aesthetics, stripped bare of the spiritual, of the humanistic ideal of unity. Mayröcker dissolves the artist-figure into the materiality of the painting itself, into its colors, shapes, and lines.[90] In the process of coupling sensations, Van Gogh's yellow becomes the "relational matrix"[91]—that is, the *metacolor* of Van Gogh's work and its afterlife.

---

[88] Referring to Bacon's own words, Deleuze remarks: "Every sensation and every figure is already 'accumulated,' 'coagulated' sensation as in a limestone figure. Hence the irreducibly synthetic character of sensation" (Deleuze, *Francis Bacon*, 134).

[89] "There is indeed a creative taste in color, in the different regimes of color, which constitute a properly visual sense of touch, or haptic sense of sight" (Deleuze, *Francis Bacon*, 123).

[90] The reduction and dehumanization of the mythological figure reveals Mayröcker's artistic process of *décollage*, with which she creates a parallel with the cutting technique of Van Gogh himself.

[91] Manning, *Politics of Touch*, xiii.

The afterlife of Van Gogh: Antonin Artaud, Alain Resnais and Akira Kurosawa

Throughout the twentieth century, the artist-figure of Van Gogh has embodied the idea of self-destruction. This is expressed no more explicitly— nor more powerfully—than in Antonin Artaud's pamphlet "Van Gogh, Man Suicided by Society," which indicts what he sees as the social and institutional forces responsible for Van Gogh's suicide. The brotherly identification with Van Gogh allows Artaud to articulate his artistic principles in the form of an outcry against social ills.

Writing in response to an exhibition of Van Gogh, which, in Artaud's view, commodified the Van Gogh myth, Artaud finds himself compelled to expose the destructive forces threatening Van Gogh and his work (as well as his own). Artaud's demonstration of Van Gogh as being "suicided by society" leads to a deconstruction of the spiritual notion of "breath" as inspiration (the Greek term *enthousiasmos* means the "breathing in" of the divine). However, it is Van Gogh's breathing organ, the throat itself, that Artaud dramatizes as being tortured when he describes Van Gogh's "magic force of a thought" as a "sulphurous insemination" of a nail that is "turning in the gullet of the only passage with which van Gogh, tetanized, van Gogh, suspended over the chasm of breath, painted."[92] Physically tortured and dehumanized, the breath of inspiration is demystified, as it were, and yet is also thematized through the torturous nail with which Artaud seems to evoke the carving and cutting technique that Van Gogh introduced to painting. The chiasmic entanglement of external forces (nail, cutting, carving) and internal forces (the breath of inspiration) describe visionary powers that transgress the medium of representation.

Artaud refuses to comment directly on Van Gogh's paintings. Instead, he comments on Van Gogh's own descriptions of his paintings, formulated in his letters—descriptions that Artaud presents as being so powerful that Van Gogh's texts are becoming his paintings, while his paintings appear to be more natural than nature itself. In Artaud's view, Van Gogh does not render nature artistically; his paintings become nature:

> So I shall not describe a painting of van Gogh after van Gogh, but I shall say that van Gogh is a painter because he recollected nature, because he respired it and made it sweat, because he squeezed onto his canvases

[92] Antonin Artaud, "Van Gogh, the Man Suicided by Society," in *Antonin Artaud: Selected Writings*, ed. Susan Sontag (Berkeley and Los Angeles: University of California Press, 1988), 493.

in clusters, in monumental sheaves of color, the grinding of elements that occurs once in a hundred years, the awful elementary pressure of apostrophes, scratches, commas, and dashes which, after him, one can no longer believe that natural appearances are not made of.[93]

The forcefulness with which Artaud sees Van Gogh creates a syntax of apostrophes and commas on the canvas, which transform the media of writing and painting, and even of representation, by becoming nature. Representations and appearances of nature are de-structured, laying bare the underlying forces.

Equipped with a visionary lucidity, Van Gogh thus achieves in Artaud's view a metaphysical transformation by confronting the cruelty of the world with his own cruelty, following the Gnostic principle of adding evil to evil, thereby overcoming or transcending it:

A stormy sky,
A chalk-white field,
Canvases, brushes, his red hair, tubes, his yellow hand, his easel, but all the lamas of Tibet gathered together can shake out of their skirts the apocalypse they will have prepared, van Gogh will have given us a whiff of its nitrogen peroxide in advance, in a painting which contains just enough of the sinister to force us to reorient.[94]

With the reference to "red hair" and a "yellow hand," Artaud dramatizes Van Gogh in the colors of Tibetan Buddhist monks (differentiating the two major schools of the "Red Hats" and the "Yellow Hats"); however, even more important than the color pattern is the chemical set-up, Van Gogh's "whiff of its nitrogen peroxide," with which rockets are fueled; for it burns on contact without a separate ignition source. Van Gogh embodies the fire of the apocalypse: Artaud transforms his appearance with red hair and yellow hands into the appearance of a flame, evoking the burning of the world around him.

Artaud's intertwinement of inner and outer worlds undoes both painting and writing in a performance of Van Gogh, the artist and man, as the embodiment of an apocalyptic vision, a body in flames—an image that inspired the short film *Van Gogh* (1948) by French director Alain Resnais, which he was completing at the time of Artaud's death.[95] By focusing solely on Van Gogh's paintings, following Van Gogh's path from The Netherlands to the South of France, dramatized through a rhythmic montage of close-ups

[93] Ibid., 499.
[94] Ibid., 503.
[95] See Dudley Andrew, *Opening Bazin* (Oxford: Oxford University Press, 2011), 162.

and travelling shots, Resnais's film leads to an increasing acceleration that culminates in black film. In this acceleration, focusing on Van Gogh's last paintings, Resnais's shot-reverse-shot technique dramatizes the relationship between hand and eye, bringing inner (vision) and outer worlds into closer and closer proximity: in close-up shots of Van Gogh's eyes (as depicted in his self-portraits), of the reaper's and the sower's hand, and of the raised hand of Martha at the deathbed of Lazarus (in one of Van Gogh's adaptations of Rembrandt's paintings), the montage inhabits the interstice between eye and hand, external and internal forces, until inner and outer worlds collapse, when, moving with the clouds of *Wheatfield with Crows*, the camera falls into darkness—fade to black. However, it is on the black screen that the after-image of the yellow motifs of wheat, sunflowers, and the sun continue to glow and burn in the spectator's eye.

Another, more recent, cinematic engagement with Van Gogh is Akira Kurosawa's 1990 film *Dreams* (1990), composed of eight vignettes. The one entitled "Crows" depicts a Japanese art student who follows Van Gogh (played by Martin Scorsese) into the vibrant world of his paintings from the Arles period (the student literally walks into and through Van Gogh's paintings). On an open wheatfield under the burning sun, the student meets Van Gogh, who explains to him how the sun and the landscape compel him to paint: "And then, as if it is in a dream, the scene just paints itself for me. Yes, I consume this natural setting. I devour it completely and whole. And when I am through, the picture appears before me complete. But it is so difficult to hold it in the eye." While staring into the sun, the Japanese student asks: "What do you do?" And Van Gogh answers: "I work, I slave, I drive myself like a locomotive." Van Gogh's look into the sun is at that moment intercut with close-ups of the turning wheels of a locomotive and a steam engine. Although this all takes place in a rural setting, Kurosawa drama-tizes Van Gogh's drive to paint, his vision, as framed by industrialization, as driven by the power of the machine. Close-ups of thick layers of bright, mostly yellow, colors culminate in an animation of circular brushstrokes depicting a sun, whirling like the wheels of a locomotive.

The end of the vignette features a close-up of a burning sun, setting up the theme of the nuclear holocaust that characterizes the two following vignettes. This juxtaposition reveals Van Gogh as a visionary who prefigured Japan's post-nuclear landscapes in his paintings. Van Gogh's wound, his pain, his cutting technique, and his compulsive focus on the sun find their fulfillment in Kurosawa's nuclear nightmare.

2

The Scandal of Yellow Books: From the Yellow Nineties to Modernism

His eye fell on the yellow book that Lord Henry had given him. What was it, he wondered. [...] After a few minutes he became absorbed. It was the strangest book that he had ever read. It seemed to him that in exquisite raiment, and to the delicate sound of flutes, the sins of the world were passing in a dumb show before him.[1]

More than any other phenomenon, the avant-garde periodical *The Yellow Book*, first published on April 15, 1895, defined the era of what came to be known as the "Yellow Nineties." As Katherine Mix observes:

On the morning of April 15, London suddenly turned yellow as the new periodical with its bright daffodil cover and staring black Beardsley design materialized on newsstands and book shops [...] "creating such a mighty glow of yellow at the far end of Vigo Street that one might have been forgiven for imagining for a moment that some awful portent had happened, and that the sun had risen in the West."[2]

The glorification of the first edition of *The Yellow Book*, edited by John Lane and illustrated by Aubrey Beardsley, was part of its marketing strategy: half-book, half-magazine, it was the review's novelty of presentation that the editors highlight in their programmatic introduction:

The aim [...] of *The Yellow Book* is to depart as far as may be from the bad old traditions of periodical literature, and to provide an Illustrated Magazine which shall be beautiful as a piece of bookmaking. [...] It will be charming, it will be daring, it will be distinguished. It will be a book—a book to be read, and placed upon one's shelves, and read

---

[1] Oscar Wilde, *The Picture of Dorian Gray*, in *The Complete Works of Oscar Wilde, Volume 3*, ed. Joseph Bristow (Oxford: Oxford University Press, 2005), 274.

[2] Katherine Lyon Mix, *A Study in Yellow: The Yellow Book and its Contributors* (Lawrence, University of Kansas Press, 1960), 81.

again; a book in form, a book in substance, a book beautiful to see and convenient to handle; a book with style, a book with finish; a book that every book-lover will love at first sight.[3]

The emphasis on the materiality of the book and its style—in particular the value of its exterior appearance—joins a style of visual reading with a disdain for modern commercial printing. Directed against what Edgar Allen Poe already in 1848 called "yellow-back pamphleteering" (the serial production of cheap novels with garishly yellow covers sold mainly at railway stations), it instead aligned itself with the French tradition of publishing modern writers with literary cachet, from Emile Zola to the Goncourts, in yellow backs. However, while the yellow backs were meant to signify the innovative and often risqué style of the French modernists, the illustrated covers of *The Yellow Book* indicated its hybrid status as both book and magazine, thereby shifting the focus to a visual style, or more precisely to a theatrical style, that dramatizes the act of reading as a kind of spectacle.

Long before Guy Debord's theoretical engagement with mass culture in *The Society of the Spectacle* (1967) and Michel Foucault's notion of the modern spectacle as a form of surveillance (*Discipline and Punish*, 1975), the shift towards the spectator as object of the spectacle (of mass media and mass consumerism) was already thematized in *The Yellow Book*. As a platform for contemporary art, *The Yellow Book* was meant to provoke or challenge the repressive bourgeois morality of the Victorian age—thereby realizing Oscar Wilde's vision of a yellow book, which he had already formulated in 1891 in *The Picture of Dorian Gray* as a book in which "the sins of the world were passing in a dumb show before him."

The color of the hour: Beardsley's *Yellow Book*

From the moment of its conception, *The Yellow Book* presents itself as having a close relationship with the culture of scandal; it is, in fact, one of the progenitors of this culture. Situating itself midway between low and high art, between the late nineteenth-century aestheticist tradition and the sensationalist style of modern mass media, *The Yellow Book* sought to create a kind of fusion between the contemporary avant-garde and the emergence of mass culture.

[3] Quoted in Mix, *A Study in Yellow*, 79. Mix quotes from *Daily Chronicle*, April 16, 1894, 3.

The birth of the idea of *The Yellow Book* can be traced to a meeting of the American-born transatlantic writer Henry Harland with the graphic designer Aubrey Beardsley on New Year's Day 1894. As Harland recalled:

> [In] one of the densest and soupiest and yellowest of all of London's infernalest yellow fogs, Aubrey Beardsley and I sat together the whole afternoon before a beautiful glowing open coal fire, and I assure you we could scarcely see our hands before our faces, with all the candles lighted, for the fog, you know. [...] We declared each to each that we thought it quite a pity and a shame that London publishers should feel themselves no longer under obligation to refuse any more of our good manuscripts. "Tis monstrous, Aubrey," I said. "Tis a public scandal," said he. And then and there we decided to have a magazine of our own. As the sole editorial staff we would feel free and welcome to publish any and all of ourselves that nobody else could be hired to print. That was the first day of January ... and the next day we had an appointment with Mr. John Lane.[4]

Beardsley proposed the title *The Yellow Book*, and the periodical soon became a forum for 138 authors and 106 visual artists, many of whom, presumably, could not find other venues for their work.[5] Although Harland's and Beardsley's reference to the monstrous and to public scandal nominally refers to the fact that their work was underappreciated, the idea of the scandalous (the Greek etymology means "stumbling block" [*skandalon*]) was to remain an important ingredient of the culture of *The Yellow Book*, whose ethos was by and large defined by Beardsley's illustrations.

The Yellow Book greatly contributed to the color yellow becoming, as Holbrook Jackson writes in *The Eighteen Nineties* (1913), "the color of the hour, the symbol of the time-spirit. It was associated with all that was bizarre and queer in art and life, with all that was outrageously modern."[6]

---

[4] Quoted in *The Yellow Book: Quintessence of the Nineties*, ed. Stanley Weintraub (New York: Anchor Books, 1964), ix–x.

[5] The appearance of *The Yellow Book* was greeted with great fanfare in 1894.

[6] Quoted in Weintraub, *The Yellow Book: Quintessence of the Nineties*, viii. Richard Le Gallienne, a prolific contributor to *The Yellow Book*, entitles one of his prose fancies "The Boom in Yellow," which he presents as a Romantic version of the decadent *art de vivre*: "Let us dream of this: a maid with yellow hair, clad in yellow gown, seated in a yellow room, at the window a yellow sunset, in the grate a yellow fire, at her side a yellow lamplight, on her knee a Yellow Book. And the letters we love best to read—when we dare—are they not yellow too? No doubt some disagreeable things are reported of yellow. We have had the yellow fever, and we have had pea-soup. The eyes of lions are said to be yellow, and the ugliest cats—the cats that infest one's garden—are always yellow. Some medicines are yellow, and no doubt there are many other yellow disagreeables; but we prefer to dwell upon the yellow blessings" (Richard Le Gallienne,

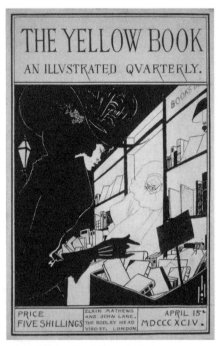

Figure 1   Aubrey Beardsley, *The Yellow Book Prospectus*. Pen and Ink, 1894. Victoria and Albert Museum, London, UK. Photo Credit: V&A Images, London/Art Resource, NY.

One of the ways in which Beardsley stages the "outrageously modern" is in the images that come to be known as "Beardsley's women." The front cover of the first edition of *The Yellow Book* features a female reader of books; elegantly stylized, this reader is at the same time staging herself as a spectacle—celebrating the New Woman of the *fin de siècle*, the independent woman and the *femme fatale* (almost never accompanied by men), with a potential for scandal.

As Emma Sutton observes:

> Many of the journal's images are set on the stage and within theatres, and the architectural background of some of the drawings—such as

Prose Fancies (Second Series) [London: H. S. Stone & Company, 1896], 88). Ironically commenting on the turn to the bright side of yellow, Le Gallienne continues to perform his intoxication with a catalog of yellow blessings, as when he intensifies the scenario of a yellow maid, dressed in yellow, reading *The Yellow Book*, asking: "Is it possible to say anything prettier for yellow than that?" (ibid., 89).

Beardsley's *Night Piece* and *Frontispiece for Juvenal*—resemble sets, or incorporate theatres into the landscape; even the *Portrait of Himself*, representing Beardsley under a bed's elaborate baldacchino, suggests an opulent theatre box. *The Yellow Book* was, then, a publication dominated by images of women and of the theatre. The disparate genres, national traditions, and types of performance to which Beardsley alluded were united by his emphasis on spectacle, artifice, and women.[7]

The theatricality of Beardsley's style, gesturing towards the transgression of traditional gender roles, soon becomes the face—quite literally—of the quarterly, with yellow as its medium. The medium of yellow exposes the theatricality that Samuel Weber has defined as characteristic for the way types of bodies (such as the icon of the New Women), as opposed to singular bodies, are staged in modern media, in which the body is perceived as "something other than an organic whole, as something other than a container of the soul."[8] Referring to Walter Benjamin's discussion of Brecht's epic theatre, Weber describes the notion of a citational gesture (which is characteristic of Brecht's staging of types rather than of characters endowed with individuality):

> Gesture, then, replaces the aesthetic concept of form in Benjamin's rethinking of theatricality. With the notion of form, however, it shares the attribute of being "fixed" and "delimited": "Unlike human actions and undertakings, [gestures have] a definable beginning and a definable end. This strict, frame-like enclosing of every element in a posture (*Haltung*) that as a whole is caught up in a living flux is one of the basic dialectical phenomena of gesture. From this an important conclusion can be drawn: gestures are obtained all the more someone engaged in an action (*einen Handelnden*) is interrupted."[9]

Using his *nom de plume* "The Yellow Dwarf" for his biting satires, Henry Harland offered an editorial note at the beginning of each issue that parodied the previous one. Max Beerbohm's illustration of the Yellow Dwarf, equipped with arrows and a mask (in the ninth volume of *The Yellow Book*; it refers to the French Nain Jaune, a cruel fairy tale character) highlights the recurrent accessories of Beardsley's theatrical style, which Beardsley marketed in the so-called "Beardsley button"; in the form of an oval we see a scene of sexual

7   Emma Sutton, *Aubrey Beardsley and the British Wagnerism in the 1890s* (Oxford: Oxford University Press, 2002), 92.
8   Samuel Weber, *Theatricality as Medium* (New York: Fordham University Press, 2004), 48.
9   Ibid., 46. Weber quotes Walter Benjamin from "Was ist episches Theater?" in *Gesammelte Schriften* 2, no. 2 (1980): 521.

perversion: a woman in a dress decorated with chrysanthemums is whipping a young man who is kneeling down. The hitting power of whips, the targeting of arrows, become the citational gesture of an art that is masking and unmasking, veiling and unveiling the lure of the scandalous, the monstrous, and the seductive. The chaos that is veiled under the beauty of lines and decorum is part of the pointing gestures; the scandal itself is only pointed to, endlessly deferred.

Scandal: The arrest of Oscar Wilde

In 1894, shortly before *The Yellow Book* was published, Beardsley became known for his illustrations of Wilde's play *Salome*. (The play was first published in French in 1893, and an English translation with Beardsley's illustrations by John Lane appeared in 1894). However, the collaboration had created tension between Wilde and Beardsley; Wilde had rejected Beardsley's translation of *Salome* in favor of one by Alfred Douglas, with whom he was having an affair at the time. Wilde's rejection had an impact on Beardsley's illustrations, which suddenly started to use biting satire, alluding to Wilde's coded references to Salome as a transsexual figure (in overtly sexual terms, in fact, featuring Wilde's own physique in the depiction of one of the female characters of the play, *The Woman in the Moon*). Wilde shot back, calling the illustrations "the scribbling of a young boy." The row resulted in Wilde's being barred from publishing in *The Yellow Book*, despite the fact that he was the most famous and provocative writer of the time, identified with both aestheticism and decadence, and was thus a natural fit for the plucky periodical. It is therefore not surprising that Wilde's public statements about *The Yellow Book* were hardly positive: he called it "dull" and—perhaps worst of all—"not yellow at all."[10]

Nonetheless, when Wilde was arrested in 1895, after the Marquess of Queensberry publicly accused him of sodomy, the sensationalist press reported: "Arrest of Oscar Wilde, *Yellow Book* under his arm."[11] The conjunction of "arrest" and "Yellow Book" in the same sentence is designed to underline both the scandalous nature of the accusation and the dubious reputation of the accused. Though it was not in fact Beardsley's *The Yellow Book* that he was carrying (as the newspaper assumed) but Pierre Louÿs's novel *Aphrodite*,[12] the yellow color of the cover was seemingly proof enough

---

[10] Weintraub, *The Yellow Book*, xvi.

[11] Quoted in Mix, *A Study in Yellow*, 142. Mix quotes from the *Westminster Gazette*, July 20, 1894. Wilde was sentenced to two years in prison on charges of homosexuality.

[12] Known as an author of erotic literature that explored female (lesbian) sexuality, Pierre Louÿs published the novel *Aphrodite* (1896), one of the best-selling novels of its time. A

of Wilde's deviant morals to set off "the angry, righteous mob."[13] As Sally Ledger remarks:

> as far as the newspapers were concerned, Wilde was accompanied to his trial by *The Yellow Book*, and [...] media reports cemented in the cultural imagination of the 1890s an association between *The Yellow Book*, aestheticism and Decadence and, after April and May 1895, homosexuality.[14]

Thus in the cultural imagination of its time, *The Yellow Book* was not only linked to the decadent movement, but also to homosexuality; the avant-garde had always been suspected of homosexual tendencies, and yellow had also been a color that stigmatized sexual deviance (in the Middle Ages, prostitutes were forced to wear yellow signs).

Further emphasizing the "literary" nature of the scandal, the court, in its charges of indecency levelled against Wilde, also referred to what it understood to be the homosexual content of *The Picture of Dorian Gray*. This scandal, whose only link to *The Yellow Book* was the color yellow, proved to be too much for the periodical, which soon ceased publication:

> [Wilde's arrest] heralded not only the demise of Wilde as a writer but also threatened the very existence of *The Yellow Book*. Beardsley was removed from his post and the journal survived for only nine more issues. Another magazine called *Savoy* took over where *The Yellow Book* so ignominiously left off. Interestingly, the first issue of *Savoy* came out in January 1896 with no less a person than Aubrey Beardsley as its art editor. *The Yellow Book*, at least during Beardsley's editorship, was seen as "the quintessential expression of the *fin-de-siècle* spirit."[15]

Ironically, *The Picture of Dorian Gray*, published in 1891, thus three years before *The Yellow Book*, had referred to a "yellow book":

> His eye fell on the yellow book that Lord Henry had sent him. What was it, he wondered. [...] After a few minutes he became absorbed. It was the strangest book that he had ever read. It seemed to him that in exquisite raiment, and to the delicate sound of flutes, the sins of the world were passing in dumb show before him. Things that he had dimly dreamed of were suddenly made real to him. Things of which he had never dreamed

mixture of a love and a crime story, *Aphrodite* depicts courtesan life in Alexandria, offering a decadent, sensual vision of Egypt in classical times. Louÿs knew Wilde personally.

13 Weintraub, *The Yellow Book*, xvii.
14 Sally Ledger, "Wilde Women and *The Yellow Book*: The Sexual Politics of Aestheticism and Decadence," *English Literature in Transition, 1880–1920* 50, no. 1 (2007): 5.
15 Http://www.carrickhill.sa.gov.au/british_augustus_john.html [accessed July 12, 2011].

were gradually revealed. [...] The style in which it was written was that
curious jewelled style, vivid and obscure at once, full of argot and of
archaisms, of technical expressions and of elaborate paraphrases, that
characterizes the work of some of the finest artists of the French school
of Symbolists. There were in it metaphors as monstrous as orchids and
as subtle in colour. The life of the senses was described in the terms of
mystical philosophy. One hardly knew at times whether one was reading
the spiritual ecstasies of some mediaeval saint or the morbid confessions
of a modern sinner. It was a poisonous book.[16]

The imagery of a yellow book and its relationship to a dumb show of
sins passing by exposes the novel itself as a secret spectacle: the secretive
appearance of the yellow book in the novel marks the moment of Dorian's
corruption. Although its content is not revealed, the yellow book, which
Dorian receives from Lord Henry in order to console him after the suicide
of his first love, marks the moment of Dorian's devotion to Lord Henry, his
falling under the spell of a predominantly immoral influence.

The yellow hue of the book is the medium of spectacle, which is characterized by its duplicity; both monstrous and subtle, spiritual and ecstatic,
medieval (or ancient) and modern, it shifts between extremes in a movement
that is always potentially transgressive. However—and most importantly—
Wilde dramatizes the movement towards moments of transgression as a
form of spiritual awakening, awakening a sense of the "sins of the world." The
close proximity Wilde establishes between the spiritual and the scandalous,
through an ecstatic notion of sinfulness, exposes the dual, scandalous and
spiritual nature of yellow itself. However, the rapprochement between the
sins of the world and the color yellow in *The Picture of Dorian Gray* was
much more radical than the actual content of *The Yellow Book*, which
appeared three years later.

As previously noted, the premises of the legal case against Wilde were
based in part on *The Picture of Dorian Gray*, a novel about an author who
writes himself into a painting to achieve immortality.[17] Wilde's own downfall
and death were in fact interpreted by later critics as already scripted into his
novel: "Wilde reputedly said that Dorian Gray was what he wanted to be,
Lord Henry Wotton what people thought he was, and Basil Hallward what
he was in reality."[18] This complex set of (also homosexual) correspondences
emphasizes the ambiguous reconfigurations of the novel and of the life of the

[16] Wilde, *Dorian Gray*, 274.
[17] Elena Gomel, "Oscar Wilde, *The Picture of Dorian Gray*, and the (Un)Death of the
      Author," *Narrative* 12, no. 1 (2004): 80.
[18] Ibid., 85.

artist, reconfigurations that would later become part of Wilde's trial, where his art was used as proof against him. To escape what Wilde called in *The Decay of Lying* "the prison-house of realism," he deploys, as Sean Latham argues, the *roman à clef* throughout his writing, challenging the distinction between the realm of facts and the realm of fiction.[19]

The function of the yellow book parallels that of the dandy that Wilde canonized in Dorian Gray:[20] it connects the artist with the criminal; the artist thus becomes a "charismatic outsider"[21] to society. His rebellion is a form of aesthetic opposition, which Wilde performs, *à la* Des Esseintes in Huysmans's *Against Nature* (*A rebours*, 1884), through the displacement of his interior decorum into the Orient. "Yellow silk damask"[22] and "elaborate yellow Chinese hangings"[23] create in "myriad sensations"[24] a sensual intensity, which expands into the East End of London. In "the labyrinth of grimy streets,"[25] Dorian explores "the real secret of life" in a "mapless space which both repels and seduces Dorian."[26] However, it is not a matter of a romanticized Orient kept at a distance, but rather of a displaced Orient, which becomes a platform, as Nicholas Mirzoeff has argued, for Wilde's "coded reference to his queer sexuality."[27] (Homo)sexuality and Jewishness are disguised and displaced into an Orient, where the yellow of saffron, of silk, topazes, and chrysanthemums is fashioned as an Oriental yellow; yellow's ambivalent character as both attractive and repulsive is thereby enhanced through the addition of this positive valence. The structure of reversal alternating between repulsion and attraction, between the artistic and the criminal, leads to a moment of transgression, the scandal of the murder and the resurrection of the author in the work of art.

In his preface to Dorian Gray, Wilde expresses his support for the ideology of *l'art pour l'art*: "There is no such thing as a moral or immoral book. Books are well written, or badly written. That is all. [...] No artist has ethical sympathies. An ethical sympathy is an unpardonable mannerism of

[19] Sean Latham, *The Art of the Scandal* (Oxford: Oxford University Press, 2009), 61.
[20] See Karl Heinz Bohrer's chapter "Die Subversion des Ästhetizismus: Hermetik, Dandy, Verbrechen," in Bohrer, *Die Ästhetik des Schreckens* (Münich and Vienna: Hanser Verlag, 1978), 35.
[21] Helmut Kreuzer, *Die Bohème. Analyse und Dokumentation der intellektuellen Subkultur vom 19. Jahrhundert bis zur Gegenwart* (Stuttgart: Metzler, 1971), 327.
[22] Wilde, *Dorian Gray*, 285.
[23] Ibid.
[24] Ibid., 288.
[25] Ibid., 211.
[26] Matt Cook, *London and the Culture of Homosexuality* (Cambridge: Cambridge University Press, 2003), 107.
[27] Nicholas Mirzoeff, "Disorientalism: Minority and Visuality in Imperial London," *The Dramatic Review* 50, no. 2 (2006): 56.

Figure 2   Dumas, *Read the Yellow Journal*. French anti-Semitic journal cover, 1941. Photo Credit: Snark/Art Resource, NY.

style. [...] All art is quite useless."[28] However, as Pericles Lewis has pointed out, "Wilde's downfall seemed to taint aestheticism with a flavor not just of uselessness, but of immorality."[29] That is, Wilde had become something of an *immoralist* as opposed to simply an amoralist. Though *Dorian Gray* was used against Wilde, Wilde was not prosecuted for his writings, but for his sexual conduct. Lewis observes:

> Nonetheless, the trials had an impact on British literary life, and especially on the theater. Wilde's own plays, while not touching on homosexuality, had dealt irreverently with the question of marriage. These were no longer produced [...] As the critic Sir Arthur Wing Pinero has observed, "It was as though the Victorian age, in its last years, had determined to be relentlessly Victorian while it could."[30]

[28] Wilde, Preface, *Dorian Gray*, 167.
[29] Pericles Lewis, *The Cambridge Introduction to Modernism* (Cambridge: Cambridge University Press, 2007), 56.
[30] Ibid., 55.

While Wilde himself became a public spectacle, it was, more importantly, Wilde's vision of a yellow book (as a show of sins passing by) that was on trial. In the eyes of the public, Wilde's vision of a yellow book had materialized itself, ironically, at the moment when Wilde himself was seen with a yellow book during his arrest. Wilde's vision of the yellow book became the prefiguration of his own scandal.

We should also mention in this context that in the 1940s, the tradition of the yellow book, as it originated in France, is transformed into anti-Semitic propaganda in *Le Cahier jaune* (*The Yellow Journal*), a French anti-Semitic monthly that was published between 1941 and 1943. It is not the new or the risqué that the front cover announces, but rather the stereotypical image of the Jew, with hooked nose, bulbous eyes, and a menorah inserted into his head. The *fin-de-siècle* culture of the yellow book is thus inverted; for instead of connoting scandal chic, the yellow of the book is here simply reduced to its stigmatic origin.

Salome's yellow veils

As was observed above, the scandal that surrounded Wilde's arrest also severely damaged the reputation of *The Yellow Book*. Beardsley's designs were no longer featured, and two years later the quarterly ceased publication altogether. Its publisher, John Lane, remembers the shocking news of Wilde's arrest: "It killed *The Yellow Book*, and it nearly killed me," he said years later.[31] Thus only a consideration of the intertwinement of these two icons of the *fin-de-siècle* period, Beardsley and Wilde, can yield an understanding of what this period meant in terms of the sobriquet Yellow Nineties.

Their brief collaboration on Wilde's play *Salome*, which became a public scandal in its own right, certainly contributed to the aura of scandal and lawsuits that plagued Wilde in the years building up to his trials and arrest. While Beardsley's illustrations emphasize the transsexual character of Wilde's Salome figure, which appears only as the muted story of Wilde's play, it is the Oriental setting and dramatization of the Jewess Salome in yellow veils that takes center stage in the performance history of Wilde's play. The biblical story of Salome revolves around the seductive dance of the virgin, which arouses her stepfather and uncle, Herod. Overwhelmed by her seductive moves, he offers her anything in exchange. Following her mother's advice, Salome demands John the Baptist's head on a platter. (John the Baptist had condemned Salome's mother's marriage to Herod as incestuous; thus Salome is carrying out her mother's revenge). It is Wilde's innovation to

---

[31] Quoted in Mix, *A Study in Yellow*, 142.

present Salome as fiercely lusting herself after John the Baptist, culminating in the kiss of the decapitated head, with which Wilde transforms the famous dance of seven veils into Salome's own ecstasy.[32]

By staging Salome as fiercely lustful as Herod himself, Wilde undoes Salome's femininity. Her heightened celebration of Iokanaan's body-parts, which she dissects in a male fashion, fetishizing not only his mouth but also his hair, exposes a transgression of gender roles that belongs to the "muted" story of the play[33]—a story that dominates Beardsley's illustrations, which emphasize Salome's manly appearance with phallic symbols. In the eyes of the public, Beardsley's illustrations of Salome defined the relation between the two artists, Wilde and Beardsley. However, Wilde imbued the play with another muted story, which immediately became part of English theatrical history, namely the way in which Salome, a Jewess, came to be seen as a yellow icon.

The actress who came to be most identified with Wilde's Salome was the legendary Jewish actress Sarah Bernhardt, who, as Sander Gilman comments, "more than anyone else, came to represent the embodiment of this destructive stereotype" of a "Jewish woman." Sarah Bernhardt was, moreover, "one of the least conventional and most self-consciously masculine female entertainers and an adamant advocate of women's rights."[34] Shortly after Bernhardt had begun rehearsals at the Palace Theatre in the West End, Lord Chamberlain disapproved of the performance of the play, ostensibly because it represented biblical figures on stage (though this was most probably a pretext).

Bernhardt seemed to be an ideal embodiment of Salome, with her Oriental look (which was caricatured or idealized in numerous portraits), her mysterious appearance, and her self-stylization as a diva. She was, however, also

---

[32] However, the double climax (of the seductive dance and the shockingly monstrous kiss) is part of the poetic structure of Wilde's version of the play, where the reversal into opposites leads to transgression and scandal. Veiled in yellow, her dance unveils not only a lustful Herod, but also a lustful Salome, culminating in the kiss.

[33] However, it is the far less muted story of Beardsley's illustrations: the unfeminine look of Salome herself, the phallic symbolism emphasizes the androgynous (if not masculine) appearance of the "tragic daughter of passion," to which Wilde is merely alluding. The reversal of gender roles, however, belongs to the narrative structure of reversal and transgression itself, which we analyzed in its build-up to the climactic moment of Salome's kiss. It is Beardsley's illustration of this climactic scene, which itself accentuates the moment of reversal and transgression, that situates the figure of Salome as she holds Iokanaan's decapitated head: "at the top of the drawing Beardsley accentuates the long line of blood that ironically connects (flowing down from, or rising up to) the severed head and the lilies that seem to feed on the blood" (Chris Snodgrass, *Aubrey Beardsley: Dandy of the Grotesque* [Oxford: Oxford University Press, 1995], 145).

[34] Gail Finney, *Women in Modern Drama: Freud, Feminism, and European Theater at the Turn of the Century* (Ithaca, NY: Cornell University Press, 1991), 67.

described in anti-Semitic terms. Wilde had imagined her performance as a spectacle in monochrome yellow. As designer Graham Robertson recounts, "every costume of some shade of yellow, from clearest lemon to dark orange, with here and there just a hint of black."[35] The costumes thus emphasized the overall yellow appearance of the play, which also dominated its reception, although there is only one stage direction mentioning Salome's yellow veil.

The image of the "Divine Sarah," as Bernhardt was also called, merged with her role in the artistic imagination. Hans Makart, a prominent Viennese painter at the time, painted a portrait of Bernhardt as Salome. When Makart withdrew the painting from an exhibition, because it had been criticized for its yellow appearance, Bernhardt's reaction, which she formulated in a letter to Makart, reveals the anti-Semitic sensitivity surrounding the figure of Salome in *fin-de-siècle* culture:

> Yellow on yellow was the color of Henri Regnault, the late master from Paris, when he painted his Salome—shouldn't the famed Sarah not also be permitted to be yellow? [...] Yes, Mr. Makart, even though my statue has been rescued from the Ring Theater fire, my portrait must now be driven away. And yet my head and arms are so beautifully made up, the gown, the table cloth, the embroidery, the palm fan, everything is so beautifully yellow. Take assurance that I, too, have become truly yellow from gall, because you, whom I held to be my friend, betrayed me, after you painted me yellow.[36]

Bernhardt's response shows her awareness of yellow's stigmatizing potential. The painting to which Bernhardt refers, *Salomé*, 1870 (Color Plate 9), by the Orientalist Henri Regnault, comes from a long tradition of visual adaptations of Salome, from Caravaggio to Odile Redon, Gustave Moreau, and Gustav Klimt. Without, however, suggesting a yellow of decay, the intense yellow of the painting stands out through its saturatedness, its vitality. Unlike the golden glitter of the ornamental that dominates Moreau's and Klimt's Salomes, expressing her excessiveness, Regnault's yellow cloth is far less abstract; it is rather corporeal in its appearance, emphasizing the liveliness of the yellow cloth. Salome's posture, referring to a moment after her dance, with the platter on which she received John the Baptist's head on her lap, seems far removed from the ecstatic spectacle, and further emphasizes her rather beastlike appearance, which Regnault himself describes as a "tamed

---

[35] W. Graham Robertson, *Time Was* (London: Hamish Hamilton, 1931), 126.

[36] Sarah Bernhardt, quoted in Sander L. Gilman, "Salome, Syphilis, Sarah Bernhardt, and the Modern Jewess," in *The Jew in the Text: Modernity and the Construction of Identity*, ed. and intro. Linda Nochlin and Tamar Garb (London: Thames and Hudson, 1995), 114.

black panther, though still savage and cruel."[37] While the image of an actual black panther faces Moreau's Salome as she dances, the panther in Regnault's Orientalist vision is embodied by Salome herself; she exemplifies the colonial fantasy of a feminized and savage Orient.

The yellow veils thus become like the cover of the yellow book in *The Picture of Dorian Gray*: the framework for a theatricality of transgression and scandal, which Wilde dramatized, in both yellow and in Oriental settings, as the "(imaginary) place where Jews and queers were imbricated in the Western imagination." Thus, already in Wilde's work, the Orient, Jewishness and homosexuality all become closely intertwined through the multivalent figuration of yellow.

Wilde's "Symphony in Yellow"

In what could be called in retrospect Wilde's poetic manifesto, "Symphony in Yellow" (1889), we find an Orientalized London imagined in yellow. Criticizing London for its stifling stiffness, the poem, under its impressionistic cover, is in fact a phallic parody of stiffness:

> An omnibus across the bridge
> Crawls like a yellow butterfly,
> And, here and there, a passer-by
> Shows like a little restless midge.
>
> Big barges full of yellow hay
> Are moored against the shadowy wharf,
> And, like a yellow silken scarf,
> The thick fog hangs along the quay.
>
> The yellow leaves begin to fade
> And flutter from the Temple elms,
> And at my feet the pale green Thames
> Lies like a rod of rippled jade.[38]

The yellow stream of images dramatized in the buzzing sounds of insects is gradually silenced, coming to a standstill in a static image of the river Thames. Once the Thames is reached, the perspective of the poet is

---

[37] *Correspondance de Henri Regnault*, ed. Arthur Duparc (Paris: Charpentier, 1872), 357.

[38] Wilde, "Symphony in Yellow," in *The Complete Works of Oscar Wilde, Volume 1, Poems and Poems in Prose*, ed. Bobby Fong and Karl Beckson (Oxford: Oxford University Press, 2000), 168.

identified, a hyper-masculine Goliath figure known for wearing "a spear with a shaft like a weaver's rod."[39] The green color of the Thames and the "rod of rippled jade" invert the regular movement of the colors of nature (yellow to green instead of green to yellow) and seem to lead back to the opening imagery of omnibuses compared to yellow butterflies.

The greenish stone of jade is in China a powerful symbol that has historically been used to attract love. As a "rippled stone" in the phallic form of a rod, it releases the wave-like movement of the yellow flow of images, inverting the flow orgiastically. The poet is both the spectator and object of his own arousal. The greenish color of the Thames/rod decorated with a scarf of yellow silk orientalizes the city while moving down to the lower part of the poet's body (evoking Oriental imagery associated with sexuality). The inversion of the natural succession from green to yellow culminates in the color (green), which has also (like yellow) been associated with homosexuals (as Judith Grahn has shown in *Another Mother Tongue*).[40] Thus Salome offers a "little green flower" to one of the Syrian guards when she asks to have Iokanaan brought to her, a telltale sign to those familiar with the code and one of Wilde's veiled references, unveiling, as it were, Salome in disguise asking for a forbidden love. *The Green Carnation* was also the title of a novel anonymously published in 1894, the same year as the English version of *Salome*. A great success on both sides of the Atlantic, the scandal-ridden novel by Robert Hitchens was based on Oscar Wilde's liaison with Lord Alfred Douglas. The popularity of the novel indicates the public interest in Wilde's persona even prior to the scandal of his arrest and trials.

Wilde and the dispersion of scandal in Joyce's *Ulysses*

Wilde's intertwinement of life and art unfolds in the "culture of yellow" Wilde helped to establish and of which he became an icon. Despite, or perhaps because of its tragic consequences, Wilde's arrest and fall from grace became a literary *topos* in the great epic novels of the 1920s, namely Marcel Proust's *In Search of Lost Time* and James Joyce's *Ulysses*.

---

[39] 2 Samuel 21:19. 2, New International Bible (NIV), Biblica, Inc., 2011, http://www.biblegateway.com/passage/?search=2+Samuel+21&version=NIV [accessed February 13, 2012].

[40] This was revived by Wilde's trademark green-dyed flower, which he wore in his buttonhole—a subversive sign that Wilde publicized in theatrical gestures, as when he had green carnations thrown into the audience after the premiere of *Lady Windermere's Fan* in 1892.

A public scandal itself—*Ulysses* was subjected to charges of obscenity in the United States—Joyce's mock-epic was first published by Sylvia Beach in 1922 in Paris, but banned until the 1930s in the United Kingdom. Although Joyce confronts Wilde's art of the scandal, he rejects its major characteristic, namely the emphatic moment of transgression (characteristic of Wilde's work as well as of his life). Instead, it could be said that Joyce opts for a dispersion of the "Wilde phenomenon" throughout his novel and across its major characters, fragmenting the moment of transgression into exhaustion, dissemination, and decay. What holds the dispersion of Wilde's scandal together is the color yellow; yellow stigmata repeatedly resurface and are dispersed in a "yellow glow,"[41] "yellow habits,"[42] and a "mellow yellow."[43] However, it is in their very fluidity that yellow stigmata (of Jews, cuckolds, homosexuals) dissolve and materialize at the same time.

Joyce confronts us with modern wanderers in a world of overstimulation: Leopold Bloom is an ad seller, and Stephen Dedalus a budding writer. The newspaper is, in its fragmented format, a model for recording everyday business, as Bloom comments while on the toilet and we are exposed to his bowel movements: "They print everything today"—just as Joyce writes about everything, including the mundane and the disgusting. Nevertheless, as Joyce remarked to Djuna Barnes: "a writer should never write about the extraordinary. That is for the journalist."[44]

In an article entitled "Oscar Wilde: The Poet of 'Salomé'" (1909), Joyce treats the extraordinary or sensational elements of Wilde's life, not his work, thereby isolating the "Wilde phenomenon" from Wilde's oeuvre (something that Wilde himself was incapable of doing). Joyce's essay focuses on the reception of the scandal and its aftershocks:

> His howl was greeted by a howl of puritanical joy. On hearing of his condemnation, the mob that was gathered in front of the courthouse began to dance a pavane in the muddy street. The newspaper journalists were admitted into the prison and, through the window of his cell, were able to feed on the spectacle of his shame. White bands covered over his name on theatre billboards; his friends abandoned him; his manuscripts were stolen while he underwent his prison sentence of two years' hard labour. His mother died under the shadow of shame; his wife died. He

[41] James Joyce, *Ulysses: A Critical Synoptic Edition*, ed. Hans Walter Gabler (New York, London: Garland Publishing, 1984), I, 20.
[42] Ibid., II, 1078.
[43] Ibid., III, 1626.
[44] Quoted in Margot Gayle Backus, "'Odd Jobs': James Joyce, Oscar Wilde, and the Scandal Fragment," *Joyce Studies Annual* (2008), 112.

was declared bankrupt, his belongings were auctioned off and his sons were taken away from him. When he came out of prison, thugs urged on by the noble Marquis of Queensbury were waiting in ambush for him. He was driven, like a hare hunted by dogs, from hotel to hotel. Hotelier after hotelier drove him from the door, refusing him food and shelter, and at nightfall he finally ended up under the windows of his brother, weeping and babbling like a child.[45]

Joyce stylizes Wilde in his essay into the figure of an Irish martyr, exposed to a form of new journalism that not only reports on incidents, but also inflames passions, in effect passing judgment in a kind of archaic, non-judicial manner. It is this media-induced spectacle, rather than the legal conviction, that effectively made Wilde an outsider, chased everywhere he went by an angry mob.

Dedalus's "yellow stick" and Bloom's "yellow habit"

In the opening of *Ulysses*, the spectacle that the medical student Buck Mulligan makes of himself in his advances towards Stephen Dedalus echoes aspects of the "Wilde phenomenon." The increasingly tense relationship between Dedalus and his friend Mulligan unfolds with respect to their opposing views of Wilde, who, in the view of the arch classicist Mulligan, is a role model for the Hellenization of Ireland, while Dedalus attempts to re-establish Wilde as an Irish artist against his representation by the British press as "an aristocratic monster of perversion."[46] Both Mulligan's view of Wilde together with his erotic advances to Dedalus are in the course of the epic novel debunked by Dedalus himself, who distances himself from the gilded rhetoric and pretentious appearance of his patronizing friend.

Mulligan enters the stage dressed in yellow as a priest,[47] ridiculing Dedalus, in a mock-mass:

---

[45] James Joyce, "Oscar Wilde: The Poet of 'Salomé,'" in *The Critical Writings of James Joyce*, ed. Ellsworth Mason and Richard Ellmann (New York: The Viking Press, 1959), 213.

[46] Backus, "'Odd Jobs'," 122.

[47] Interestingly, in the famous color scheme Stuart Gilbert offered twenty years after the first publication of *Ulysses*, he does not list yellow at all. Instead "white, gold" is mentioned as the color scheme for the "Telemachus" episode, and green for the "Proteus" episode. As we will see, yellow is clearly the dominant color of the "Proteus" chapter, introduced in the first episode through the character of Mulligan. See Stuart Gilbert, *James Joyce's Ulysses* (New York: Vintage Books, 1961, 8th edn), 41. See also J. Colm O'Sullivan, *Joyce's Use of Colors:* Finnegans Wake *and the Earlier Works* (Ann Arbor, MI: UMI Research Press, 1987), 26. O'Sullivan also points to the "Proteus" episode as "the most colorful episode of *Ulysses*" (ibid., 27).

> STATELY, PLUMP BUCK MULLIGAN CAME FROM THE
> STAIRHEAD, bearing a bowl of lather on which a mirror and a razor
> lay crossed. A yellow dressing gown, ungirdled, was sustained gently
> behind him by the mild morning air. He held the bowl aloft and intoned:
> —Introibo Ad Altare Dei.[48]

Mulligan's appearance is staged on an altar, from which he speaks down to Dedalus during his morning toilette, taking him to task for his Greek name and his inferior standing in terms of class and education, whereas Mulligan later claims, in their contest over the ownership of Wilde, "Wilde as an exemplar of his own Oxonian Hellenism and as a guarantor of his class-inflected standards of aesthetic taste."[49] However, the moment Mulligan evokes Wilde, he gets his reference to the artist wrong, and his priestly appearance in a yellow dressing gown is literally dissolved by his object of desire, Dedalus, who deconstructs his stilted and pretentious rhetoric.

Zooming in on the appearance of Mulligan's "white teeth glistening here and there with gold points. Chrysostomos,"[50] Dedalus points to the decay under the golden crowns in his mouth, dismantling his colonizing rhetoric ("Hellenise"[51] Ireland) and his priestly garb ("yellow dressing gown, ungirdled").[52] With his dissecting look, Dedalus is not only dissecting body parts but also Mulligan's *habitus*, his gilded rhetoric, "superficially gilded with mirth,"[53] which he despises. Through Dedalus's perception, Joyce is creating a yellow medium, in which the visceral sensation of scorn comes to the fore. Seen from Dedalus's perspective through smoke and grease, Mulligan's "yellow glow"[54] slowly dissolves during the course of "Telemachus." Floating like the "fumes of fried grease," Mulligan's face appears in Dedalus's perception "like a hairy oval";[55] Mulligan's body is fragmented, a cracked image that refers back to the cracked mirror that Mulligan holds in his hands:

> Laughing again, he brought the mirror away from Dedalus's peering
> eyes.

[48] Joyce, *Ulysses*, I, 3.
[49] Backus, "'Odd Jobs,'" 122.
[50] Joyce, *Ulysses*, I, 2.
[51] Ibid., I, 10.
[52] Ibid., I, 2.
[53] Annie Atura and Lee Dionne, "Color in 'Proteus,'" *The Modernism Lab at Yale University*, http://modernism.research.yale.edu/wiki/index.php/%22Proteus%22 [accessed July 12, 2011].
[54] Joyce, *Ulysses*, I, 20.
[55] Sara Danius, *The Senses of Modernism: Technology, Perception and Aesthetics* (Ithaca, NY: Cornell University Press, 2002), 154.

—The rage of Caliban at not seeing his face in a mirror, he said. If Wilde were only alive to see you!

Drawing back and pointing, Stephen said with bitterness:

—It is a symbol of Irish art. The cracked looking-glass of a servant.[56]

However, for Dedalus, the cracked looking-glass becomes the "symbol of Irish art" that Wilde used (in *The Decay of Lying*) to examine English society. Dedalus is redefining Wilde in his marginalized role as an Irish servant, or, as Joyce will later say, a "jester to the English courthouse." In *Ulysses*, Mulligan is eventually degraded to a clown-like role. Although he still appears elevated on top of the tower in the "Circe" chapter, the buttered scone in his hands and the "dress of puce and yellow" reveal a ridiculous and repulsive appearance:

(FROM THE TOP OF A TOWER BUCK MULLIGAN, IN PARTICOLOURED JESTER'S DRESS OF PUCE AND YELLOW AND CLOWN'S CAP WITH CURLING BELL, STANDS GAPING AT HER, A SMOKING BUTTERED SPLIT SCONE IN HIS HAND).[57]

Mulligan's flamboyant entrance in a yellow gown and his project to "Hellenise" Ireland is here summarily debunked as a "jester's dress of puce and yellow." After Dedalus explicitly reflects on and rejects the role of a "jester," he chooses his own path.

However, what remains is his aestheticism and scorn directed at bourgeois society—Wildean features, emblematized in his "stick," a Wildean accessory (and also Joyce's own for that matter), which Joyce calls a "yellow stick": "LYNCH: Damn your yellow stick. Where are we going?"[58] The yellow color of his stick[59] stands out like the yellow color of Mulligan's jester garb; they form a color code, through which the Wilde scandal is at once pointed to and dispersed at the same time, creating a subplot, a book within a book, a yellow book, as it were, inside *Ulysses*.

---

[56] Joyce, *Ulysses*, I, 10.

[57] Ibid., II, 1266.

[58] Ibid., II, 934.

[59] The yellow color of Dedalus's stick links him, interestingly, not only to Wilde's stick, but also to the yellow flower that is a trademark of Mulligan's appearance in "Proteus." Moreover, the *topos* of the yellow flower also unfolds with respect to Bloom and the construction of his Jewish identity. Thus, both homosexuality and Jewish identity (yellow stigmata) are very much a part of the yellow topography that leads through *Ulysses*. With respect to Ira B. Nadel's argument, that Dedalus's self-hatred is modeled after Jewish self-hatred, his trademark of the "yellow stick" links him even more directly to his Jewish friend, Bloom. See Ira B. Nadel, *Joyce and the Jews: Culture and Text* (Gainesville: University of Florida Press, 1996), 153.

Only *ex negativo*, in the role of a jester, is Wilde identified, in a role that Dedalus refuses to play. In his rejection of Mulligan in "Proteus," Dedalus reflects on Wilde's trial: "Staunch friend, a brother soul: Wilde's love that dare not speak its name. His arm. Cranley's arm. He now will leave me. And the blame?"[60] Dedalus refuses Mulligan's advances towards him (like Cranley does in *A Portrait of the Artist as a Young Man*), with one of the most often-quoted lines from Wilde's trial about the love that "dare not speak its name." The prosecutor confronts Wilde, who quotes from a love poem that Alfred Douglas wrote for him entitled "Two Loves" (1894):

> Charles Gill (prosecutor): What is "the love that dare not speak its name?"
> Wilde: "The love that dare not speak its name" in this century is such a great affection of an elder for a younger man as there was between David and Jonathan, such as Plato made the very basis of his philosophy, and such as you find in the sonnets of Michelangelo and Shakespeare.[61]

Dedalus's reference to "Wilde's love that dare not speak its name" appears within the context of Joyce's satire on the modern culture of trials and libel suits, which he represents through Dedalus's counterpart, Bloom, thus dispersing the "Wilde phenomenon" even further.

Bloom, who is himself presented as the reformer of a social purity movement,[62] hides the telltale signs of his private affairs (a yellow flower and a yellow bar of soap) wrapped up in a newspaper, the very medium in which Bloom's own trials (accused of his sexual affairs, and thus a victim of his own social purity movement) will be made public. One of the most direct allusions to Wilde's trial unfolds in a Wildean language of flowers.[63] It thereby thematizes, as Margot Backus has argued, the Wildean style of

---

[60] Ibid., I, 99–100.

[61] Wilde, "Testimony of Oscar Wilde," quoted in Douglas O. Linder, *An Account of the Three Trials of Oscar Wilde*, UMKC School of Law, http://law2.umkc.edu/faculty/projects/ftrials/wilde/Crimwilde.html [accessed March 22, 2012].

[62] The Wildean trial, his language of flowers, refers here, however, to a larger discourse on social purity, which Katherine Mullin has analyzed with respect to evangelical Protestant ideologies that actively promoted notions of social purity during the years of Joyce's residence in Dublin as a young man. See Katherine Mullin, *James Joyce, Sexuality and Social Purity* (Cambridge, New York: Cambridge University Press), 2003.

[63] "In his poetry and love letters, Wilde prettifies the grosser specifics of sexual embodiment with references to flowers, particularly roses. In Lord Henry Wotton's famous revelation to Dorian Gray of Dorian's own inchoate thoughts and feelings, Wotton constitutes Dorian as both object and subject of sexual desire through rose imagery: 'You, Mr. Gray, you yourself, with your rose-red youth and your rose-white boyhood, you have had passions that have made you afraid, thoughts that have filled you with terror, day-dreams and sleeping dreams whose mere memory might stain your cheek with shame'" (Backus, "'Odd Jobs,'" 139).

self-commodification (through flowers): "He opened the letter within the newspaper. A flower. I think it's a yellow flower with flattened petals. Not annoyed then? What does she say?"[64] The yellow flower he carries in his pocket, the telltale sign of his affair, links his ancestral Jewish history with his current affairs. For his name, *Bloom*, is a translation of the original Hungarian family name, *Virag*, which means flower; in his extramarital affair and exchange of love letters Bloom calls himself Henry Flower.

However, the language of the yellow flower that surrounds Bloom's "sweet sins," his affair, literally dissolves in the context of a Jewish ritual bath,[65] which is both a parody of Bloom's infertility, his "limp" yellow trunk ("He saw his trunk and limbs riprippled over and sustained, buoyed lightly upward, lemonyellow"),[66] as well as a parody of his active involvement in a social purity movement against prostitution, while engaging in extramarital affairs himself.

Both stigmatized and stigmatizing, Bloom is subject and object of a culture of scandal, and, like Wilde himself, is put on trial. In his defense, "Brother Buzz" asks for forgiveness, evoking the (medieval) Christian imagery of the persecution of Jews, stigmatized in yellow—a parallel of Mulligan's degradation to a jester in a yellow dress:[67]

BROTHER BUZZ: (INVESTS BLOOM IN A YELLOW HABIT WITH EMBROIDERY OF PAINTED FLAMES AND HIGH POINTED HAT. HE PLACES A BAG OF GUNPOWDER ROUND HIS NECK AND HANDS HIM OVER TO THE CIVIL POWER, SAYING) Forgive him his trespasses.[68]

Brother Buzz evokes what he describes through his name, namely a buzzing sound, through which medieval stigmata burst forth again in modern society, disseminated and dispersed in quotidian practices that structure social life.

[64] Joyce, *Ulysses*, I, 154.
[65] As Ariela Freedman has pointed out, the bath "marks the transition between the state of ritual purity and impurity. More significantly for the purpose of this narrative, it marks a transition from a period of menstruation and abstinence, for seven days after the cessation of the menstrual cycle, and the beginning of a period of sexual intercourse and fertility" ("Did it Flow?: Bridging Aesthetics and History in Joyce's *Ulysses*," *Modernism/modernity* 13, no. 1 [2006]: 860).
[66] Ibid., I, 174.
[67] In "Proteus," Mulligan's trademark was a golden-yellow primrose at his waistcoat, a reflection of his Oxford manners. See O'Sullivan, *Joyce's Use of Colors*, 37. The yellow primrose is also known in England as the favorite flower of Benjamin Disraeli, Britain's only prime minister of Jewish birth. The Primrose League was founded in his memory in 1893, to spread Conservative Principles in Britain. Neil R. Davison discusses Disraeli's significance in his *James Joyce, Ulysses, and the Construction of Jewish Identity* (Cambridge: Cambridge University Press, 1988), 29.
[68] Joyce, *Ulysses*, II, 1079.

Ironically, it is Mulligan who warns Dedalus of the advances of the Jew Bloom: "The wandering Jew, Buck Mulligan whispered with clown's awe. Did you see his eye? He looked upon you to lust after you."[69] Reversing his own lusting after Dedalus, he warns Dedalus of Bloom being "Greeker than the Greeks," undermining his own project to "Hellenise" Ireland.[70] Between Mulligan's yellow dresses, Bloom's yellow flowers, and Dedalus's yellow teeth, a spectrum of yellow is unfolding, defining a space between the personal and the collective, the private and the public, into which the "Wilde phenomenon" is dispersed.

---

[69] Ibid., I, 468.

[70] Jean-Michel Rabaté comments in *James Joyce and the Politics of Egoism* (Cambridge: Cambridge University Press, 2001, 165) that "if, indeed, the 'jewgreek is greekjew' in *Ulysses*, then the perversion of the two positions culminates in snide suggestions of homosexuality and incest, suggestions that spare absolutely no one in the novel."

3

Yellow Passions

The color is repellent, almost revolting; a smouldering unclean yellow,
strangely faded by the slow-turning sunlight.
— Charlotte Perkins Gilman

Dictionnaire de mélancolie et de crime was the title Charles Baudelaire
had originally contemplated for his seminal lyric sequence *Les Fleurs
du Mal* (*Flowers of Evil*, 1857). Traditionally, melancholia, the color of
artistic inspiration, is associated with blue; thus Baudelaire's change of title
announces a broader shift in color schema, in which dirty-yellow returns as a
stigmatic yellow, as in his poem "The Seven Old Men" ("Les sept vieillards"):
"Suddenly an old man whose tattered yellow clothes / Were of the same color
as the rainy heavens, [...] Appeared to me. One would have said his eyes
were drenched / With gall." Baudelaire bases the break with conventional
poetic forms on the ancient model of humor pathology,[1] marking a shift
towards the choleric temperament, which has historically been associated
with yellow bile. In such moments of shock and rupture, what Baudelaire
called "correspondences" (*les correspondances*) become manifest.

Inspired by Emanuel Swedenborg's cosmology, in which the human
microcosm replicates the macrocosm, Baudelaire saw the poet as the
decipherer and revealer of correspondences between the material and the
spiritual world.[2] These structure a synthetic vision that comes to the fore in

[1] Humoral theory formed the basis of Western medicine and often contributed to the
creation of characters in drama and fiction. In *Anatomy of Melancholy* (1621), Robert
Burton describes the qualities of the four humors. In the twentieth century, Rudolph
Steiner's embrace of the therapeutic use of color based on humor theories had a strong
impact on the reflections on color in artists such as Andrei Bely and Wassily Kandinsky
(see Chapter 5). See Rudolph Steiner, *The Anthroposophical Approach to Medicine*
(London: Steiner Press, 1951).

[2] Baudelaire expressed his idea of "correspondences" emblematically in the first two
quatrains of his eponymous poem. See Baudelaire, "Correspondences," trans. Frances
Cornford, in *Baudelaire in English*, ed. Carol Clark and Robert Sykes (London, New
York: Penguin Books, 1997), 16. Fellow symbolist Arthur Rimbaud added a performative dimension to Baudelaire's conception of synaesthesia in his poem entitled *Vowels*:

moments of ecstatic rapture, moments in which, as Walter Benjamin writes in *On Some Motifs in Baudelaire*, the poet transcends "earthly existence."[3] Benjamin emphasizes the role of this mystical dimension in Baudelaire's concept of synaesthesia: "the *correspondances* record a concept of experience which includes ritual elements."[4] According to Benjamin, these ritualistic elements allow Baudelaire to connect the mystical experience of correspondences between senses, nature, and the cosmos, on the one hand (what Baudelaire calls a "forest of symbols"), and the modern experiences of shock and *frisson*, on the other. While the idea of "correspondences" is explicitly synaesthetic, the experience of shock (an overstimulation of the senses) that Benjamin sees at the center of Baudelaire's work is, one could argue, an implicit concept of synaesthesia: in moments of shock, the overstimulation either provokes or is a function of the crossing of the senses, providing us with a new understanding of modern experience.[5]

The yellow of contempt: Baudelaire, Tristan Corbière, František Kupka

In Baudelaire's "The Seven Old Men" the return of yellow's stigmatizing potential is dramatized as being physically remembered ("And his long shaggy beard, like that of Judas") and at the same time multiplied in an atmosphere of hostility and anger, in which the poet asks himself: "Of what infamous plot was I then the object?" The poet is subjected to the multiplication of the "sinister old men" and their "wickedness" on his voyage through the city, which is presented in its yellow atmosphere as a kind of hell; and yet, Baudelaire transforms this atmosphere of disgust, bitterness, and

---

"A black, E white, I red, U green, O blue: vowels" (A noir, E blanc, I rouge, U vert, O bleu: voyelles). Rimbaud's approach to synaesthesia is based on his research into medical studies that point to a delirious state of the senses, an acute confusional state in which body and thought are deranged, liberating forms of sensual thinking that provoke visions of bliss, thereby revealing structures ordering the world (such as the alphabet in its aural and visible as well as haptic dimensions).

[3]　Walter Benjamin, "On Some Motifs in Baudelaire," in Benjamin, *Illuminations: Essays and Reflections*, ed. Hannah Arendt, trans. Harry Zohn (New York: Schocken Books, 1968), 182.

[4]　Ibid., 181.

[5]　Ancient color theories consider chiasmic relationships between physiological colors (in Hippocrates the humor phlegm is white, blood is red, bitter bile is yellow and sharp bile is black) and the colors of the elements (fire, earth, air, water), which create correspondences between macrocosmic and microcosmic dimensions. See J. L. Benson, "Greek Color Theory and the Four Elements," in ScholarWorks@UMass (Amherst: University of Massachusetts), 46.

anger into an idyllic moment, a moment of an eternal beauty, activating the vision of an artificial paradise. However, the moment of reversal creates the intensity of a discontinuous moment, not a moment of fulfillment, but rather the experience of a rupture, the sudden experience of an irretrievable loss. Karl Heinz Bohrer, however, has argued in his interpretation of Baudelaire's poetics that the aesthetic experience of leave-taking (*Abschied*) radicalizes the experience of melancholy.[6] Against Benjamin's reading of Baudelaire, Bohrer emphasizes the experience of loss as an a priori negative experience that cannot be retrieved for historical or autobiographical reasons; Bohrer instead insists on the category of intensity.

Tristan Corbière's response to Baudelaire some twenty years later in his collection of poems *Les amours jaunes* (*Yellow Passions*, 1873) can be characterized as cynical, as when he dismisses the Romantic return to the cholerical temperament of humor pathology as a mere fashion. His tone is bitter throughout the collection, describing the modern condition surrounding him as a "yellow sauce from chic and contempt." Using black humor to attack the "whole fabric of nineteenth century French poetry"[7] as well as his own status as a poet, Corbière transforms into "depoetized" moments of "prosaic under-statement" Baudelaire's attempts to capture fugitive moments emerging from evil and decay.[8] The self-declared Tristan figure is suffused with a bitter-yellow atmosphere throughout; he sees his life as an "adulterous mixture": each possibility is canceled out by its opposite—an "artless artist," an "actor, who did not know his role."[9] Pathos itself is ridiculed through "yellow laughter" (*le rire jaune*), the French expression for "sour smile," with which Corbière establishes his cynical gestures.

Similarly cynical is artist František Kupka's visual portrait of Baudelaire, which he entitled *The Yellow Scale*, 1907 (Color Plate 10). The Czech painter based his portrait on one of Nadar's daguerreotype photographs of Baudelaire. The poet, imagined as a sick man on an Oriental lounge chair, appears tortured by the spiritual malaise he himself named *ennui*, with one hand clasping a yellow book (the reading of which appears to have just been interrupted) and the other languorously clutching a cigarette. Baudelaire literally *embodies* the yellow tonalities that reveal his sickly appearance. Kupka captures Baudelaire's deteriorating health (due to frequent exposure

---

[6] Karl Heinz Bohrer, *Der Abschied. Theorie der Trauer* (Frankfurt am Main: Suhrkamp, 1997), 107.

[7] Ibid., 39.

[8] Albert Sonnenfeld, "The Yellow Laugh of Tristan Corbière," *Yale French Studies* 23 (1959): 41.

[9] Tristan Corbière, *Selections from Les Amours jaunes* (Berkeley and Los Angeles: University of California Press, 1954), 39.

to alcohol, opium, and hashish) as a kind of self-fulfillment of his negative vision of lust and decay, which became the reality of Baudelaire's own life, darkened by sickness and despair. Kupka mixes a realistic portrait of the poet with an abstraction in monochrome yellow, saturating, as it were, with the narrative of decline that encapsulates the artist, his psychological and physiological state, as well as his work (the yellow book). As in Corbière's *Yellow Passions*, the yellow of light and enlightenment is here transformed into the yellow of decadence, bitterness, and contempt.

On the verge of leaving naturalistic representations behind to make his mark in abstract art, Kupka celebrates with *The Yellow Scale* a decadent tradition associated with Baudelaire's oeuvre and life, which Kupka will transform, in his later work, into a celebration of speed (inspired by the Futurists) and simultaneity in "pure paintings." The French poet and art critic Guillaume Apollinaire, who coined the term *Orphism* at the *Salon de la Section d'Or* (1912), in reference to works such as Kupka's *Amorpha: Fugue in Two Colors*,[10] saw these paintings as anti-figurative as music.[11] However, in *The Yellow Scale* the color yellow is a figure of materiality itself, of the creaturely (the sick body) as well as of the spiritual (Baudelaire's yellow book as an artistic expression of the spiritual malaise he embodies). The negativity of yellow emphasizes its materiality, which shows itself towards the end of the nineteenth century and the *fin de siècle* as a means of artistic self-reflection. The yellow of sickness and decay functions as the canvas of reflections on correspondences between inner and outer conditions, both of which point to an understanding of the present moment as a moment of crisis, namely the crisis of the individual in an age of mass society and

[10] The art critic and member of the Bloomsbury Group in England, Roger Fry points to the equation of abstraction with music in the catalog to the "Second Post-Impressionist Exhibition" in 1912, which is most likely "a debt to the contemporaneous work of Kupka," as Richard Cork comments in *Art Beyond the Gallery in Early 20th Century England* (New Haven, CT: Yale University Press, 1985), 172. The shift towards abstraction and the emphasis on form in the Second Post-Impressionist Exhibition is part of Virginia Woolf's dialogue with Fry and her reflection on a language of color, as we will see towards the end of this chapter.

[11] Apollinaire published for the catalog of Robert Delaunay's one-man show in Berlin in 1913 the poem *Les Fenêtres* (*The Windows*) as a commentary on the painter's theories of simultaneity. The famous opening line and refrain of the poem "Du rouge au vert tout le jaune se meurt" (From red to green all the yellow dies) presents a "poetic transformation of the kind of color theory that Delaunay attacked. According to Eugène Delacroix and Michel-Eugène Chevreul, red and green are complementary colors, whereas red and yellow form a dissonance and should not be juxtaposed; thus according to Chevreul's color wheel, yellow 'dies' en route from red to green" (Anne Hyde Greet and S. I. Lockerbie in their commentary on Guillaume Apollinaire, *Calligrammes: Poems of Peace and War (1913–1916)* [Berkeley and Los Angeles: University of California Press, 1991], 351).

industrialization. The fact that this crisis is imagined in yellow prefigures the mass phenomena of the "yellow peril" and "yellow journalism" towards the end of the nineteenth century.

The yellow of disgust: Charlotte Perkins Gilman's "The Yellow Wallpaper"

The physicality and materiality of a sickly, unclean and inflamed yellow becomes a central theme (the theme of a *pattern*) in one of the most famous stories ever written about the color yellow, Charlotte Perkins Gilman's "The Yellow Wallpaper." Composed in 1890 and published in 1892 in *The New England Magazine*, the short story recounts the experiences of a woman supposedly suffering from "temporary nervous depression." Confined to a room by her doctor-husband in the belief that this "treatment" will ameliorate her condition and with no other outlet for her feelings—even writing is forbidden and must be done furtively—she becomes obsessed with "The Yellow Wallpaper" that adorns the walls of her room. The story describes the protagonist's increasing anxiety and progressive descent into madness as she transforms the wallpaper into the stage on which she performs her political and social vision.

"The Yellow Wallpaper" has been primarily interpreted as a kind of feminist manifesto. I contend, however, that lurking behind the feminist critique of a debilitating paternalism lies a "yellow passion" that smacks of both racial and media politics. Gilman's way of unleashing the narrator's temper in reflections on the color yellow entails a performative dimension, namely, the enactment of a fundamental shift in perspective inspired by a new perception of yellow as color of light-as-medium, namely, photography.

In this context, I will also discuss a 1917 short story by Virginia Woolf entitled "The Mark on the Wall," which recalls aspects of Gilman's piece, in particular the way in which the narrator analyzes a "film of yellow light" projected on the wall of her room. In spaces enclosed by walls marked in yellow, both Gilman and Woolf reveal the significance of yellow as a stigmatizing force through an ecstatic temporality that resonates on multiple levels: aesthetic, psychological, sociological, technical, and medical.[12] I contend

---

[12] Woolf emphasizes in her definitions of the task of modern fiction her commitment to multi-perspectivism and the role of the modern artist at the margins of established authority, very much along the lines of Baudelaire's assertion, as Angeliki Spiropoulou points out, that the artist is like a mirror "as vast as the crowd itself," as well as of Benjamin's notion of the ragpicker. See Angeliki Spiropoulou, *Virginia Woolf, Modernity and History: Constellations with Walter Benjamin* (New York: Palgrave Macmillan, 2010), 34.

that it is through the extra-literary tools employed by these two authors, in particular the techniques of painting, photography, and film, that the multivalent figuration of yellow is made manifest in a moment of illumination, a "luminous moment," as Jane Goldman observes, which is at the same time an "historical intervention."[13]

In the "The Yellow Wallpaper," Gilman anticipates the full spectrum of uses of yellow as they unfold half a decade later in politics, media, and art. Participating in contemporary debates about wallpaper designs (an important element of the movement of aestheticism and its association with yellow motifs), Gilman evokes the themes of journalism and racism, which were about to be named in yellow ("yellow journalism" and the "yellow peril"). However, by capturing a moment in time just before these yellow phenomena were explicitly named, Gilman's reflection on yellow patterns remains closely linked to the materiality of yellow itself, which she dramatizes as yellow's ability to constantly change its appearance depending on the light. Yellow is also associated with the Romantic *topos* of poetic inspiration (symbolized by the moonlight), but in the form of a violent confrontation with questions of politics and gender as well as of artistic creation.

Gilman intended for her piece to be taken allegorically, i.e. as a piece of propaganda. As Gilman herself explains in a letter to W. D. Howells, who asked her for permission to reprint the story in his collection "Little American Masterpieces of Fiction" in 1919:

> I am pleased and honored that you should wish to use "The Yellow Wallpaper" in the book as you ask. Did you know that that one piece of "literature" of mine was pure propaganda? I was once under Dr. Weir Mitchell's treatment, at 27. He sent me home to "Live as domestic a life as possible; have your child with you all the time; lie down an hour after each meal; have but two hours of intellectual life a day (!); and never touch pencil, brush, or pen as long as you live." I tried it one summer, and went as near lunacy as one can and come back.[14]

Gilman was at the time of "The Yellow Wallpaper" already an accomplished writer and lecturer, as well as editor of her own periodical, *The Forerunner Magazine*. It nevertheless took Gilman two years to get her piece published.

---

[13] Jane Goldman, *The Feminist Aesthetics of Virginia Woolf: Modernism, Post-Impressionism and the Politics of the Visual* (Cambridge: Cambridge University Press, 1998), 8.

[14] Charlotte Perkins Gilman, "Letter to W. D. Howells," 17 October 1919, in *Charlotte Perkins Gilman's "The Yellow Wallpaper" and the History of Its Publication and Reception: A Critical Edition and Documentary Casebook*, ed. Julie Bates Dock (University Park: Pennsylvania State University Press, 1998), 96.

One editor rejected her with the comment: "I could not forgive myself if I made others as miserable as I have made myself!"[15] Gilman herself called the piece, in a letter to a friend, an "awful story" and notes in her diary that it was written in two days, "with the thermometer at one hundred and three—in Pasadena, Cal[ifornia]."[16]

The urgency with which Gilman describes the writing of the story is reflected in its structure: divisible into 12 sections or entries (indicated through changes in perspective and light conditions), Gilman's text performs the staging of a female perspective, which is first and foremost characterized by its optic hapticality, that is, its emphasis on touch and contact as the medium of sensuous communication. Indicating her belief in superstition (in opposition to her husband's "intense horror of superstition"), the number 12, as a magic number, points to the organization of time (12 hours of the clock, 12 months of the year), of measurement (a dozen) and spirituality (Jesus's 12 disciples). However, it is the temporal dimension that both structures and drives the narrative.

The heated and sickly atmosphere of the story is transmitted through the feverish analysis of a repulsive wall pattern and its yellow color, which initiates a kind of revolt in the protagonist, an inner revolt that by the end of the story is bursting forth to the outside. The following is the first description of the wallpaper in the story:

> The paint and paper look as if a boys' school had used it. It is stripped off—the paper in great patches all around the head of my bed, about as far as I can reach, and in a great place on the other side of the room low down. I never saw a worse paper in my life. One of those sprawling flamboyant patterns committing every artistic sin. It is dull enough to confuse the eye in following, pronounced enough to constantly irritate and provoke study, and when you follow the lame uncertain curves for a little distance they suddenly commit suicide—plunge off at outrageous angles, destroy themselves in unheard of contradictions. The color is repellent, almost revolting; a smouldering unclean yellow, strangely faded by the slow-turning sunlight.[17]

What is striking is the "flamboyance" of the yellow pattern of the wallpaper, which the narrator describes as committing "every artistic sin." Once she starts to familiarize herself with the pattern, starts even to mimic its appearance, the yellow pattern will develop the revolting impact that she

---

[15] Horace E. Scudder to Gilman, ibid., 91.

[16] Gilman, ibid., 85.

[17] Ibid., 30–1.

detected in its appearance from the outset ("the color is repellent, almost revolting"). We should also note that the reference to a "boys' school" at the beginning of the passage marks the yellow pattern, from the outset, in terms of a nexus between gender and aesthetics, part of a multivalent figuration that will expand to include medical, political, and ethical dimensions.

Trained as a graphic designer at the Rhode Island School of Design, Gilman was certainly aware of the debates over wallpaper design in the 1880s; thus the narrator of "The Yellow Wallpaper" knows "a little of the principle of design." And: "I know this thing was not arranged on any laws of radiation, or alternation, or repetition, or symmetry, or anything else that I ever heard of."[18] William Morris's yellow wallpaper designs were hotly debated in the 1880s, and, later in her life, Gilman visited Morris himself, while on a lecture tour through England. The use of the color yellow as an index of aestheticism was also associated with Oscar Wilde, who, in his lectures in the United States in the 1880s and early 1890s, noted (in regard to Whistler's painting of a blue and yellow room) that "one keynote of color should predominate."[19] However, the artistic sins that the narrator in "The Yellow Wallpaper" notices are not a function of art, but are rather due to a kind of vandalism or prurience, as the opening of the above-quoted passage emphasizes: "The paint and paper look as if a boys' school had used it." Gilman's point of criticism, as she will articulate in her own lectures against the idea of *l'art pour l'art* (1894) and in her *The Man-Made World, or, Our Androcentric Culture* (1911), is the male excess that she also detected in the art movements of decadence, which she considered to be simply another expression of patriarchy. Gilman's argument is that "art is human," but needs to be "feminized first," to achieve the "conditions in which human art can be produced."[20]

"The Yellow Wallpaper" is very much a story about the achievement of such conditions, and is therefore not only a manifesto of a "new female aesthetics" but also a political manifesto, or rather a manifesto on political art. As Ann Heilmann has argued, Gilman turns in her story "the two signifiers of aestheticism (the color yellow and the flower tapestry made famous by William Morris) into the central metaphor [...], juxtaposing these with a woman's centered politics and perspective, the central female consciousness of her text."[21] Indeed, the narrator ridicules the concern with domestic issues

---

[18] Ibid., 34.
[19] Oscar Wilde, "The House Beautiful," quoted in Ann Heilmann, "Overwriting Decadence: Charlotte Perkins Gilman, Oscar Wilde, and the Feminization of Art in 'The Yellow Wallpaper,'" in *The Mixed Legacy of Charlotte Perkins Gilman*, ed. Catherine J. Golden and Joanna Schneider Zangrando (Newark: University of Delaware Press, 2000), 182.
[20] Ibid., 184.
[21] Ibid., 178.

when she mentions her sister-in-law's complaints about the staining power of the yellow wallpaper: "Then she said that the paper stained everything it touched, that she had found yellow smooches on all my clothes and John's, and she wished we would be more careful!"[22] The sexual excess that the sister implies is dismissed by the narrator as the conventional perspective of women concerned with home and marital life.

The staining materiality of "The Yellow Wallpaper" points emphatically outside the domestic realm, to the revolting character of the yellow patterns, which "plunge off at outrageous angles, destroy themselves in unheard of contradictions"—descriptions that point to Gilman's frequent attacks on sensationalist journalism and the corruption of print culture, as Sari Edelstein has shown.[23] Although yellow journalism only received its name after the battle over the comic strip "The Yellow Kid" in 1897,[24] sensationalist reporting had been associated with the color yellow since the 1880s. This was partly due to the quick yellowing of the paper, to which Gilman also seems to point, as when she emphasizes the fading of the unclean yellow ("strangely faded by the slow-turning sunlight"). Strongly opposed to the pointlessness and sensationalism of the publishing industry, Gilman made it her mission to create with *Forerunner*, the periodical she published from 1909 to 1916, what she called a "special medium,"[25] which she defines in the opening issue in the form of a poem:

> "Then This"
> The news-stands bloom with magazines,
> They flame, they blaze indeed;
> So bright the cover-colors glow,
> So clear the startling stories show,
> So vivid their pictorial scenes,
> That he who runs may read.[26]

The blazing flamboyance of sensationalist newspapers, meant to be read on the run, requires a fundamental change in direction: not backward, but forward. This sense of a forward movement, which takes on the new,

---

[22] Gilman, *Charlotte Perkins Gilman's "The Yellow Wallpaper,"* 38.

[23] "In the context of Gilman's experiences with the press, the story's vilification of paper can be seen as a professional critique of the newspaper industry as well as a personal and feminist response to her own exploitation" (Sari Edelstein, "Charlotte Perkins Gilman and the Yellow Newspaper," *Legacy: A Journal of American Women Writers* 24, no. 1 [2007]: 81).

[24] See my discussion in the Introduction to this book.

[25] Quoted in Edelstein, "Charlotte Perkins Gilman and the Yellow Newspaper," 72.

[26] Gilman, "Then This," in Cynthia Davis, *Charlotte Perkins Gilman: A Biography* (Stanford, CA: Stanford University Press, 2010), 293.

resembles, in its outrageous angles and horizontal lines and columns, the sensationalist arrangement of a newspaper page. As Gilman writes in "The Yellow Wallpaper":

> But, on the other hand, they connect diagonally, and the sprawling outlines run off in great slanting waves of optic horror, like a lot of wallowing seaweeds in full chase. The whole thing goes horizontally, too, at least it seems so, and I exhaust myself in trying to distinguish the order of its going in that direction.[27]

The "optic horror" resists ordering principles; it rather overcomes in waves, resembling the front page of a newspaper, which, driven by sensationalist headlines, is also spreading out in columns that are arranged vertically as well as horizontally. Gilman's description of an uncontrollable force moves thereby from the experience of an "optic horror" to a bodily sense of being overwhelmed and exhausted by the yellow pattern as a constant presence, which Gilman dramatizes as inescapable and haunting.

With the visceral sense of an unclean and repellent yellow, we are confronted with Gilman's racial politics. As Susan Lanser has suggested:

> Despite her socialist values, her active participation in movements of reform, her strong theoretical commitment to racial harmony, her unconventional support of interracial marriages, and her frequent condemnation of America's racist history, Gilman upheld white Protestant supremacy; belonged for a time to eugenics and nationalist organizations; opposed open immigration; and inscribed racism, nationalism and classism into her proposals for social change.[28]

The perception of an "unclean," "smoldering," and "repellent" yellow must thus be reinterpreted within the context of Gilman's writings. Many of her views are conventional for the era, linked as they are to the racial ideology of the late nineteenth century, which explains their presence in a writer who was viewed—and who viewed herself—as a progressive thinker. The yellow pattern that the narrator of "The Yellow Wallpaper" sees spreading like a "fungus" all over her room resonates with racist rhetoric in which the color "'yellow' applied not only to the Chinese, Japanese, and light-skinned African-Americans, but also to Jews, Poles, Hungarians, Italians, and even the Irish."[29] Although the term "yellow peril" was coined only in 1895, five years after Gilman wrote her short story, the negative imagery of yellow as a

---

[27] Gilman, *"The Yellow Wallpaper,"* 34.
[28] Susan Lanser, "Feminist Criticism, 'The Yellow Wallpaper,' and the Politics of Color in America," *Feminist Studies* 15, no. 3 (1989): 429.
[29] Ibid., 426.

color stigmatizing immigrants from the East and the South had already been established, an imagery driven especially by notions of impurity, unclean-liness, bad odour, and associated with such terms as "human garbage" and "pollutants."[30] The distrust of immigrants was particularly strong in California, where Gilman had just moved in 1890, the year she wrote "The Yellow Wallpaper."

In *The Forerunner*, "yellow" groups are frequently singled out as "lazy old Orientals," pointing to the "criminal conditions" in Chinatown and the "unhealthy social practices" of the Chinese.[31] Describing the presence of African-Americans as the existing "problem" of the country, Gilman sees the "inflow" of China's "oppressed" as endangering the American "national" character. In her book *Concerning Children* (1900), Gilman argues for the supremacy of American children, and emphasizes that the "more subversive races"—in her view "the Chinese and the Hindu, where parents are fairly worshipped and blindly obeyed"—are therefore inferior to the "races of free and progressive thought and healthy activity."[32] Paradoxically, Gilman's rhetoric against the "yellow" races is to a certain degree reflected in the condition in which the narrator of "The Yellow Wallpaper" finds herself—a fact that is transformed in a dramatic twist of the story, in which passivity and obedience, as well as repulsion, are reversed.

Camera Lucida: Gilman and Albrecht Dürer

The negative and even threatening appearance of the yellow wallpaper is reversed when the restlessness of the narrator develops into a counter-force; analyzing resemblances and correspondences, the narrator recognizes elemental connections between the yellow pattern of the wallpaper, its irritable appearance, and her own irritable state of mind:

> On a pattern like this, by daylight, there is a lack of sequence, a defiance of law, that is a constant irritant to a normal mind.
> The color is hideous enough, and unreliable enough, and infuriating enough, but the pattern is torturing.
> You think you have mastered it, but just as you get well underway in following, it turns a back-somersault and there you are. It slaps you in the face, knocks you down, and tramples upon you. It is like a bad dream.

[30] Ibid.
[31] Ibid., 430.
[32] Quoted in ibid.

> The outside pattern is a florid arabesque, reminding one of a fungus. If you can imagine a toadstool in joints, an interminable string of toadstools, budding and sprouting in endless convolutions—why, that is something like it.
>
> That is, sometimes!
>
> There is one marked peculiarity about this paper, a thing nobody seems to notice but myself, and that is that it changes as the light changes.
>
> When the sun shoots in through the east window—I always watch for that first long, straight ray—it changes so quickly that I never can quite believe it.[33]

The torturous pattern shows itself in daylight as an aggressor; its color is hideous; it defies laws, and even starts to act violently against the narrator; it is, however, the experience of the yellow pattern as a personal threat that causes the animation of the pattern ("it slaps you in the face") and prompts an active engagement with its aggressive appearance. Unable to control the violent threat, the narrator performs a change of perspective by stepping back, perceiving the yellow pattern now from a distance as "florid arabesque"—not as a human threat anymore, but threatening nonetheless. The narrator compares the appearance of the arabesque to a fungus, more specifically to the poisonous fungus of a toadstool with its umbrella-shaped body. What is thus spreading in "endless convolutions" are not the geometric patterns of arabesques, which extend, in their potentially infinite structure, beyond the visible material world, but the pattern that is spreading and sprouting and that is described in terms of decomposition, as a kind of parasitic organism. As a form of Oriental imagery, it shows itself as a degeneration from its original decorative and spiritual power.

However, the rhetoric of the increasing degeneration and dramatization of the yellow pattern as an uncontrollable force is interrupted by the remark: "That is, sometimes!"—which indicates that the yellow patterns are not one-dimensional; other times of the day will in fact offer moments of inspiration. The shift is dramatized as a change of light, which is revealed through the (increasingly proximate) relation between the self-perception of the narrator and the perception of the yellow color and its violent patterns.

When the moonlight appears, the effects of the spreading violence and decomposition are reversed into the recognition of a structure, the impression of a personal attack into a sympathetic engagement, and the dehumanizing force into a human encounter:

---

[33] Gilman, *"The Yellow Wallpaper,"* 37.

> By moonlight—the moon shines in all night when there is a moon—I
> wouldn't know it was the same paper.
> At night in any kind of light, in twilight, candle light, lamplight, and
> worst of all by moonlight, it becomes bars! The outside pattern I mean,
> and the woman behind it is as plain as can be.
> I didn't realize for a long time what the thing was that showed behind,
> that dim sub-pattern, but now I am quite sure it is a woman.[34]

To be sure, this doubling of the subject (*Doppelgänger*) is a staple of the
horror genre (into which "The Yellow Wallpaper" is sometimes assimilated).
The uncanny effects are no doubt intended, but curiously this is also a
humanizing moment. What during daytime has paralyzing effects possesses
at night a transformative power. The narrator not only recognizes in the
pattern a woman in a similar condition to her own, but identifies with her
and initiates a revolt against the conditions of the "revolting" paper; she thus
starts to "creep" like the "creepy" appearance of the pattern: "I always lock the
door when I creep by daylight. I can't do it at night, for I know John would
suspect something at once." The opposition between day and night, symbol-
izing rationality (John, sunlight) and irrationality (moon, madness ["lunatic"
derives from "lunar"], darkness, superstition) respectively, dissolves behind
closed doors, while the narrator is conquering the room as her own, claiming
a space, which she recognizes as her space of (self-)illumination.

For what the dramatic shift in perspective at night entails first and
foremost is a change in methodology. The narrator, who had already given
up writing, does not attempt to read the pattern any more; instead, the visual
approach of an analysis from a distance has been replaced by direct sensual
contact with what is perceived as an undecipherable pattern.

> As soon as it was moonlight and that poor thing began to crawl and
> shake the pattern, I got up and ran to help her.
> I pulled and she shook, I shook and she pulled, and before morning we
> had peeled off yards of that paper.
> A strip about as high as my head and half around the room.
> And then when the sun came and that awful pattern began to laugh at
> me, I declared I would finish it to-day![35]

With the reappearance of the sun, the narrator formulates her declaration,
which is to tear the paper from the wall "to-day," to overwrite it with her
own body, creeping eventually on top of the paper along the walls of the
room. The narrator has developed sensuous correspondences with the

[34] Ibid.
[35] Ibid., 40.

paper and its yellow pattern, namely by looking for similarities (at night), becoming Other by virtue of the process itself, instead of looking for laws and principles, that is, for non-sensuous, rational correspondences. Gilman here appears to formulate a fundamental critique of rational thought and processes of abstraction, which, in her view, fail to account for the modern (feminine) condition. Rather, the linkage between her own (irritating, irrational) condition and those of the woman on the other side is realized at night in the changing appearance of the yellow pattern, in a medium capable of recording change. Yellow, as the color of light, becomes the narrator's medium of illumination. By moonlight, she is becoming Other herself, getting out of the pattern that is torturing her: "I hate to see it sometimes, it creeps so slowly, and always comes in by one window or another. John was asleep and I hated to waken him, so I kept still and watched the moonlight on that undulating wall-paper till I felt creepy."[36]

She starts to feel the creepiness of the paper herself, and, at the end of the story, she creeps in circles along the walls of the room day and night, like the woman behind the prison-bars of the paper; in effect, she is becoming as "revolting" as the color of the paper, overwriting in the process her doctor's analysis and prescription not to write at all, but to rest ("he said we came here solely on my account, that I was to have perfect rest and all the air I could get").[37] However, the narrator does not revolt by turning against the wall; her biting and scratching at the wallpaper is not an attempt to get outside; on the contrary, she sees her confinement as an impetus to go farther inside by becoming more and more like "The Yellow Wallpaper" itself, not through reading or deciphering, not by way of analysis, but by going outside of herself, through the strong urge, as Benjamin observes in *The Work of Art in the Age of Mechanical Reproduction*, "to get a hold of an object at very close range by way of its likeness, its reproduction."[38] The narrator is, on the one hand, reproducing the properties of the yellow pattern and, on the other, creating a sensuous connection between herself and the paper, engaging herself physically in a mimetic process.

Indeed, what presents itself in Theodor Adorno as the "born again mimetic faculty of modernity"[39] also seems to be at work in Gilman's imagery of the darkened room, in which likenesses and similarities reveal the narra-

---

36 Ibid., 36.
37 Ibid., 30.
38 Benjamin, *Illuminations*, 223.
39 Gertrude Koch in "Mimesis and the Ban on the Graven Images" refers to Adorno's suggestion that modernity has affinities with the "earliest period of childhood prior to the ego having taken a definite shape," as Michael Taussig points out in "Physiognomic Aspects of Visual Worlds" (*Visual Anthropology Review* 8, no. 1 [1992]: 21).

tor's ability to recognize connections to the inhospitable atmosphere that "The Yellow Wallpaper" creates in the room of her confinement. Distinctions between inside and outside, self and other, begin to break down in a network of correspondences and dialectical movements between extremes:

> There are always new shoots on the fungus, and new shades of yellow all over it. I cannot keep count of them, though I have tried conscientiously.
>
> It is the strangest yellow, that Wallpaper! It makes me think of all the yellow things I ever saw—not beautiful ones like buttercups, but old foul, bad yellow things. [...] It used to disturb me at first. I thought seriously of burning the house—to reach the smell. But now I am used to it. The only thing I can think of that it is like the *color* of the paper! A yellow smell.[40]

The strategy Gilman presents is driven by a process of familiarization and the search for mimetic faculties. Instead of burning the house, a cholerical gesture (in humor pathology the "choleric" is identified with the element of fire), the narrator compares the smell, and reaches the conclusion that smell and color are related, as interwoven with each other as the narrator is with the woman behind the paper. Her immersion in the yellow physiognomy of the room expands and slowly begins to transcend the prison-world of her confinement; by becoming more and more immersed in yellow, she liberates herself from the pattern that captured her. The color yellow is a "mimetic" medium, in the sense that the narrator learns "to become similar and to behave mimetically," as Benjamin states in "On the Mimetic Faculty."[41] Her own metamorphosis unites her with the yellow imagery of the room, which takes her outside of herself, to the point where she develops a new sensorium, a "sixth" sense, as Michael Taussig has called the ability to notice in mimetic faculties a specific sense on the basis of which resemblances and correspondences are generated: "No proposition could be more fundamental to understanding the visceral bond connecting perceiver to perceived in the operation of mimesis."[42] The sensuous contact that the mimetic operation entails is also fundamental to Gilman's way of dramatizing the transformation of a space of confinement. The similarities recognized between the yellow pattern and her own condition initiate a movement that transports the narrator out of herself and, paradoxically, further inside her confinement.

---

[40] Gilman, "*The Yellow Wallpaper*," 39.

[41] Walter Benjamin, "On the Mimetic Faculty," in *Walter Benjamin: Selected Writings 1931–1934*, ed. Michael William Jennings (Cambridge, MA: Harvard University Press, 2005), 720.

[42] Taussig, *Mimesis and Alterity: A Particular History of the Senses* (New York: Routledge, 1993), 39.

Gilman's focus on the transformative process inside the room of her confinement points to the room's transformation into a stage. The narrator becomes a spectacle to herself, liberated and captivated at the same time; she is "self-sculpting" (an expression used by Roger Caillos in the 1930s, reflecting on mimetic aspects of magic);[43] that is, she is her own path of resistance on the torn-off pieces of the yellow wallpaper, striving to liberate herself from the rest-cure through a form of active resistance, which she performs ritualistically by circling around the four walls of the room.

The negativity of yellow, which unfolds during daytime, is transformed, under different lighting conditions, at nighttime (activating the Romantic association between moonlight and creative inspiration). At night, the yellow wallpaper is recognized as light-sensitive material, thereby opening up the imagery of a photochemical reaction—literally "drawing with light" (evoking the Greek word *photo-graphein*) in the "darkroom" of her confinement. Gilman thus stages resistance as a performative act, using the yellow pattern of the wallpaper as material to write on. Inscribing herself with her whole body, the narrator performs an act of self-transformation characteristic of a magic show:

> I don't like to *look* out of the windows even—there are so many of those creeping women, and they creep so fast.
> I wonder if they all come out of that Wallpaper as I did?
> But I am securely fastened now by my well-hidden rope—you don't get ME out in the road there!
> I suppose I shall have to get back behind the pattern when it comes night, and that is hard!
> It is so pleasant to be out in this great room and creep around as I please!
> I don't want to go outside. I won't, even if Jennie asks me to.
> For outside you have to creep on the ground, and everything is green instead of yellow.
> But here I can creep smoothly on the floor, and my shoulder just fits in that long smooch around the wall, so I cannot lose my way.[44]

Gilman's narrator is presented as being part of a movement; her creeping on all fours is reflected in the movement of the fast-creeping women outside, as a first step of resistance to and liberation from the (patriarchal) pattern,

---

[43] "In this dizzying journey through insect biology, aesthetics, early anthropology of magic, and the body as a self-sculpting camera, Caillois concludes that mimesis is a 'being tempted by space,' a drama in which the self is but a self-diminishing point midst others, losing its boundedness" (Taussig, "Physiognomic Aspects of Visual Worlds," 27).

[44] Gilman, *"The Yellow Wallpaper,"* 41–2.

thereby escaping the domestic sphere. However, Gilman's narrator insists on what she now understands as her privileged role inside the darkened yellow room, on staying in her *camera lucida*. Instead of creeping outside together with the other women ("there are so many"), she prefers to creep inside what is now a "room of her own."

The preference for yellow (inside) over green (outside), for creeping inside ("securely fastened") over gazing outside, is a preference for the transformed space of confinement and its yellow conditions, which the narrator describes as a space that corresponds to her psychological and physiological make-up ("and my shoulder just fits in that long smooch along the wall"). The radical shift that Gilman dramatizes here is a shift in perspective, or more precisely, a shift in perspectivism itself; the classical set-up of creating perspective by creating a framework, the famous look through the window frame that has defined Western perspectivism since the Renaissance, is here put into question ("I don't like to look out of the window"), replaced by a sensuous performance of creeping, emphasizing the senses of smell ("yellow smell") and touch ("smoothly"), rather than the ocular sense of distance and objectification (looking).

Throughout the story, which announces itself as a story about visual design, Gilman replaces the terminology of looking with an emphasis on the *knowledge* that the narrator *senses*: "a thing nobody seems to notice but myself";[45] "there are things in that paper that nobody knows but me, or ever will";[46] "I am determined that nobody shall find it out but myself!"[47] Eventually peeling off the yellow pattern from the wall, the narrator begins to literally grasp its disturbing color and, more importantly, to grasp (metaphorically) the correspondences to her own condition. Following the dictum that Gilman will formulate a few years after writing "The Yellow Wallpaper"—that art must first be feminized—the emphasis on the female perspective as a perspective driven by a haptic notion of color and light, rather than by purely optical and visually constructed patterns, reverses the classical notion of perspectivism itself, most famously expressed in Albrecht Dürer's reflections on perspectivism and proportionality.

In *Artist drawing a Model*, Dürer presents the depiction of the female nude as it is perceived through patterns from a distance. In "The Yellow Wallpaper," the theme of the female nude as the object of the male gaze is itself inverted: "there is a recurrent spot where the pattern lolls

---

45 Ibid., 37.
46 Ibid., 35.
47 Ibid., 38.

Figure 3 Albrecht Dürer, *Artist Drawing a Model in Foreshortening through a Frame Using a Grid System*. Woodcut from "Unterweysung des Messung" (Treatise on Perspective), Nuremberg, 1527. Photo Credit: Foto Marburg/Art Resource, NY.

like a broken neck and two bulbous eyes stare at you upside down."[48] However, with the reversal of perspectives, the emphasis also shifts to a focus on light and color; as Svetlana Alpers comments, regarding Dürer's perspective machine, "sight or vision is defined geometrically in this art. It concerns our measured relationship to objects in space rather than the glow of light and color."[49] Light and color are, however, the parameters that determine the narrator's perspective in "The Yellow Wallpaper"—in opposition to the rational geometry of patterns that the appearance of the yellow wallpaper defies. The constantly changing conditions of light make the idea of a controlling perspective (which Dürer frames in his sketch, equating spectatorship with "a controlling patriarchal perspective")[50] impossible; instead, Gilman stages the female perspective as constantly shifting, as moving along with the changing appearance of color and light. The technical device of the *camera obscura*, as a perspective machine, is transformed—to invoke Roland Barthes—into a *camera lucida*:[51] a theatrical performance of self-transformation. Barthes's emphasis on the development of photography out of the arts of the stage (such as the

[48] Ibid., 32.
[49] Svetlana Alpers, "Art History and Its Exclusions: The Example of Dutch Art," in *Feminism and Art History: Questioning the Litany*, ed. Norma Braude and Mary D. Garrard (Boulder, CO: Westview, 1982), 186.
[50] Barbara Freedman, *Staging the Gaze: Postmodernism, Psychoanalysis, and Shakespearean Comedy* (Ithaca, NY: Cornell University Press, 1991), 2.
[51] Roland Barthes, *Camera Lucida: Reflections on Photography*, trans. Richard Howard (New York: Hill and Wang, 1982). Barthes's emphasis on the spectator who sees the dead in the "lifelike" face of the photographic object goes back to the development of photography as an art of the stage, a form of animated light-show (ibid., 29). The moment of the animation of the dead also marks the turning-point of "The Yellow Wallpaper," that is, the moment that the paper itself comes to life, when it "slaps you" in the face.

magic lantern) echoes Gilman's emphasis on the performative dimension of the narrator's engagement with the yellow pattern that surrounds her. Her active engagement reverses the passivity of the painterly object, as emblematized in Dürer's *Artist drawing a Model*. Like Dürer's figure of Melancholia, who is stuck with one foot in superstition (the magic square at the wall) and one foot in modern science (exposing the globe, the circle as her *instrumentarium*), Gilman's narrator creates her own space. Its yellowish color provokes the *revolt* of the narrator—a choleric gesture, as it were, in contrast to the melancholic temperament traditionally associated with the arts and with contemplation.

The literalness of Gilman's style links back repeatedly to yellow motifs, which she identifies as the key to the story, as when the narrator advises her husband that he can find the key to her locked door under the leaves of a banana tree, also called "plantain":

> How he does call and pound!
> Now he's crying for an axe.
> It would be a shame to break down that beautiful door!
> "John dear!" said I in the gentlest voice, "the key is down by the front steps, under a plantain leaf!"
> That silenced him for a few moments.[52]

It is the doctor-husband's own behavior that now appears to be hysterical: pounding on the door, screaming for an axe, he appears to be playing the role of a madman. However, the narrator herself is determined on her path, crawling over her husband's body, on top of the yellow wallpaper. The reversal of roles is the culmination point of a series of reversals that Gilman inscribes in the narrator's engagement with the yellow pattern. The repulsive and unclean materiality of yellow is not decoded, but rather performed in its wide-ranging and constantly changing appearance, opening in the last installment a reference to yellow as the color of an exotic fruit, of bananas. Thus both literally and figuratively Gilman refers to the key to the story as being hidden under the banana tree. The key leads to the story about the narrator herself becoming yellow, not through the "yellow smooches" (being intimate with her husband), but through an aggressive act of liberation from her imprisonment in a pattern.

We might here cite the narrative model of the "Madwoman in the Attic" to which Gilman's short story appears to conform. This model was first proposed in Sandra Gilbert's and Susan Gubar's well-known study *The Madwoman in the Attic: Woman Writers and the Nineteenth Century*

[52] Gilman, "*The Yellow Wallpaper*," 42.

Imagination, which derived its central idea from Charlotte Brontë's novel *Jane Eyre* (1847). Jane is dreaming of leaving Thornfield mansion to roam freely in society; however, Rochester's mad wife Bertha stays locked in the attic, until she eventually burns down the mansion, throwing herself into the flames. Bertha's Creole features (she was brought to England from the West Indies), her eyes, and her madness, crawling on all fours, suggest close ties to the woman Gilman's narrator recognizes behind the bars of the pattern as well as to her own behavior. However, Bertha's dramatic suicide is overwritten with Gilman's narrator's decision not to jump out of the window: "I am getting angry enough to do something desperate. To jump out of the window would be admirable exercise, but the bars are too strong even to try." Liberation in Gilman's "Yellow Wallpaper" is, paradoxically, only possible through an active engagement with the abjection of yellow; for it is through the repulsiveness of the color yellow that the revolt is initiated against patterns. As the color of light-sensitive material, yellow becomes the medium in which Gilman stages the transformation into a "new mode of truth-seeking and reality-testing," which Benjamin saw as the basis for the development of the potential that he ascribed to the medium of film. Benjamin saw this medium as tearing our "prison-world asunder by the dynamite of a tenth of a second, so that now, in the midst of its far-flung ruins and debris, we calmly and adventurously go traveling."[53] Benjamin's image of debris (which Gilman also uses to visualize a room with torn-off wallpaper pieces on the floor) is supposed to be a function of the filmic apparatus itself. With its close-ups, its montage techniques, the filmic apparatus emphasizes the body of the perceiver, not just the mind's eye. The shift to optical tactility is the central shift that Gilman performs in the realm of yellow, converting the optical perception of a color into its tactile perception; in other words, it transforms the perception of the color yellow into an image of debris, as it were, where it confronts the modern implications of gender, race, and media politics. The visual politics of yellow, so disturbing in Gilman's own political comments throughout her career, both as an artist and an intellectual, becomes the medium where the "uncleanliness" of modern times shows itself, where the "unheard of contradictions"[54] unfold.

Emphasizing the significance and singularity of the female perspective throughout her piece, Gilman insists on the yellow pattern as a culturally generated phenomenon. Five years prior to the appearance of

---

[53] Benjamin, *Illuminations*, 236.
[54] Gilman, *"The Yellow Wallpaper,"* 31.

Aubrey Beardsley's and John Lane's *The Yellow Book* and anticipating the decade that would come to be named the "Yellow Nineties," Gilman is, in effect, overwriting the decadent movement, which had yet to declare yellow as its emblematic color.

While, as we saw in the previous chapter, decadent yellow is itself a yellow of transgression, ever gesturing towards the scandalous and self-consciously playing with yellow's stigmatizing potential, Gilman connects the color yellow to the pressing political issues of her time. Typically read as a manifesto for the formation of a feminist perspective, "The Yellow Wallpaper" also expresses a more conventional—and more disturbing—attitude toward race and the mass phenomena of its time (mass immigration, mass media).

A "film of yellow light": Virginia Woolf's "The Mark on the Wall"

Almost three decades after the publication of "The Yellow Wallpaper," Virginia Woolf, in her short story "The Mark on the Wall" (1917), similarly reflects on the act of writing in a space of enclosure, which Woolf will call a few years later in her eponymous lecture series "a room of one's own": "For women have sat indoors all these millions of years, so that by this time the very walls are permeated by their creative force."[55] The confrontations with the walls of the room, which reveal a creative space while at the same time they are "marked out by patriarchy,"[56] invite a feminist perspective. Peggy Kamuf writes that there is both "recognition and an infringement of the place of a creative subject which is no longer or not yet a 'one.'"[57] Written during the time of the Great War, the inevitable intrusion into the interior space of the war raging outside creates "some collision with reality,"[58] which unfolds in a "film of yellow light."[59]

---

[55] Virginia Woolf, *A Room of One's Own* (London: Hogarth Press, 1929), 131.
[56] Goldman, *The Feminist Aesthetics of Virginia Woolf*, 10.
[57] Peggy Kamuf, "Penelope at Work: Interruptions in *A Room of One's Own*," *Novel* 16 (1982): 17. Goldman uses Kamuf's notion of "intervention" for her investigations of Woolf's central tropes of light, shade, and color (Goldman, *The Feminist Aesthetics of Virginia Woolf*, 10). While Goldman offers towards the end of her study a more specific reading of Woolf's allusions to suffrage colors, my interpretation of the role of yellow in "The Mark on the Wall" (and in *Mrs. Dalloway*) also insists on the political context (yellow journalism, the Great War).
[58] Virginia Woolf, "The Mark on the Wall," in *The Complete Shorter Fiction of Virginia Woolf*, ed. Susan Dick (New York: Harcourt Brace Jovanovich Publishers, 1985), 88.
[59] Ibid., 77.

Recalling the beginning of Leonardo da Vinci's *Treatise on Painting* (1651),[60] in which the Renaissance artist suggests focusing on a stain, a mark on a wall, for inspiration, Woolf dramatizes the mark on the wall as a way of bringing an unstoppable flow of images to a halt, of interrupting "old fancies" to fix a moment in time, or space-time:

> Perhaps it was in the middle of January in the present year that I first looked up and saw the mark on the wall. In order to fix a date it is necessary to remember what one saw. So now I think of the fire; the steady film of yellow light upon the page of my book; the three chrysanthemums in the round glass bowl on the mantelpiece. Yes, it must have been winter time, and we had just finished our tea, for I remember that I was smoking a cigarette when I looked up and saw the mark on the wall for the first time.[61]

The description of the mark on the wall evokes a cinematic set-up: the round glass bowl is the projecting lens and the fire the light source, projecting the motif of the three chrysanthemums. "The mark on the wall seems also to project from the wall," observes the narrator, thereby turning the living room into a cinema. Observing the projections on the wall inside her room, the protagonist sits passively, a spectator to the play of images. (One could also cite Plato's Allegory of the Cave in this context).[62] The "film of yellow light" that is reflected from the mark on the wall onto the page of her book is a film of golden, radiating matter (in Greek: *chrysa*), which is the theme of the three chrysanthemums. However, Woolf does not mention the fashionable use of chrysanthemums in the Yellow Nineties (used as decoration on vases and in wallpaper designs, and which made a room appear twice its size, as Richard Le Gallienne observes in one of his contributions to *The Yellow Book*).[63] Nor

---

[60] Sue Roe in "The impact of post-impressionism" (in *The Cambridge Companion to Virginia Woolf*, ed. Sue Roe and Susan Sellers [Cambridge: Cambridge University Press, 2000], 177) juxtaposes "The Mark on the Wall" with Leonardo's *Treatise*, which he opens with the advice to study marks on walls, and not only marks, but also clouds, embers of fire, mud, etc. Roe's comparison of Leonardo's lists of inspiring objects and Woolf's lists that move from the organic world into interiors show Woolf's movement into the "mind's most vibrant manifestations: the imagination, or what we sometimes call the mind's eye."

[61] Woolf, "The Mark on the Wall," 77.

[62] Plato, *The Republic*, Book VII. In this text, the projected shadows of the fire are contrasted with the full illumination of the sun upon emerging from the cave.

[63] "Yellow is becoming more and more dominant in decoration—in wallpapers, and flowers cultivated with decorative intention, such as chrysanthemums. And one can easily understand why: seeing that, after white, yellow reflects more light than any other colour, and thus ministers to the growing preference for light and joyous rooms. A few yellow chrysanthemums will make a small room look twice its size, and when the sun comes out upon a yellow wallpaper the whole room seems suddenly to expand, to open

does she mention the use of chrysanthemums in graveyards as tributes to the dead (a tradition imported from Japan at the turn of the century and greatly influenced by the publication of Pierre Loti's travelogue on Japanese manners, *Madame Chrysanthemum*, 1887). Instead, the motif of the three chrysanthemums structures, in an abstract form, the repeated failed attempts to focus on the mark on the wall, leading the protagonist to "sink deeper, away from the surface, with its hard separate facts."[64] The three chrysanthemums keep reappearing in the form of three dots, marking each renewed attempt to focus on the mark on the wall—seventeen times—which also indicates the time when the story was written, the time of the 1914–1918 war.[65]

Indeed, the war dead haunt Woolf's story, not as fallen heroes, but rather as phantoms, which Woolf figures through a yellow detail in which the color of the chrysanthemums reappears:

There is a rule for everything. The rule for tablecloths at that particular period was that they should be made of tapestry with little yellow compartments marked upon them, such as you may see in photographs of the carpets in the corridors of the royal palaces. Tablecloths of a different kind were not real tablecloths. How shocking, and yet how wonderful it was to discover that these real things, Sunday luncheons, Sunday walks, country houses, and tablecloths were not entirely real, were indeed half phantoms, and the damnation which visited the disbe-liever in them was only a sense of illegitimate freedom. What now takes the place of those things I wonder, those real standard things? Men perhaps, should you be a woman; the masculine point of view which governs our lives, which sets the standard, which establishes Whitaker's Table of Precedency, which has become, I suppose, since the war half a phantom to many men and women, which soon—one may hope, will be laughed into the dustbin where the phantoms go, the mahogany sideboards and the Landseer prints, Gods and Devils, Hell and so forth, leaving us all with an intoxicating sense of illegitimate freedom—if freedom exists…[66]

---

like a flower. When it falls upon the pot of yellow chrysanthemums, and sets them ablaze, it seems as though one had an angel in the room. Bill-posters are beginning to discover the attractive qualities of the colour" (Richard Le Gallienne, "The Boom in Yellow," in *British and European Aesthetes, Decadents, and Symbolists in the Victorian Web*, http://www.victorianweb.org/decadence/lagalliene1.html [accessed December 1, 2011].

64 Woolf, "The Mark on the Wall," 85.

65 "The Mark on the Wall" "marked," as the title suggests, a new direction in Woolf's writing: "the new machine had created the possibility of the new story," as Hermione Lee has observed (*Virginia Woolf* [New York: Vintage Books, 1999], 359).

66 Woolf, "The Mark on the Wall," 86.

The "little yellow compartments" in a tablecloth stage a non-event (which Woolf pits against the event of the Great War), leading to a reflection on gender, life, and freedom. Through an almost imperceptible yellow detail, the perception of history and of humanity is presented as mechanized and constructed, and as such put into question and dissolved. "Little yellow compartments" relate the absurdity of domestic rules to the absurdity of standards set by patriarchal society. However, the shift in perspective for both men and women is caused by the war losses, turning "men of action" into colorless "phantoms," which are "laughed into dustbins." Nowhere do the dead or dying materialize themselves; rather they fade from a yellow detail into dust, a pale version of the initial image that merges with the yellow light of the fire, the chrysanthemums, and the cigarette smoke, thereby forming a politically charged, yellow atmosphere—an allusion to warmongering yellow journalism.

Colors in Woolf remain fleeting and in transition, and as such they represent a heightened form of perception, which Woolf frequently expresses through a language of flowers, as in her short story "Kew Gardens" (1919), where flowers pronounce colors like tongues. Both "Kew Gardens" and "The Mark on the Wall" were illustrated by Woolf's sister, Vanessa Bell, in woodcuts that echo the merging of interior and exterior environments.[67] A colorist whose work was shown at the Second Post-Impressionist Exhibition in London (1912),[68] Bell shares with Woolf a notion of color that enables a form of "collective communication":[69] "Woolf shares her sister's aesthetic preoccupations: they both try to show non-physical experiences as formal realities, at the same time emphasizing and illuminating feminine

---

[67] Diane Filby Gillespie has researched the cooperation and dialogue between Vanessa Bell and Virginia Woolf. With respect to Bell's illustration of "The Mark on the Wall," Gillespie writes: "As the natural world fills the narrator's thoughts, so it mingles with the furniture and teacup in the woodcut. Both Woolf and Bell blur the distinction between interior and exterior environments. This theme and the reference to tea are reinforced by a small woodcut of fruit on an oval plate placed beneath the passage from the story" (Gillespie, *The Sisters' Arts: The Writing and Painting of Virginia Woolf and Vanessa Bell* [Syracuse, NY: Syracuse University Press, 1988], 139).

[68] Goldman notes Woolf's emphasis on color in the context of Post-Impressionist Exhibitions in 1910 and 1912. Whereas the Second Post-Impressionist Exhibition shifted its focus to the significance of form, Woolf "stays with earlier interpretations of Post-Impressionism, developing an interest in color closely related to the aesthetic practice of her sister Vanessa, who exhibited at the Second Post-Impressionist exhibition" (Goldman, *The Feminist Aesthetics of Virginia Woolf*, 123). Roger Fry, who coined the term Post-Impressionism and was, like Woolf, a member of the Bloomsbury Circle, was strongly influenced by the theories of Julius Meier-Graefe, to which I referred in Chapter 1, on Van Gogh. Meier-Graefe's discourse on color as a form of modern aesthetic enlightenment becomes in Woolf, as Goldman suggests, "a source of feminist, political enlightenment" (ibid., 126).

[69] Ibid., 149.

experiences. Both show communication between people as material events. Both relate this to color."[70] While Woolf's tropes of color are, on the one hand, inspired by "the new language of Post-Impressionist color"[71] (in its radical departure from naturalism, especially in its use of expressive, even transgressive colors),[72] they are at the same time linked to a feminist-political discourse. As we have already seen in "The Mark on the Wall" with respect to the "three chrysanthemums" and the "yellow compartments," colors play a structural role, and yet, colors are also overflowing and ecstatic—like the "film of yellow light" itself. Colors in Woolf are, I would argue, synaesthetic in Eisenstein's sense: that is, based on collective rather than subjective forms of perception, exposing a "system of imagery"[73] that, in "The Mark on the Wall," is linked towards the end of the story to the act of writing in time of war.

The "film of yellow light" dissolves entirely at the end of the story, when the mark turns out to be the mark of a snail. In its gliding and transparent manner, the mark of the snail, an emblem of slowness, creates an upheaval because it is noticed on the way to the newspaper stand, to an encounter with the medium that encapsulates fast-paced life and hard, cold facts:

> There is a vast upheaval of matter. Someone is standing over me and saying—
> "I am going out to buy a newspaper."
> "Yes?"
> Though it's no good buying newspapers ... Nothing ever happens. Curse this war; God damn this war! ... All the same, I don't see why we should have a snail on our wall.
> Ah, the mark on the wall! It was a snail.[74]

Although the snail reveals the mystery of the mark, it does not seem to bring the narrator's "train of thought," with which she is resisting the "rapidity of

---

[70] Ibid., 150.

[71] Ibid., 168.

[72] Woolf writes in her essay "Old Bloomsbury": "The Post-Impressionist movement had cast—not its shadow—but its bunch of variegated lights upon us. We bought poinsettias made of scarlet plush; we made dresses of printed cotton that is especially loved by negroes; we dressed ourselves up as Gauguin pictures and careered around Crosby Hall [at the Ball of the Second Post-Impressionist Exhibition of 1912]. Mrs. Whitehead was scandalized" (Woolf, "Old Bloomsbury," in *Moments of Being*, ed. Jeanne Schulkind [New York, London: Harcourt Brace, 1985], 200). Michael Taussig discusses Woolf's description of costumes in terms of Gauguin's paintings as a "licensed transgression" that confronts the body as much as the mind. See Michael Taussig, *What Color is the Sacred?* (Chicago: The University of Chicago Press, 2009), 11.

[73] Eisenstein, *The Film Sense*, 151.

[74] Woolf, "The Mark on the Wall," 89.

life," to a standstill. Too much is happening in the desperate attempt to "sink deeper under the surface of things"; while the raging war outside does not bring any news, the war-machine marches implacably on.

The narrator resists the war-machine in her resistance to movement *tout court*; it is through the "film of yellow light" that Woolf creates a state of flux in which the "hard facts" dissolve into matter that "becomes expressive," as Deleuze and Guattari write in *What is Philosophy?*, with respect to the creation of a flow of life that modernists such as Woolf and Joyce establish in their works. In this state of flux, life and time are, as Claire Colebrook comments, "beyond mechanized experience [...] plunging into chaos and returning with a renovated order."[75]

In Woolf, the notion of luminosity, heated imagination, and inward contemplation determines the "film of yellow light" that pervades her work as a stage on which she performs the "collision with reality."[76] The yellow atmosphere of "The Mark on the Wall" materializes itself, as it were, in the luminous body of a snail, which deconstructs the phenomenon (fast-paced news) that it contests as an embodiment of slowness.[77]

Social concerns such as the Great War clash with an attempt to contemplate; however, Woolf resists the Wildean notion of looking at the concerns of society through the "cracked looking glass" of an artist. Woolf, in fact, obliquely questions Wilde's notion of the looking glass in "The Mark on the Wall":

> Suppose the looking glass smashes, the image disappears, and the romantic figure with the green of forest depths all about it is there no longer, but only that shell of a person which is seen by other people— what an airless, shallow, bald, prominent world it becomes! A world not to be lived in. As we face each other in omnibuses and underground

---

[75] Claire Colebrook, *Deleuze: A Guide for the Perplexed* (London, New York: Continuum, 2006), 96.

[76] Woolf, "The Mark on the Wall," 88.

[77] Especially in her analysis of *The Fish and the Sun*, Goldman focuses on Woolf's transformative use of suffrage colors, thus establishing a link to Woolf's feminist aesthetics. Goldman concludes her extensive study of color and visual politics in Woolf as follows: "In exploring Woolf's tropes of light and color in relation to iconographic colorist and suffragist traditions and contexts, I have sought to revise the critical emphasis on aesthetic emotion, psychological volume, and significant form, as characteristic of her Post-Impressionism; and to identify in the dominant discourse a green oasis, perhaps. A prismatic, materialist, feminism may be at work in Woolf's Post-Impressionism. Exploiting both the 'interaction and [the] inevitable tension between spheres of "feminism" and "aesthetics," ' Woolf's feminist aesthetics utilizes the politics of the visual by engaging with art both on gallery walls and on the street" (Goldman, *The Feminist Aesthetics of Virginia Woolf*, 207).

railways we are looking into the mirror that accounts for the vagueness, the gleam of glassiness, in our eyes.[78]

The "gleam of glassiness in our eyes" moves us away from the dualities of male/female, art/politics, past/future, outside/inside, nature/artifice that structure Wilde's aesthetic architecture as he formulates it in *The Decay of Lying*; the "gleam of glassiness" reveals a new form of perception, which Woolf also celebrated as the perception of the camera-eye, in her fascination with photography and experimental film. In the notion of the "glassiness of the eye," a celebration of the camera-eye comes to the fore, thus anticipating the revolutionary hope that the Russian director Dziga Vertov formulated in his idea of the "Kino-eye": "Kino-eye means the conquest of time (the visual linkage of phenomena separated in time). Kino-eye is the possibility of seeing life processes in any temporal order or at any speed inaccessible to the human eye."[79] As close as Woolf's temporal concept of linking "separate moments"[80] in time comes to Vertov's cinematic utopia of the camera-eye, especially in his emphasis on the camera's ability to capture what remains invisible to the human eye, Woolf's way of writing the "film of yellow light" that her narrator remembers seeing on the page of her book is not characterized by a form of "absolute writing in film," but rather by its vagueness. In the lightness of a "film of yellow light" an atmosphere of contemplation is created, which in its inwardness clashes with the facticity of reality. The moment of collision itself is dramatized in the medium of yellow, in which Woolf attempts to capture her revolt against the "men of action," their culture and their wars. Woolf announces her revolt in "The Mark on the Wall" as a revolt of the "non-event" against the warmongering of a patriarchal culture.

The "film of yellow light" is thereby part of a photology that is characteristic of Woolf's work at large: from *Night and Day* to *To the Lighthouse*,[81] solar eclipses and the reemergence of light and color out of darkness are recurrent themes. For example, confronting the impact of the Great War in *Mrs. Dalloway*, Woolf lashes out against the treatment of the mentally ill through the character of a war veteran, Septimus Warren Smith. An evocation of the "film of yellow light" appears just before Septimus's death:

---

[78] Woolf, "The Mark on the Wall," 85.

[79] Sara Danius, *The Senses of Modernism: Technology, Perception, and Aesthetics* (Ithaca, NY: Cornell University Press, 2002), 169.

[80] Maggie Humm points to Woolf's "account of film especially as a space which subverts chronology" (*Modernist Women and Visual Cultures: Virginia Woolf, Vanessa Bell, Photography, and Cinema* [New Brunswick, NJ: Rutgers University Press, 2003], 76).

[81] See Goldman's extensive discussion of Virginia Woolf's heliotropics in Goldman, *The Feminist Aesthetics of Virginia Woolf*, 13.

Going and coming, beckoning, signaling, so the light and shadow which now made the wall grey, now the bananas bright yellow, now made the Strand grey, now made the omnibuses bright yellow, seemed to Septimus Warren Smith lying on the sofa in the sitting-room; watching the watery gold glow and fade with the astonishing sensibility of some live creature on the roses, on the wallpaper. Outside the trees dragged their leaves like nets through the depths of the air; the sound of water was in the room and through the waves came the voices of birds singing. Every power poured its treasures on his head, and his hand lay there on the back of the sofa, as he had seen his hand lie when he was bathing, floating, on the top of the waves, while far away on shore he heard dogs barking and barking far away. Fear no more, says the heart in the body; fear no more.[82]

Shifting between the yellow of the omnibuses passing by outside, the bananas inside, and the reflection of the "gold glow" of the ocean on the wallpaper, Woolf creates a "film of yellow light," a zone between inside and outside, a zone of floating movements that surround and transport the traumatized character into a state of flux; his body (outside shell) and his fear (inside) disperse in a yellow reflection. The lightness of the "film of yellow light" is inscribed in the potential weight that freights every moment. Woolf's use of yellow's luminosity reflects a darkness it refuses to name.

---

[82] Virginia Woolf, *Mrs. Dalloway* (London: CRW Publishing, Collector's Library, 2003), 155–6.

4

"The little patch of yellow wall": Proust

*His dizziness increased; he fixed his gaze, like a child upon a yellow
butterfly that it wants to catch, on the precious little patch of wall. "That's
how I ought to have written," he said. "My last books are too dry, I ought
to have gone over them with a few layers of colour, made my language
precious in itself, like this little patch of yellow wall."*

—Marcel Proust

One of the most iconic scenes in Proust's epic novel *In Search of Lost Time*
(*À la recherche du temps perdu*, 1913–27) is the death of the writer Bergotte
in the fifth volume, entitled *The Captive* (*La Prisonnière*). While visiting a
Dutch art exhibit, the elderly Bergotte stops in front a painting by Johannes
Vermeer entitled *View of Delft*, and, while examining a detail of the painting,
the "little patch of yellow wall" (petit pan de mur jaune), he experiences
vertigo and dies. The convergence of a famous painting, the death of one of
the most important figures in Proust's novel, and the mysterious repeated
phrase "little patch of yellow wall" makes this one of the most iconic and
contested scenes in the critical literature on Proust. Most importantly, it
reinforces the existential significance of Proust's novel, for, as the critic
Anthony Bailey has observed, "through Vermeer Proust meditated his own
end."[1]

I offer in this chapter a new and comprehensive interpretation of this
scene, drawing out the specificity of yellow as it relates to the major themes
of Proust's novel and to the "culture of yellow," namely, the multivalent
figuration that develops in and through yellow and that connects the
aesthetic with other registers and conceptual fields (physiology, politics,
religion). Nowhere is this multivalence better illustrated in Proust than in
the repeated motif of the "little yellow patch of wall."

I begin by considering an intertextual reference that will set up my
reading of Proust: the repeated motif of the "patch of wall" (*pan de mur*)

[1] Anthony Bailey, *Vermeer: A View of Delft* (New York: Henry Holt & Company, 2001),
248.

in Honoré de Balzac's first best-seller *Eugénie Grandet* (1833). Balzac's novel is interesting not only for this motific connection, but also for its systematic use of the color yellow, which prefigures many of the themes of this study.

"I love yellow": Balzac's *Eugénie Grandet*

Eugénie Grandet is the story of a French provincial miser (Monsieur Grandet) whose singular passion for money, particularly in its material form of gold, puts him at odds with his family—principally with his daughter Eugenie, who embodies spiritual values—leading to a tragic result. Monsieur Grandet is presented as a stereotypical figure of the new capitalist society that emerges during the Restoration and flourishes after 1830, while the innocent Eugenie symbolizes the traditional religious attitude threatened by a nascent modernity.

The phrase "patch of wall" first appears as a kind of screen on which the young female protagonist, Eugenie, projects the "thousand thoughts" that she faces as she is overwhelmed by feelings of love for her cousin Charles, who is visiting from Paris:

> When the sun reached an angle of the wall where the "Venus-hair" of southern climes drooped its thick leaves, lit with the changing colors of a pigeon's breast, celestial rays of hope illumined the future to her eyes, and thenceforth she loved to gaze upon that *piece of wall* [*pan de mur*], on its pale flowers, its blue harebells, its wilting herbage, with which she mingled memories as tender as those of childhood. The noise made by each leaf as it fell from its twig in the void of that echoing court gave answer to the secret questionings of the young girl, who could have stayed there the livelong day without perceiving the flight of time. Then came tumultuous heavings of the soul. She rose often, went to her glass, and looked at herself, as an author in good faith looks at his work to criticize it and blame it in his own mind. "I am not beautiful enough for him!" Such was Eugenie's thought—a humble thought, fertile in suffering. The poor girl did not do herself justice; but modesty, or rather fear, is among the first of love's virtues.[2]

The patch (or piece) of wall functions here for Eugenie, as it will for Proust's Bergotte, as a kind of wellspring for reflection in a moment of awakening:

[2]　Honoré de Balzac, *Eugénie Grandet*, trans. Roberts Brothers (Boston: Roberts Brothers, 1887), 82 (my emphasis).

for Eugenie, it is the awakening of her amorous being, the beginning of her adult life, which is also the beginning of an illusion that is destined to be lost; whereas for Bergotte, the moment occurs at the end of life, and the awakening involves a recognition of failure, of what-might-have-been. The motif of the illuminated patch of wall is a detail that contains a world; yet the detail is not the fragment of a fulfilled world (as the German Romantics had affirmed). Rather the opposite is the case; Balzac's attention to the "patch of wall" in *Eugénie Grandet* figures a world that is falling apart, while in Proust, the repetition of "little patch of yellow wall" signifies the downfall of the individual artist Bergotte.

The details of the "patch of wall" mirror Eugenie's multifaceted appearance: on the one hand, pale and almost wilting at her young age (like some of the flowers overgrowing the patch), due to her constricted and piteous life in her parents' home; on the other hand, a blossoming young woman, Venus-like. The patch manifests all the potentialities of her awakening passion, the potential of a fulfilled love, but also the suffering and disappointment to follow.

Another repetition of the "patch of wall" in *Eugénie Grandet* reveals a similarly contemplative dimension:

> In the mornings she sat pensive beneath the walnut-tree, on the worm-eaten bench covered with gray lichens, where they had said to each other so many precious things, so many trifles, where they had built the pretty castles of their future home. She thought of the future now as she looked upward to the bit of sky which was all the high walls suffered her to see; then she turned her eyes to the *old patch of wall* [*le vieux pan de muraille*], and to the roof above the room in which he had slept. Hers was the solitary love, the persistent love, which glides into every thought and becomes the substance, or, as our fathers might have said, the tissue of life.[3]

Persistently, Eugenie is reviving the moments of a confession that had long ago lost its grounding in the reality outside her estate, where the man who confessed his love to her and for whom she is waiting has long since moved on. Eugenie becomes a paragon of spiritual love and faithfulness. The "worm-eaten" bench from where Eugenie can see her "future castle" is falling apart, like the patch of wall itself. Its materiality contrasts with a spirituality that remains untouched by the passage of time. In the Proust passage analyzed below, the passage of time is similarly imagined as a rotting process; however, it is the "worm-eaten body" of Vermeer that the narrator compares

---

[3]   Ibid., 205 (my emphasis, translation modified).

to the refinement and immortality of his work, emblematized in the detail of the "little patch of yellow wall."

Eugenie's spirituality is portrayed as a dangerous counter-force to the materialism that surrounds her, particularly that of her father, marked by the negativity (and materiality) of yellow. When Eugenie's cousin Charles first enters the Grandets' estate, he is repulsed by the "yellow, smoke-stained walls of the well of the staircase," which sobers his expectations of a supposedly rich uncle. The yellow here is a sign of decay, poverty, and neglect, in stark contrast to the Grandets' actual wealth, which is kept hidden from view. Though they share a moment of spiritual closeness, Eugenie is diametrically opposed to the Charles who returns from the East, who now closely resembles her father—all money—just as the very name of Eugenie's father, *Grandet*, is an anagram of *d'argent*, meaning "money" in French. Thus the "patch of wall," as a spiritual value for Eugenie, is contrasted with the precious pieces of (yellow) gold that drive the materialism of the male protagonists (and the patch of wall in Proust will also be an index of value, of "preciousness").

Monsieur Grandet's obsession with gold is exemplified in the exclamation "J'aime le jaune" (I like/love yellow).[4] It is almost as if Grandet were attracted more to the material appearance of gold, as epitomized by its color, than to its monetary (exchange) value: "Monsieur Grandet had a private treasure, some hiding-place full of louis, where he nightly took ineffable delight in gazing upon great masses of gold."[5] The very touchstone of value, gold (at once a color, a metal, and a monetary vehicle) is treated by Balzac as tinged with an inexpugnable negativity, thereby joining the opposing poles of yellow: the pole of value with the pole of death, disease, and decay. This is in fact the crux of Balzac's critique of capitalism: the corruption of true worth or value. For value becomes indistinguishable from greed; the fusion of passion with absolute value results in *Eugénie Grandet* in a parody of the sacred. Grandet's religious form of greed—an asceticism to be sure, but also a kind of idolatry—is ultimately a self-contradictory and self-destructive force that imprisons the characters within the walls of Grandet's estate.

The mother's yellow appearance ("dry, thin woman, as yellow as a quince, awkward, slow, one of those women who are born to be down-trodden") attracts Monsieur Grandet's passion for yellow ("you are a bit yellow, that's true; but I like yellow, myself"),[6] thereby emphasizing the increasingly

---

4   Ibid., 199.
5   Ibid., 10.
6   Ibid., 215.

deadly spiral precipitated by the absolute nature of the passion for the yellow metal. Eugenie's equally obsessive character transforms her father's imprisoning walls into the walls of a cloister. The "patch of wall" epitomizes this world of imprisonment as an illuminated detail. The illuminated "patch" thus serves as a screen of projection for thoughts of disillusionment, exposed in the negative turn of the color of light into color of decay, dirt, and greed.

Although the avaricious Monsieur Grandet is not Jewish, his passion for gold suggests a confusion with the Jewish motif of the moneylender, a motif that becomes progressively more prevalent in the course of Balzac's novel cycle, the *Comédie Humaine*. Already in *Eugénie Grandet*, the fixation on gold activates a Jewish stereotype. Monsieur Grandet is presented as an apprentice of a Jew and his business strategies, namely the stutter that he employs in all his negotiations and that becomes an essential part of his public persona:

> Some years earlier, in spite of his shrewdness, he had been taken in by an Israelite [*Israélite*], who in the course of the discussion held his hand behind his ear to catch sounds, and mangled his meaning so thoroughly in trying to utter his words that Grandet fell a victim to his humanity and was compelled to prompt the wily Jew with the words and ideas he seemed to seek, to complete himself the arguments of the said Jew, to say what that cursed Jew ought to have said for himself; in short, to be the Jew instead of being Grandet. When the cooper came out of this curious encounter he had concluded the only bargain of which in the course of a long commercial life he ever had occasion to complain. But if he lost at the time pecuniarily, he gained morally a valuable lesson; later, he gathered its fruits. Indeed, the good man ended by blessing that Jew for having taught him the art of irritating his commercial antagonist and leading him to forget his own thoughts in his impatience to suggest those over which his tormentor was stuttering.[7]

Interestingly, Balzac says that Grandet *becomes* a "Jew" ("to be the Jew instead of being Grandet") by adopting the Jew's conniving ways. Balzac thus presents Monsieur Grandet's business shrewdness as being imitative, imitative to the point of becoming being. Indeed, the fact that the stutter is an "act" is unknown to most everyone who comes into contact with Grandet; they consider it to be part of his "nature."

---

[7]   Ibid., 145.

The association between greed and the figure of the Jewish money-lender (particularly Gobseck)[8] is present in many of Balzac's novels, such as *Lost Illusions* (*Les Illusions perdues*, 1837–43), where Balzac describes the "yellow forehead" and "yellow hand" of a Jewish moneylender, even questioning his status as a human being: "if indeed Salomon could be called a man."[9] As Frances Schlamowitz Grodzinsky argues in her study of Balzac, *The Golden Scapegoat*, Balzac's revival of yellow stigmata with increasing intensity in the *Comédie Humaine* is connected with two distinct types of Jewish characters: those who do not assimilate and succeed; and those who do attempt to assimilate and fail. Grandet, however, is merely driven by his instincts, "obsessive, devoured by ambition and greed, but without the intellect and will power of the Jew to control it," writes Grodzinsky.[10] Thus in the larger context of the *Comédie Humaine*, Grandet's passion for the yellow metal of gold emphasizes the opposition between the greedy, almost animal-like Jew, who is in the end self-destructive, and the successful Jew, the "refined product: the person who has succeeded in turning the dross of his existence into a purer form. The authentic Jew, like the true alchemist and artist, transforms his life by the nature of his inner vision that guides him towards his goal."[11] Thus, in Balzac's vision of modernity, the "refined Jew" becomes, like the artist, the *golden scapegoat*, at first scorned and then rewarded by society. Grandet is presented as the apprentice of a Jew; he incorporates the Jew's techniques—a reversal of Jewish assimilation. By attributing to a non-Jew features stereotypically ascribed to Jews, the revival of anti-Semitism becomes part of a free-floating stigmatism grounded in the color yellow.

Balzac's use of yellow in *Eugénie Grandet* is one of the first and most powerful examples in modern literature of a revitalized modern form of stigmatization as well as a commentary on the corruption of value. Thus Proust's use of the phrase "little yellow patch of wall" can be neither innocent nor coincidental (particularly given Proust's great admiration for Balzac). It also brings out a similar multivalent figuration, situating yellow in the current of late modernity.

---

[8] This character appears in many of Balzac's novels, but especially in *Gobseck* (1830).

[9] Honoré Balzac, *Lost Illusions*, trans. Herbert J. Hunt (New York: Penguin, 1971), 428–9.

[10] Frances Schlamowitz, *The Golden Scapegoat: Portrait of the Jew in the Novels of Balzac* (New York: Whitston Publishing, 1989), 86.

[11] Ibid.

Proust and Vermeer's *View of Delft*

In 1921, Proust attended an exhibition of Dutch paintings at the Jeu de Paume museum in Paris, where he could contemplate his favorite painting, Vermeer's *View of Delft*, 1658 (Color Plate 11), which he had seen almost twenty years earlier during a visit to The Hague.[12] Proust's faithful servant Celeste Albaret recounts:

> In the year 1921, [Proust's] only memorable outing was to visit, in the company of the writer Jean-Louis Vaudoyer, whom he liked so well, the exposition of Dutch painting that was being held at the Jeu de Paume that spring [...] and it was mainly to see again the paintings of his dear Vermeer, notably the little patch of yellow wall. Jean-Louis Vaudoyer had come to pick him up in the morning at the stroke of eleven. As far as I can remember, he returned sometime early in the evening, exhausted. He had had vertigo during the visit of the exposition.[13]

It is interesting that Albaret refers to the "little patch of yellow wall" as if it were a kind of metonymy (or perhaps even a synecdoche) for *View of Delft* itself. Most probably she was remembering this episode through the prism of Proust's retelling of it in his novel, or perhaps Proust had himself referred to the painting thus. Either way, it is a striking use of the phrase, which indicates that it possesses a larger significance than is usually assumed.

The critic Anthony Bailey narrates the same episode as follows:

> In May 1921 the exhibition of Dutch painting at the Jeu de Paume was attracting crowds, drawn to see among other things, Vermeer's *View of Delft* and *Girl with a Pearl Earring*. According to George Painter's biography of him, Proust had read in the Paris press articles on the Vermeers by Lèon Daudet and Jean-Louis Vaudoyer. At last he decided he had to go and see them. At nine one morning, a time when he is usually just going to sleep, Proust sent a message to Vaudoyer asking him to accompany him to the Jeu de Paume. Leaving the apartment he had a terrible attack of giddiness, and recovered from it and went on down stairs. At the exhibition, Vaudoyer steadied the writer's shaky progress towards the *View of Delft*. Proust was apparently revived by Vermeer, for he managed to go on to the Ingres exhibition and then to lunch at the Ritz before returning home, though according to Painter he

---

[12] Proust visited The Hague in 1902, at the height of the Dreyfus affair, a visit that affected him greatly.

[13] Quoted in Marcel Proust, *Ecrits sur l'art*, ed. Jérôme Picon (Paris: Flammarion, 1999), 10 (my translation).

was still "shaken and alarmed" by the attack. He never went out again. Proust soon transmuted this experience into the *Captive* [...] to which he was still making changes.[14]

The parallels between these two accounts of Proust's real-life experiences and the scene described in *The Captive* are too proximate to be merely coincidental. Indeed, the themes of "death" and "resurrection" figure prominently in the passage that describes Bergotte's encounter with the Vermeer painting. No doubt Proust (who was ailing) had sensed his own death, and wished to immortalize it in his writing; for in the death of the writer Bergotte, Proust dramatizes the very vertigo he had himself experienced standing in front of *View of Delft*.

A little over a year after seeing the Vermeer exhibit, Proust was dead.[15] *The Captive* had been published just weeks before. Like his fictive author, Bergotte, Proust would have preferred to die after seeing the Vermeer painting one last time. The posthumous publication of *In Search of Lost Time* would therefore be, as Proust says of Bergotte's books at the end of the scene, a "symbol of resurrection."

Here is the death scene in its entirety:

> The circumstances of his [Bergotte's] death were as follows. A fairly mild attack of uraemia had led to his being ordered to rest. But, an art critic having written somewhere that in Vermeer's *View of Delft* (lent by the Gallery at The Hague for an exhibition of Dutch painting), a picture which he adored and imagined that he knew by heart, a little patch of yellow wall (*un petit pan de mur jaune*) (which he could not remember) was so well painted that it was, if one looked at it by itself, like some priceless specimen of Chinese art, of a beauty that was sufficient in itself, Bergotte ate a few potatoes, left the house, and went to the exhibition. At the first few steps he had to climb, he was overcome by an attack of dizziness. He walked past several pictures and was struck by the aridity and pointlessness of such an artificial kind of art, which was greatly inferior to the sunshine of a windswept Venetian palazzo, or of an ordinary house by the sea. At last he came to the Vermeer which he remembered as more striking, more different from anything else he knew, but in which, thanks to the critic's article, he noticed for the first time some small figures in blue, that the sand was pink, and, finally, the precious substance of the tiny patch of yellow wall. His dizziness increased; he fixed his gaze, like a child

---

[14] Bailey, *Vermeer: A View of Delft*, 248–9.
[15] Proust died on November 18, 1922.

upon a yellow butterfly that it wants to catch, on the precious little patch of wall. "That's how I ought to have written," he said. "My last books are too dry, I ought to have gone over them with a few layers of colour, made my language precious in itself, like this little patch of yellow wall." Meanwhile he was not unconscious of the gravity of his condition. In a celestial pair of scales there appeared to him, weighing down one of the pans, his own life, while the other contained the little patch of wall so beautifully painted in yellow. He felt that he had rashly sacrificed the former for the latter. "All the same," he said to himself, "I shouldn't like to be the headline news of this exhibition for the evening papers."

He repeated to himself: "Little patch of yellow wall, with a sloping roof, little patch of yellow wall." Meanwhile he sank down on to a circular settee; whereupon he suddenly ceased to think that his life was in jeopardy and, reverting to his natural optimism, told himself: "It's nothing, merely a touch of indigestion from those potatoes, which were under-cooked." A fresh attack struck him down; he rolled from the settee to the floor, as visitors and attendants came hurrying to his assistance. He was dead. Dead for ever? Who can say? Certainly, experiments in spiritualism offer us no more proof than the dogmas of religion that the soul survives death. All that we can say is that everything is arranged in this life as though we entered it carrying a burden of obligations contracted in a former life; there is no reason inherent in the conditions of life on this earth that can make us consider ourselves obliged to do good, to be kind and thoughtful, even to be polite, nor for an atheist artist to consider himself obliged to begin over again a score of times a piece of work the admiration aroused by which will matter little to his worm-eaten body, like the patch of yellow wall painted with so much skill and refinement by an artist destined to be for ever unknown and barely identified under the name Vermeer. All these obligations, which have no sanction in our present life, seem to belong to a different world, a world based on kindness, scrupulousness, self-sacrifice, a world entirely different from this one and which we leave in order to be born on this earth, before perhaps returning there to live once again beneath the sway of those unknown laws which we obeyed because we bore their precepts in our hearts, not knowing whose hand had traced them there—those laws to which every profound work of the intellect brings us nearer and which are invisible only—if then!—to fools. So that the idea that Bergotte was not dead for ever is by no means improbable.

They buried him, but all through that night of mourning, in the lighted shop-windows, his books, arranged three by three, kept vigil like angels with outspread wings and seemed, for him who was no more, the symbol of his resurrection.[16]

I will now endeavor to unpack this complex scene, focusing my analyzes on the phrase that forms the emotional center of the passage: "the little patch of yellow wall."

The yellow patch: Mieke Bal and Georges Didi-Huberman

It is a singular fact that *View of Delft* is hardly ever referred to without mentioning Proust's discussion of it; yet, despite all of the attention devoted to it, there is little or no consensus as to what the "little patch of yellow wall" means, or even what it refers to in the painting (for there are many yellow points in the painting that could fit the bill). In fact, some critics, such as Mieke Bal, see no yellow at all in *View of Delft* ("the 'little yellow patch' is nowhere to be seen in the painting"),[17] thus questioning the very propriety of the phrase. However, a closer look at her conclusion reveals a problematic reading of both Proust's novel and of Vermeer's painting. While Bal allows that Proust could be referring to a little patch of light at the extreme right of the painting, she argues that this wall is far from being, as she quotes, a "little wall," but rather "a quite robust-looking wall"[18] and thus not a "little patch." Reducing the phrase "little patch of yellow wall" to "little wall," Bal misses the yellow and therefore the significance of the repetition of "the patch of yellow wall" in the text.

The wall to which Bal refers as a "rather robust-looking wall" is the wall of the New Church, which Vermeer bathes in sunlight, while depicting the Old Church in its shadow. The illuminated wall of the New Church is certainly one of the focal points of the painting. However, we must remember that Proust does not refer to it as a "little wall," but as a "little *patch* of yellow wall"—in the painting, not in reality (the referent). Seen from afar, it forms, despite the distance, the painting's most luminous spot. It is where Vermeer casts the sunlight and directs the spectator's gaze. Vermeer uses the light to emphasize the reformed church during the period of the Enlightenment

---

[16] Proust, *The Captive, In Search of Lost Time, Volume V, The Captive and the Fugitive*, trans. C. K. Scott Moncrieff and Terence Kilmartin (New York: The Modern Library, 2003), 244–5.

[17] Mieke Bal, *The Mottled Screen: Reading Proust Visually* (Stanford, CA: Stanford University Press, 1997), 260.

[18] Ibid.

(thereby revealing his ideological point of view in the painting). What Proust actually refers to with "little yellow patch," then, is *point of view*, both in terms of ideology and of artistic technique. This is, in fact, the theme of the painting—hence the title: *View of Delft*. The title points to the technique of perspectivism that is performed in the painting, the technique of creating different focal points and viewpoints on the city. (For example, the illuminated wall of the new part of the city forms only one of the focal points; others would be the figures in the foreground, or the sky with clouds in movement.)

If, as Gilles Deleuze observes, Proust prefers the "telescope, not the microscope" in his writing,[19] we can interpret Proust as emphasizing Vermeer's own concentration on the New Church in an analogous manner to the painter himself. Seen from a distance, Vermeer creates a focal point not by magnitude but by luminosity, shifting the focus away from purely spatial relationships towards temporal indicators. The new and the old parts of the city are juxtaposed beneath a cloudy sky; fleeting moments of light and shadow are reflected in the sea. However, those fleeting moments do not merely capture optical effects, but are illuminating points of view.

Art historian and theorist Georges Didi-Huberman sees the patch very differently from Bal. He defines the patch as that which "resists 'inclusion' in the picture because it makes a detonation or intrusion in it."[20] In contrast to the *detail*, which tends to create "stability and closure," the patch, in Didi-Huberman's view, is "semiotically labile and open";[21] it reveals a "process, a power, a not-yet," and in that sense disturbs or destabilizes the picture. The question in Didi-Huberman's account is whether the color yellow refers to the wall, in which case it would simply be a detail of the wall, or to the "patch," which, according to Didi-Huberman, is a kind of floating signifier, ambiguous and unstable: "it imposes itself first as non-iconic *index* of an act of paint."[22]

I contend, however, that the yellow patch is not merely a visible detail of the painting, but rather a *theme* of the painting, a theme highlighted by Proust's technique of writing, reflected upon as an "act of illumination," to paraphrase Didi-Huberman, actualizing a moment of illumination in Proust's own work. Projected on the failure of the author Bergotte, the

---

[19] Gilles Deleuze, *Proust and Signs*, trans. Richard Howard (New York: George Braziller, 1972), 113.

[20] Georges Didi-Huberman, *Confronting Images: Questioning the Ends of a Certain History of Art*, trans. John Goodman (University Park: Pennsylvania State University Press, 2005), 268.

[21] Ibid., 269.

[22] Ibid., 270.

narrator is performing a balancing act in which he puts his own aesthetic (and political) values on display, framed by the discussion of the preciousness of the "little patch of yellow wall." At stake here, then, is a technique of figuration or *inscription*, rather than what Didi-Huberman calls "painting in the act" (that is, the actualization of the act of painting itself through a detail that is set in motion). Thus, in this sense, Vermeer's painting functions as a sort of allegory of the Proustian style of representation. What he makes us see is a detail that, through its multivalent figuration, opens up a series of oblique references, which I now explore. These references recall the *fin-de-siècle* period, with its "culture of yellow" that, as we have seen, is intimately connected with stigma and scandal.

Proust and Vermeer's *The Goldweigher*

By means of the Vermeer painting, I contend that Proust is moving through late modernity, shifting from Vermeer's emphasis on the Enlightenment in *View of Delft* (the illuminated wall of the reformed New Church) towards the present, thus contrasting an era of enlightenment with an era of apparent decline and decadence. Yellow is thus the pivot point where opposing values and signs clash and are put into relief.

The figure of the pivot point is the "celestial pair of scales": "In a celestial pair of scales there appeared to him, weighing down one of the pans, his own life, while the other contained the little patch of wall so beautifully painted in yellow. He felt that he had rashly sacrificed the former for the latter." The yellow of the patch is here explicitly compared to gold as a paragon of value. Weighing his own work against that of Vermeer, the preciousness of the "little patch of yellow wall" is literally weighing him down; he starts to lose control over his body in a vertiginous experience. The balancing act itself exposes the ambivalence of the passion for yellow, its competing material-istic and spiritual values. In his last moments, Bergotte realizes that his work lacks the fluidity, the layering, and thus the preciousness that he recognizes in Vermeer's "little patch of yellow wall": "My last books are too dry, I ought to have gone over them with a few layers of color, made my language precious in itself, like this little patch of yellow wall." It is as if Bergotte were both judging himself and being judged by an atemporal "celestial" judge; the scales thus appear to be as much imposed from the outside (divine justice) as generated from within (self-criticism).

The conjuring of the scales suggests a reference to another painting by Vermeer, with which Proust would have been familiar: *The Goldweigher*. This painting is related by both color and the theme of value ("preciousness") to

Figure 4 Johannes Vermeer, *Woman Holding a Balance*, c. 1664. Oil on canvas, 39.7 × 35.5 cm, National Gallery of Art, Widener Collection, © 2013 National Gallery of Art, Washington, DC.

the "little patch of yellow wall." In *The Goldweigher*, an allegorical painting, Vermeer depicts a scene from *The Last Judgment* (in the background), which is juxtaposed with a pregnant woman weighing pearls. The biblical allegory of justice watches over the vain occupation with earthly goods. The question of earthly versus religious values is suggested through the figure of the pregnant woman, in the form of a balancing act: her gaze and hand are directed toward the decisive point of balance; verticals and horizontals divide up into squares, with the form of the square defining the logic of the painting.[23] Both

---

[23] Michel Serres, "The Woman Weighing Gold," *Samalgundi* 44–5 (1979): 73.

dimensions are self-regulating, whereas the hand of the painter disappears in a maneuver that is crucial for Vermeer's technique in *View of Delft*. Vermeer does not place the spectator in a single spot, but instead opens up multiple perspectives.

The pigment Vermeer uses for the pearls the Goldweigher is weighing reflects their value. In having Bergotte die from a urinary infection ("The circumstances of his death were as follows. A fairly mild attack of uraemia had led to his being ordered to rest"), Proust may in fact be referring to this exceptional pigment, called "monghuir piuri" (which appears for the first time in the bright yellow tones of Vermeer's *Goldweigher*), an Indian-yellow that was available for only a couple of years before being forbidden due to the unethical way of creating and producing the color (the color was produced from the urine of cows fed with mango; because this procedure caused urinary infections, it was soon prohibited).[24] This may partially explain why the color's preciousness is an index of Bergotte's sickness, the cause of his death. Paradoxically, then, the very "preciousness" of this yellow color itself involves death. The theme of value (preciousness, yellow gold) is contrasted with that of death and dying (yellowing); the dialectic increases the sensation of vertigo that conjures up the image of the scales: on one side, Bergotte can see his life, on the other, the "little patch of yellow wall." However, the theme of the refinement and value of a smallest detail is the theme of the painting itself; thus it is the self-reflexive status of the pearls (its pigments) that Proust exposes in his *ekphrasis* of the Goldweigher's scale; the value of the detail is presented as the value of its self-reflexivity.

We are confronted with a range of health problems relating to Bergotte's person: digestion problems, a urinary infection, hypothermia, and insomnia. Bergotte's actual preparation for the journey to the Vermeer exhibition involved eating only potatoes, which he connects with the vertigo he suddenly experiences in front of the Vermeer painting. The freshness of the potatoes, their rawness—Bergotte remembers them as being "under-cooked"—dramatizes physiologically the fear that he experienced previously, namely that of being the subject of the day's news: "I shouldn't like to be the headline news of this exhibition for the evening papers." In other words, he does not want to be a topic of scandal, of trivial *faits divers*.

In his *On Some Motifs of Baudelaire*, Walter Benjamin commented on the role of newspapers in Proust, which he sees as an example of the inability to process data and information in modern life, an inability that drives Proust's efforts to restore the figure of the storyteller: "The principles of journalistic

---

[24] See Margarete Bruns, *Das Rätsel der Farbe: Materie und Mythos* (Stuttgart: Metzler, 1998), 93.

information (freshness of news, brevity, comprehensibility, and, above all, lack of connection between the individual news items) contribute as much to this [inability to assimilate data by way of experience] as does the make-up of the pages and the paper's style."[25] The lack of connection between news items characteristic of a newspaper's presentation mirrors Bergotte's perception of the "little patch of yellow wall," which remains a scattered detail that he appreciates, but that he is unable to integrate into the whole; instead, it remains a stumbling block (the literal meaning of the Greek *skandalon*), both mentally and physically. Indeed, while focusing on the "little patch of yellow wall," Bergotte stumbles into his own death.

The death of Bergotte and the resurrection of the author

Bergotte's relation to the "little patch of yellow wall" is also captured through references to modern fashion, as when the "little patch of yellow wall" appears to him "as precious in itself as a Chinese artwork." As Jan Hokenson points out, Bergotte is throughout the novel "relegated to an arid Orientalism, quite notably not *Japoniste*."[26] Proust uses Japanese art contrastively with *chinoiserie*, which connotes the superficiality of decorative art (i.e. fashion). Hokenson writes:

> The artist-figures, for instance, rise and fall in Japoniste terms. Because Marcel must become the only great writer, the literary equivalent of Elstir in painting and Vinteuil in music, Marcel twice reports that the painter spent years studying Japanese art [...] But the novelist Bergotte is not allowed a Japoniste period, being instead insistently associated with mere "Chinoiserie."[27]

This contrastive use of Chinese and Japanese art as it plays out in the figure of Bergotte is especially instructive with respect to the "little patch of yellow wall." For here Proust exposes one of the prime examples of a Japanese way of seeing in his work, that is, a "bringing to consciousness" by rendering fugitive impressions (such as childhood memories), which Proust evokes through the yellow butterfly that Bergotte tries to catch: "he fixed his gaze,

[25] Walter Benjamin, "On Some Motifs in Baudelaire," in *Illuminations, Essays and Reflections*, ed. Hannah Arendt, trans. Harry Zohn (New York: Schocken Books, 1978), 158–9.

[26] Jan Hokenson, "Proust's *japonisme*: Contrastive Aesthetics," in *Marcel Proust (Bloom's Modern Critical Views)*, ed. Harold Bloom (New York: Chelsea House Publications, 2004), 98.

[27] Ibid.

like a child upon a yellow butterfly that it wants to catch, on the precious little patch of wall."[28] Bergotte's failure to catch the yellow butterfly describes the challenge of the narrator: to be a *japoniste* as an artist (to capture the fugitive), a challenge paralleled in life through his futile attempt to capture the figure of Albertine, the very epitome of a fugitive.[29]

Proust dramatizes Bergotte's last viewpoints on the "little patch of yellow wall" in a falling movement:

> He repeated to himself: "Little patch of yellow wall, with a sloping roof, little patch of yellow wall." Meanwhile he sank down onto a circular settee; whereupon he suddenly ceased to think that his life was in jeopardy and, reverting to his natural optimism, told himself: "It's nothing, merely a touch of indigestion from those potatoes, which were undercooked." A fresh attack struck him down; he rolled from the settee to the floor, as visitors and attendants came hurrying to his assistance. He was dead. Dead forever?

The "fall" of Bergotte is thus both literal and figurative; the literal fall evokes the figurative dimension. Death is mentioned twice in this passage (as a statement and in the form of a question), continuously performing the polarity of the color yellow itself, shifting between decay/death and brightness/value/illumination.[30]

For, after Bergotte's death, the narrator reflects on the concept of the "afterlife," commenting that:

> there is no reason inherent in the conditions of life on this earth that can make us consider ourselves obliged to do good, to be kind and thoughtful, even to be polite, nor for an atheist artist to consider himself obliged to begin over again a score of times a piece of work the admiration aroused by which will matter little to his worm-eaten body, like the patch of yellow wall painted with so much skill and refinement by an artist destined to be forever unknown and barely identified under the name Vermeer.

The preciousness of the "patch of yellow wall" is now seen from the

---

28 Proust, *The Captive*, 245.
29 See the discussion of Albertine at the end of this chapter.
30 In his chapter "Cardiac Fatigue" in *What Color Is the Sacred?*, Michael Taussig refers to Bergotte's death scene in *In Search of Lost Time* as an example where transparency, the kind of "subdued luminosity" characteristic of Vermeer's paintings, is itself *actualized* (in Benjamin's sense, as opposed to reflected on): "Transparent color," Taussig writes, "is but another name for polymorphous magical substance, that metamorphosing medium midway between body and mind, not visual but colored [...]" (Michael Taussig, *What Color Is the Sacred?* [Chicago: University of Chicago Press, 2009], 208).

perspective of the narrator, in a spiritual dimension, reflecting on the immortality of art, which he contrasts with the reality of the decay and decomposition of the artist's body and perhaps even of the disappearance of his name. The mortality of the worm-eaten body of the artist himself is contrasted with the immortality of the "patch of yellow wall," the figure of ultimate *value*. Proust makes the contrast more explicit in the last line of the passage: "They buried him, but all through that night of mourning, in the lighted shop-windows, his books, arranged three by three, kept vigil like angels with outspread wings and seemed, for him who was no more, the symbol of his resurrection."[31] According to René Girard, the introduction of Christian imagery here (as elsewhere in the novel) is sincere, without "disturbing the external positive and 'realist' order" of Proust's work.[32] That is, artistic resurrection and spiritual resurrection are one in Proust. The disembodied voice of the narrator inscribes his vision of resurrection into Bergotte's death, thereby countering the falling movement with a rise. The narrator, that is, the writer Marcel, is projecting his vision onto Bergotte's downfall; he reunites the scattered patches in a Christian vision. However, it is also a vision of a book. Its spiritual (angelic) character appears in stark contrast to the somatic description of Bergotte's dying body, thereby developing a dynamic movement from abject mortality to a glorious vision of immortality—one associated with art itself.[33] The color yellow (in the "lighted shop-windows") becomes the force through which the transition between the material (somatic) and immaterial (spiritual) is expressed. But it is of course a vision of the artist as resurrected in his work that Proust is attempting to conjure here, with Christian-themed references to books "arranged three by three" that resemble angels "with open wings."[34]

The actual moment of the author's death is thereby opened up and put into question, undone in a dialectic of death and resurrection, which unfolds by inscribing reflections on the "little patch of yellow wall" and its relationship to Bergotte's work back into Vermeer's *View of Delft*. Oscar Wilde established the motif of the death of the author in his *The Picture of Dorian Gray*, a novel about an author who writes himself into a painting to

---

[31] Proust, *The Captive*, 244–5.

[32] René Girard, *Deceit, Desire and the Novel*, trans. Yvonne Freccero (Baltimore: Johns Hopkins University Press, 1965), 313 (translation modified).

[33] This passage "reminds of Wordsworth's *Intimations of Immortality from Recollections of Early Childhood*" (Elliott Coleman, *The Golden Angel: Papers on Proust* [New York: Coley Taylor, 1954], 64). Coleman is referencing Charlotte Haldon's study on the intertextual reference to Wordsworth's *Ode*.

[34] This is one of Hokenson's intriguing conclusions, which he draws from his discussion of Proust's *japonisme*. See Hokenson, "Proust's *japonisme*: Contrastive Aesthetics," 91.

achieve immortality.[35] His ideal is presented to him by the painting that he stabs at the end of the novel: "Lying on the floor was a dead man, in evening dress, with a knife in his heart. He was withered, wrinkled, and loathsome of visage."[36] Dorian Gray's portrait remained as perfect as it was before the attack, indestructible. The author enters, as Roland Barthes will famously state, "his own death":

> Writing is the destruction of every voice, of every point of origin. Writing is that neutral, composite, oblique space where our subject slips away, the negative where all identity is lost, starting with the very identity of the body writing. [...] [T]he voice loses its origin, the author enters into his own death, writing begins.[37]

The "death of the author" is in Barthes's sense the beginning of immortality, the "afterlife" of writing. Bergotte's voice is also lost, undone by the narrator's vision of his books. However, in its volatile oscillation between image and word, the "little patch of yellow wall" brings the flow of time to a stop in a vision that appears to be detached from both Bergotte's and the narrator's perspective—detached as the "little patch of yellow wall" itself, which, through the intensity of its repetition (mentioned eight times in the space of a few pages), develops a dynamic of its own, thereby surpassing the moment it is supposed to encapsulate, that of Bergotte's death. By inscribing Bergotte's death into the "little patch of yellow wall," Proust is, paradoxically, bringing the "little yellow patch of wall" to life. The detail of the "little yellow patch of wall," on which Bergotte focuses while he is dying, illuminates his work (and its failure)—which serves as a screen of projection for imagining the immortal work of art.

Proust's two (open) secrets

The scandal of the Dreyfus affair reverberates in many sections of *In Search of Lost Time*. As the narrator announces at the beginning of *The Captive*, "the Dreyfus case was long since over, but 20 years later people would still talk about it, and so far only two years had elapsed."[38]

[35] See Elena Gomel, "Oscar Wilde, *The Picture of Dorian Gray*, and the (Un)Death of the Author," *Narrative* 12, no. 1 (2004): 80.

[36] Oscar Wilde, *The Complete Works of Oscar Wilde* (London: Hamlyn, 1977), 503.

[37] Roland Barthes, "The Death of the Author," in *Modern Criticism and Theory: A Reader*, ed. David Lodge (London: Longman, 1988), 170.

[38] Proust, *The Captive*, 42.

Alfred Dreyfus was a French-Jewish general unjustly accused and sentenced to life imprisonment for military treason. After his conviction, Dreyfus reportedly commented: "My only crime is to have been born a Jew."[39] The scandal became a literary *cause célèbre* in January 1898 when Émile Zola published a famous open letter to the French president entitled "J'accuse...!" in the newspaper *L'Aurore*. The letter accused the French government of the unlawful jailing of Dreyfus, and, more potently, of rank anti-Semitism. To avoid imprisonment, Zola fled to England.

In *The Captive*, Zola's flight to England is vividly discussed. One of the characters (the jeweller Cartier) comments: "if M. Zola had gone out of his way to stand his trial and to be convicted, it was in order to enjoy the only sensation he had never yet tried, that of being in prison."[40] But this is quickly denounced as an "idiotic" point of view by Oriane, one of the narrator's friends. The heated debate about the Dreyfus affair is interrupted by the narrator himself, who seeks to turn the conversation to a discussion of dresses ("a yellow dress with big black flowers")[41] and a gown "streaked with gold like a butterfly's wing,"[42] thus coloring, as it were, the topic of anti-Semitism in yellow—an ironic strategy of redirection.

As was discussed in earlier chapters, the color yellow had become fashionable at the time of the *fin de siècle*, without losing its stigmatic connotation. (This fusion of scandal and fashion can be perceived, for example, in the yellow dresses of Toulouse-Lautrec's posters of the singer and dancer "Jane Avril.")[43] In addition, in Proust the yellow coloring of clothes marks the shift from an individual to a collective consciousness, a shift reflected in the iconic figure of the butterfly. The image of the butterfly is clearly a metonymy for fashion, for the tension between the conscious individual and the collective unconscious that reveals, as Walter Benjamin remarks in the *Arcades Project*, a dream-like quality: "fashion, like architecture, inheres in the darkness of the lived moment that belongs to the dream consciousness of the collective."[44]

Significantly, Proust, in one of his longest sentences, brings together the theme of anti-Semitism with that of homosexuality, effectively marking a rapprochement between the two great "literary" scandals of the recent

---

[39] Michael Burns, *Dreyfus, A Family Affair: From the French Revolution to the Holocaust* (New York: Harper, 1992), 123.

[40] Proust, *The Captive*, 44–5.

[41] Ibid., 47.

[42] Ibid., 48.

[43] Matthias Arnold, *Henri de Toulouse-Lautrec 1864–1901: The Theatre of Life* (Cologne: Benedikt Taschen, 2000), 39.

[44] Walter Benjamin, *The Arcades Project*, ed. Rolf Tiedemann, trans. Howard Eiland and Kevin McLaughlin (Cambridge, MA: Harvard University Press, 1999), 39.

past: the Dreyfus affair and Oscar Wilde's arrest and trial. One of the most blatantly political outcries of *In Search of Lost Time*, Proust's sentence captures the shock of the news of Oscar Wilde's arrest on charges of homosexuality with moving pathos:

> Their [homosexuals'] honour precarious, their liberty provisional, lasting only until the discovery of their crime; their position unstable, like that of the poet one day fêted in every drawing-room and every theatre in London, and the next was driven from every lodging, unable to find a pillow upon which to lay his head, turning the mill like Samson and saying like him: "The two sexes shall die, each in a place apart!"; excluded even, except on the days of general misfortune when the majority rally round the victim as the Jews round Dreyfus, from the sympathy—at times from the society—of their fellows, in whom they inspire only disgust at seeing themselves as they are, portrayed in a mirror which, ceasing to flatter them, accentuates every blemish that they have refused to observe in themselves, and makes them understand that what they have been calling their love (and to which, playing upon the word, they have by association annexed all that poetry, painting, music, chivalry, asceticism have contrived to add to love) springs not from an ideal of beauty which they have chosen but from an incurable disease; like the Jews again (save some who will associate only with those of their race and have always on their lips the ritual words and accepted pleasantries), shunning one another, seeking out those who are most directly their opposite, who do not want their company, pardoning their rebuffs, enraptured by their condescension.[45]

Twenty years after Wilde's death in Paris there was "no need to name the victim. Everyone knew who the 'poet' was," writes William Carter in *Proust in Love*.[46] Even if the yellow stigma is here implicit (namely, in the association between Wilde and the *The Yellow Book*, which was discussed in Chapter 2), it nevertheless suggestively intertwines the scandal of Wilde's arrest with that of the Dreyfus affair, thereby addressing the two open secrets of *In Search of Lost Time*: homosexuality and Jewishness. In the end, however, yellow in Proust is never explicitly stigmatic—Proust was himself, of course, both homosexual and Jewish—and yet, yellow has an ambivalent relation to both identities, which reflects the ambivalence of the color yellow itself.

[45] Proust, *Sodom and Gomorrah*, 21–2.
[46] William C. Carter, *Proust in Love* (New Haven, CT: Yale Univerity Press, 2006), 89.

Vincent van Gogh, *The Yellow House*, 1888. Oil on canvas, 72 × 91.5 cm, Van Gogh Museum, Amsterdam.

Vincent van Gogh, *Piles of French Novels*, 1887. Oil on canvas, 53 × 73.2 cm, Van Gogh Museum, Amsterdam.

Vincent van Gogh, *Quinces, Lemons, Pears and Grapes*, 1887. Oil on canvas, 48.5 × 65 cm, Van Gogh Museum, Amsterdam.

Vincent van Gogh, *Sunflowers*, 1889. Oil on canvas, 95 × 73 cm, Van Gogh Museum, Amsterdam.

Paul Gauguin, *Yellow Christ*, 1889. Oil on canvas 92 × 73 cm. Cat. W 327. Albright-Knox Art Gallery, Buffalo, New York, New York State, USA. Photo Credit: Erich Lessing/Art Resource, NY.

Paul Gauguin, *Self-portrait with Yellow Christ*, 1890–91. Oil on canvas, 38.0 × 46.0 cm, Musee d'Orsay, Paris, France. Photo Credit: Erich Lessing/Art Resource, NY.

Vincent van Gogh, *Wheatfield with a Reaper*, 1889. Oil on canvas, 73 × 92 cm, Van Gogh Museum, Amsterdam.

Francis Bacon, *Study for a Portrait of van Gogh I*, 1956. Oil on canvas, h 154.1 × w 115.6 cm, acquired 1956, Robert and Lisa Sainsbury Collection, UEA 31. This image © Estate of Francis Bacon 2006. All rights reserved, DACS.

Henri Regnault, *Salomé*, 1870. Oil on canvas, 160 × 102.9 cm. Gift of George F. Baker, 1916 (16.95). The Metropolitan Museum of Modern Art, New York, NY, U.S.A. Image copyright © The Metropolitan Museum of Art, Image source: Art Resource, NY.

František Kupka, *The Yellow Scale*, 1907. Oil on canvas, 79.0 × 79.0 cm, © ARS, NY. Inv. AM4165P. Photo: Jean-Claude Planchet, Musée National d'Art Moderne, Centre Georges Pompidou, Paris, France. Photo Credit: CNAC/MINAM/Dist. Réunion des Musées Nationaux/Art Resource, NY.

Jan Vermeer, *View of Delft*, ca. 1658. Oil on canvas, 96.5 × 117.5 cm, Mauritshuis, The Hague, The Netherlands. Photo Credit: Scala/Art Resource, NY.

Wassily Kandinsky, *Sketch for Composition II*, 1910. Oil on wood, 62 × 58.2 cm, ©ARS, NY, Private Collection. Photo Credit: Visual Arts Library/Art Resource, NY.

Josef Albers, *Study for Homage to the Square: Departing in Yellow*, 1964. Oil on board, 76.2 × 76.2 cm, © ARS, NY, Tate Gallery, London, UK. Photo Credit: Tate, London/ Art, Resource, NY.

Helmut Federle, *Asian Sign*, 1980. Acrylic on canvas, 234.5 × 288.5 cm, Kunstmuseum Basel/Museum for Contemporary Art, © Helmut Federle and Pro Litteris, Zűrich, Switzerland.

Felix Nussbaum, *Self-Portrait with Jewish Identity Card*, 1943. Oil on canvas, 56 × 49 cm, Felix Nussbaum House, Osnabrück, Germany, © Artists Rights Society (ARS), New York. Photo Credit: Visual Arts Library/Art Resource, NY.

Frank Stella, *Odelsk I*, 1971. Mixed media on canvas, 228.6 × 335.3 cm, (Polish Village #11), Photo: Steven Sloman, Collection of the Artist, © ARS, New York. Photo Credit: Art Resource, NY.

Consider the ambivalent portrayal of the Baron Charlus in *The Captive*.[47] Although he is one of the most clearly homosexual characters of *In Search of Lost Time*, his homosexuality is referred to only obliquely. In the following passage, only Charlus's "yellow trousers" point to the secret of his homosexuality. The unsuspecting reader is thus easily led astray in this scene, which is presented through the eyes of the butler, who is unaware of the tearoom's secret:

> Constantly the butler would say: "I'm sure M. le Baron de Charlus must have caught a disease to stand about as long as he does in a pistiere. That's what comes of chasing the ladies at his age. You can tell what he is by his trousers [...] As I passed the pistiere in the Rue de Bourgogne I saw M. le Baron de Charlus go in. When I came back from Neuilly, a good hour later, I saw his yellow trousers in the same pistiere, in the same place, in the middle stall where he always stands so that people shan't see him."[48]

The "yellow trousers" that "tell what he is" display the open secret of homosexuality in *The Captive*. In *Sodom and Gomorrah*, the open secret is revealed beneath the tearoom walls: "Charlus remains in the closet while having sex in (almost) plain view," as Jarrod Hayes comments.[49] The color yellow in its stigmatizing potential enables the architecture of an open secret. However, the long history of yellow as a color stigmatizing Jews (which, since the *fin de siècle*, expanded to also stigmatize homosexuals) is put on display in the description of the Jewess Esther's dress, not as a secret, but as an inscription in plain view: "the yellow of her dress was spread so unctuously, so thickly, as to have acquired a kind of solidity."[50]

Albertine and the yellow butterfly

The figure who truly *embodies* yellowness in *In Search of Lost Time* is Albertine, the protagonist of *The Captive*, who creates at every turn an apocalyptic atmosphere in yellow through the passion of jaundice she unleashes. Closely associated with the artistic movement of *japonisme*,

---

[47] As Lawrence R. Schehr states in his chapter, "Un Amour de Charlus" (in *French Gay Modernism* [Urbana: University of Illinois Press, 2004], 53): "With the beginning of *Sodom and Gomorrhe* the paradigm changes completely. No longer can Marcel be in a position of nonknowledge. No longer can he feign not knowing what homosexuality is about. The visibility of the paradigm—produced through the 'blindness and insight' of invisibility—changes the game."

[48] Proust, *The Captive*, 249.

[49] Jarrod Hayes, "Proust in the Tearoom," *PMLA* 110, no. 5 (1995): 994.

[50] Proust, *In Search of Lost Time, Vol. 1, Swann's Way*, 82.

Albertine, who constantly escapes her lover, embodies the Japonist attempt to capture and accentuate fugitive moments.

At once attractive and repulsive, Albertine is energized by the figure of the yellow butterfly at the beginning of *The Captive*. Shifting the talk away from the heated debate of the Dreyfus affair ("the conversation had taken a wrong turning"),[51] the narrator talks about the dress he remembers as being "streaked with gold like a butterfly's wing"[52] (the dress that Madame Guermantes wants to give him for Albertine, during a visit to her salon, at the opening of the novel). However, just like the yellow butterfly—a reminder of his childhood—that escapes Bergotte, so too does Albertine escape the narrator. She will become a fugitive and die (but even her death will escape him).

As the embodiment of a fugitive appearance, Albertine epitomizes the narrator's challenge to capture artistically what is vanishing. Throughout the novel, the capturing of fugitive moments is reflected in the narrator's reflection on and study of Japanese art, in which he catches "nature on the wing and in the instant."[53] Hence the centrality of the instantaneous sensation of taste in the narrator's attempt to capture his lover, Albertine, who is introduced in the famous teacup scene, when a childhood memory emerges from a Japanese porcelain bowl and is captured through a reference to a Japanese children's game:

> And as in the game wherein the Japanese amuse themselves by filling a porcelain bowl with water and steeping in it little pieces of paper which until then are without character or form, but, the moment they become wet, stretch and twist and take on colour and distinctive shape, become flowers or houses or people, solid and recognisable, so in that moment all the flowers in our garden and in M. Swann's park, and the water lilies on the Vivonne and the good folk of the village and their little dwellings and the parish church and the whole of Combray and its surroundings, taking shape and solidity, sprang into being, town and gardens alike, from my cup of tea.[54]

The banal matter of paper bits is suddenly transformed into "a new order of reality, at once imaginative, imagistic, and in fluid motion,"[55] which allows

[51] Proust, *The Captive*, 46.
[52] Ibid., 48.
[53] Hokenson, "Proust's *japonisme*: Contrastive Aesthetics," 89. Hokenson points to Proust's literal reference to Hokusai's image of birds on the flight, which only appear as such upon closer examination (ibid., 95).
[54] Proust, *Swann's Way*, 64.
[55] Hokenson, "Proust's *japonisme*: Contrastive Aesthetics," 85.

the narrator to bring his childhood alive through a Japonist aesthetic: "Proust embraces particularly the evocative power of suggestion, the rendering of fugitive impressions, the crucial blanks or incompleteness—indeterminacies opening imaginative possibilities (for narrator and reader), and the sensory appeal in swift delicate strokes of line and color."[56] The narrator's sensory appeal to his lover, Albertine, is thus an appeal to her as a fugitive appearance, which she cultivates herself, not at least in her self-stylization as an exponent of *japonisme,* as when she appears in kimonos or refers to Pierre Loti's *Madame Chrysanthème* (although her reference is presented in a satirical manner).[57]

Albertine defines the principle of *japonisme* while following one of her passions—eating lemon ice-cream. (Albertine was acquainted with the painter Elstir, who is described as a Japoniste; his "butterfly signature" is like a Japanese seal).[58] The yellowish color of Albertine's ice-cream evokes Elstir's painting of a snow-landscape, which she describes in Japonist terms: "those lemon ices are still mountains, reduced to a tiny scale, but our imagination restores their dimension, like those Japanese dwarf trees which one feels are still cedars, oaks, machineels."[59] Albertine performs her emphasis on the suggestive power of Japanese art (in contrast to European illusionism and its emphasis on mimetic relationships) while eating lemon ice-cream, literally giving us a taste of that which is about to vanish. Melting the ice-cream in her mouth, Albertine is thus performing her own fugitiveness. The taste of lemon ice-cream and her aesthetic taste for *japonisme* is embodied and intensified through the color yellow, which both connects and intertwines the fugitive impressions: the narrator's way of imagining her in the dress that looks like a "yellow butterfly"; the yellowish snowscape; and the yellowish ice-cream. Albertine's cutting of the melting lemon ice-cream with her tongue "excited my jealousy," comments the narrator, interrupting her, adding yet another layer of yellow (jaundice) to the network of yellow signs surrounding Albertine: "In the same way, at the foot of my yellowish lemon ice, I can see quite clearly postillions, travellers, post-chaises over which my tongue sets to work to roll down freezing avalanches that will swallow them up."[60] The cruelty of Albertine's tongue—the unfolding of a cruel and cold landscape, of accidents with sliding carriages in yellow snow—corresponds to the violence of the scene as the narrator perceives it. Splitting mountains

---

[56] Ibid., 88.
[57] In other parts of the novel, Marcel also satirizes Albertine's references to Japanese art and abuses of *japonisme.* See ibid., 89.
[58] Ibid., 91.
[59] Proust, *The Captive,* 166.
[60] Ibid.

of ice with her tongue, Albertine becomes the synecdoche of a tongue, all tongue, with a split tongue—thereby creating throughout *The Captive* the rupturing atmosphere of jaundice, in diametrical opposition to the warm and blossoming gardens evoked in the famous passage of the Madeleine, in which Proust also introduced his *japonisme* through the sense of taste.

While Marcel's and Albertine's *japonisme* involves the sensation of taste, the epiphanic quality associated with Marcel's Japonist imagery, bringing houses, people and gardens of his childhood back to life, contrasts with the scenario of death and cruelty enacted in Albertine's tasting of the lemon ice-cream. Evoking the apocalypse, the narrator Marcel describes his relationship to Albertine as an accumulation of radiant moments:

> Sweet, gay, innocent moments to all appearance, and yet moments in which there gathers the unsuspected possibility of disaster, which makes the amorous life the most precarious of all, that in which the unpredictable rain of sulphur and brimstone falls after the most radiant moments, whereupon, without having the heart of will to draw a lesson from our misfortune, we set to work at once to rebuild upon the slopes of the crater from which nothing but catastrophe can emerge.[61]

The apocalyptic motif of scattering sulphur and brimstone is also the motif of the "little patch of yellow wall," which is scattered over Bergotte's final moments, only to be reunited by the narrator. Bergotte's decline and death functions as the screen of projection for the writer's (that is, Marcel's) own rise. Albertine's character is not further fleshed out; she remains, as Mieke Bal notes, "only a series of snapshots"[62] in the narrator's rendering of fugitive impressions with their scandalous potential.[63]

---

[61] Ibid., 98.

[62] Bal, *The Mottled Screen*, 225.

[63] Deleuze develops the "fundamental link between jealousy and homosexuality" (Deleuze, *Proust and Signs*, 123).

5

The "Yellow Peril" and the Visual Politics of Race

O Russia! Forget your former glory:
The two-headed eagle is ravaged,
And your tattered banners passed
Like toys among yellow children

—V. S. Soloviev

The French aristocrat and writer, Count Joseph-Arthur de Gobineau (1816–82), author of the infamous *An Essay on the Inequality of the Human Races* (1853–5), declared that "China fell below the West on the scale of civilizations"[1]—this despite the intense admiration of China in the previous century by Enlightenment thinkers such as Voltaire. This shift in attitude, due in large part to colonial politics and to the beginning of mass migration during the second half of the nineteenth century, was articulated early on as a warning against what would later become known as the "yellow peril." Gobineau specifically uses the color yellow in his *Essay* to conjure a threatening image. Jacques Barzun comments that "already in the *Essay*, the hordes of silent yellow men are pictured as bound to engulf the decreasing race of whites precariously perched on the peninsular tip of the Asiatic continent we call Europe."[2] In Gobineau's taxonomy of races, the yellow race was seen as the antithesis of the "negroid variety": "The yellow race is the exact opposite of this type. [...] The yellow man has little physical energy, and is inclined to apathy; he commits none of the strange excesses so common among Negroes. His desires are feeble, his will-power rather obstinate than violent."[3]

---

[1] Gregory Blue, "Gobineau and China: Race Theory, the 'Yellow Peril,' and the Critique of Modernity," *Journal of World History* 10, no. 1 (1999): 93.
[2] Jacques Barzun, *Race: A Study in Superstition* (New York: Harper Torchbooks, 1965, rev. edn.), 57.
[3] Joseph-Arthur Count Gobineau, "An Essay on the Inequality of the Human Races" [1853–5], in *Gobineau: Selected Political Writings*, ed. Michael B. Biddiss (New York: Harper and Row Publishers, 1970), 135–6.

The lack of physical strength is, in Gobineau's view, compensated for with "a love of utility and business, and respect for the law. Such qualities made the yellows superior to the Negroes, but they were still mediocre vis-à-vis the white."[4] Gobineau saw the Slavic race in terms of its miscegenation with "the yellows"—a motif I analyze later in this chapter in Andrei Bely's *Petersburg*, an epic Russian novel from the beginning of the century.

A cultural pessimist, Gobineau argued that the increased mixing of races would lead to the demise and disintegration of the Aryan race. However, although Gobineau's theories did not resonate with the French extreme Right (they were more concerned with nationalism, with "Frenchness," than with Aryanism as such), he did become famous through his later association with the composer Richard Wagner, who added his own ideas of redemption and regeneration to Gobineau's racial theories. After Gobineau's and Wagner's deaths, the Bayreuth circle was instrumental "in popularizing Gobineau in the German-speaking world,"[5] leading to the Nazi appropriation of his theories for their own racial politics.

Staging the "Yellow Peril": Richard Wagner and Wilhelm II

Fascism's recognition of the power of the spectacle as undergirding its racial politics is prefigured by the staging of the so-called "yellow peril" at the turn of the century. Dramatizing the totality of the threat, often with apocalyptic undertones, this staging is often characterized by a multimedia elaboration, drawing on ideas of synaesthetic art. Wagner's concept of the *Gesamtkunstwerk* (the "total artwork") is a case in point. Its totalizing artistic vision becomes the matrix for political representation in National Socialism. In its metaphysical aspect, Wagner's vision of the *Gesamtkunstwerk* as the "joint work of the people of the future" (as he described it in his essay *The Art-Work of the Future*) is related to the synthesis of media, the visual, and the acoustic. Philippe Lacoue-Labarthe comments as follows on the specifically political ramifications of the *Gesamtkunstwerk*.

> The political model of national-socialism is a *Gesamtkunstwerk* because, as Dr. Goebbels was well aware, the *Gesamtkunstwerk* is a

---

[4] Detmar Klein, "Gobineau, Joseph Comte de (1816–82)," in *Encyclopedia of Nineteenth-Century Thought*, ed. Gregory Claeys (London: Taylor & Francis, 2005), 245.
[5] Ibid., 246.

political project. The *Festspiel* of Bayreuth was to be for Germany what the great Dionysiads had been for Athens and all of Greece: the place where the people, gathered in its State, gives to itself the representation of what it is, and of what founds it, as such. Which does not only mean that the work of art (tragedy, musical drama) offers the truth of the *polis* or of the State, but that the political itself institutes and constitutes itself (and re-founds itself regularly) in and as a work of art.[6]

In this context the *Gesamtkunstwerk* is the very basis of an aestheticization of politics. Politics becomes less a matter of power distributed among competing forces than a total social vision that is inextricable from the affects and effects that constitute it as a mass (and self-contemplating) phenomenon.

While the notion of synaesthesia is, on the one hand, the defining idea of the total work of art, privileging especially the link between acoustic and visual media, it is, on the other hand, equally characteristic of the avant-garde works that attempt to deconstruct the Wagnerian idea of the *Gesamtkunstwerk* (in both the political as well as the artistic sense). As the simultaneous stimulation of senses in ecstatic moments, synaesthesia, according to the avant-garde, represents moments of rupture and disunity that thematize modes of mediation. Thus, while the *Gesamtkunstwerk* implies union and even regeneration in the Nazi context, in which Wagner's concept of *The Art-Work of the Future* is enthusiastically embraced,[7] in the context of avant-garde art, with its often "distant and ambiguous relationship with Wagner,"[8] the notion of the total artwork becomes a counter-strategy for realizing dystopian and entropic fantasies, as in the staging of the apocalyptic scenarios of the "yellow peril."

---

[6] Philippe Lacoue-Labarthe, *La fiction du politique* (Paris: Christian Bourgois, 1987), 97–8 (my translation).

[7] "The great United Art-work, which must gather up each branch of art to use it as a mean, and in some sense to undo it for the common aim of *all*, for the unconditioned, absolute portrayal of perfected human nature,—this great United Art-work he cannot picture as depending on the arbitrary purpose of some human unit, but can only conceive it as the instinctive and associate product of the Manhood of the Future" (Richard Wagner, *The Art-Work of the Future* [1849], The Wagner Library, http://users.belgacom.net/wagnerlibrary/prose/wagartfut.htm [accessed September 14, 2012].

[8] Anke Finger and Danielle Follett, *The Aesthetics of the Total Artwork: On Borders and Fragments* (Baltimore: The John Hopkins University Press, 2010), 14. Anke Finger and Danielle Follett explore in their study of the total artwork the increasing criticism of Wagner's aesthetics at the beginning of the twentieth century, after the enthusiastic reception of Wagner's ideas in the late nineteenth century, especially by the French symbolists, and in artists such as Arnold Schoenberg.

Instrumental in popularizing the fear of the "yellow peril" was Kaiser Wilhelm II.[9] In 1895, the Kaiser had commissioned a portrait, of his design, with the title *Völker Europas, wahrt eure heiligsten Güter! (Peoples of Europe, Guard Your Dearest Goods!)*, which Hermann Knackfuss realized in form of a *heliogravure* depicting the Archangel Michael and an allegorical Germany leading a charge against an Asiatic threat represented by a golden Buddha. The menace to the representatives of the West represents first and foremost a spiritual menace, even a cosmological threat, dramatized in an imagined clash of swords and warriors, in contrast to the almost immaterial aspect of a cloud that appears all the more dangerous in its hardly graspable form of invasion.[10]

At the time of the Boxer Rebellion (1898–1901), the term "yellow peril" was in widespread use.[11] Kaiser Wilhelm II used the term as part of his sinophobic rhetoric during his so-called "*Hunnenrede*" speeches to his troops. Wilhelm II's biggest fear was a pact between China and Japan; however, during the Boxer Rebellion, Japan did not yet have any intentions of invading the West. It was only in 1904 that Japan attacked Russia, thus realizing the West's xenophobic fears:

> When the Boxer Rebellion occurred in China and the imperial powers dispatched a punitive expedition to China, Japan sent the greatest number of troops of all. Although this did not go unnoticed in the West, the real sensation occurred when Japan declared war on its neighbor Russia and actually won it.[12]

[9] In his *The Yellow Peril 1890–1923* (New York: Arno Press, 1978), Richard A. Thompson points to the difficulty determining "where the fear of an invasion from the East first developed," but that it is "equally difficult to trace the origin of the words 'Yellow Peril'" (2). However, Kaiser Wilhelm II seems to have been instrumental in coining the term: "An English author declared in 1904 that the Kaiser started the yellow peril discussion in 1900. At the same time, a Chinese writer was certain that the phrase originated in the European newspapers in China during the Boxer Rebellion of 1900. On January 8, 1898, however, the editors of *Living Age* used the term as the title for an editorial in which they declared that the Kaiser was the first statesman to use the words 'yellow peril' in public statements. The Kaiser, the editors added, was inspired in his remarks by reading Charles Pearson's *National Life and Character*. Another writer stated simply that no one really knew who invented the term yellow peril. It was certain, however, that the Kaiser popularized it" (ibid., 4).

[10] See Jean-Pierre Lehmann, *The Image of Japan: From Feudal Isolation to World Power 1850–1905* (London: Routledge, 2010), 88.

[11] Heinz Gollwitzer emphasizes in his study *Die Gelbe Gefahr. Geschichte eines Schlagworts. Studien zum imperialistischen Denken* (Göttingen: Vandenhoeck & Ruprecht, 1962, 42) that Kaiser Wilhelm II did not use the term "yellow peril" itself before 1900, when the catchphrase was already widely used. However, the Kaiser claimed himself that it was him "who originated the phrase 'yellow peril'" (ibid., 42).

[12] Sepp Linhart, "Niedliche Japaner oder Gelbe Gefahr? Westliche Kriegspostkarten

Figure 5 *The Yellow Peril: European Nightmare*, postcard caricature by T. Bianco, c. 1900, satirizing the fear generated by Kaiser Wilhelm of the influx of Chinese laborers to Europe. Photo Credit: Kharbine-Tapabor, The Art Archive at Art Resource, NY.

During the period from the Boxer Rebellion to Japan's victory over Russia, the catchword of the "yellow peril" established itself in the popular imagination. In a series of postcards by the French cartoonist T. Bianco created in 1900 (the postcard being one of the most popular visual forms of mass media during the first half of the twentieth century), the "yellow peril" is visualized as a threat of catastrophic dimensions. One of these, entitled "The Yellow Peril: European Nightmare," shows sleeping European nations in a yellow landscape: "A countless number of yellow men stream out of the celestial empire towards several beds, in which the heads of several European states like Edward II, William II etc. are about to awake."[13]

Bianco's satire of a "European Nightmare" dramatizes the influx of Asian masses as a yellow flood of catastrophic dimensions. Four years later, in 1904, Bianco shows the still-sleeping European powers with the exception of the Russian tsar, who is awakening and ready to fight the Japanese, while masses of people are pouring out of the Asian Celestial Empire. In a third version, Bianco portrays a duel between a white bear (an allegory of Russia) and a yellow emperor, who is ready to stab the bear. Through yellow clothing

1900–1945" (Dainty Japanese or Yellow Peril? Western War-Postcards 1900–45) (Vienna, Münster: Lit Verlag, 2005), 145.

[13] Ibid., 149.

and an overall saturation of these caricatures in yellow, the catchword of the "yellow peril" is thereby established visually in its racist and apocalyptic dimension.

Generally speaking, the multivalent figuration of the "yellow peril" is based on two systems of imagery: 1) that of the mass migration of yellow hordes, overrunning the West, in a dramatic, worldwide clash of cultures; and 2) that of a singular, supernatural yellow figure, a kind of synecdoche of an uncontrollable power targeting the West from within. Examples of the latter include: Tom Edison's novel *Nugget Library* (1892), whose Chinese protagonist (alternately described as Mongolian), Kiang Ho, a sort of wizard with magic powers, is determined to destroy Western society; the fearsome crime boss Quong Lung in C. W. Doyle's *The Shadow of Quong Lung* (1900); Robert W. Chambers's novel *The Makers of the Moons* (1896), whose principal character "Man in the Moon," known by his Chinese name Yue-Lan, is the leader of a secret society. Chambers's character was seen as one of the first "yellow peril" villains; in fact, he is considered by critics to be one of the forerunners of what would become the "yellow peril" archetype and stereotype in fiction, Dr. Fu Manchu, the protagonist of a series of crime novels by Sax Rohmer, published between 1913 and 1959, which focused on the idea of an international secret society.

Sax Rohmer's Fu Manchu

The first novel in Rohmer's series, *The Mystery of Dr. Fu-Manchu* (1913, entitled *The Insidious Dr. Fu Manchu* in its American edition), exploits the fear of the superiority of the "yellow race"—a popular *topos* of detective stories and science fiction, especially after the Boxer Rebellion (during which Western missionaries were massacred in China). Fu Manchu is a Chinese super-criminal and evil genius who, along with his sadistic and cunning daughter, fights Western powers. This character inspired many imitations, the most famous being Dr. No from the eponymous James Bond novel (1958) and film (1962).

Fu Manchu is described in the novel as follows:

Imagine a person, tall, lean and feline, high-shouldered, with a brow like Shakespeare and a face like Satan, a close-shaven skull, and long, magnetic eyes of the true cat-green. Invest him with all the cruel cunning of an entire Eastern race, accumulated in one giant intellect, with all the resources of science past and present, with all the resources, if you will, of a wealthy government—which, however, already has denied all knowledge of his existence. Imagine that awful being, and you have a mental picture of Dr. Fu-Manchu, the yellow peril incarnate in one man.[14]

The last sentence makes manifest the tropic strategy of the novel: to reduce a mass phenomenon to a single figure, a synecdoche for the "yellow peril." Also called a "yellow devil"[15] or "yellow Satan"[16] and the "head of the Yellow Movement,"[17] Dr. Fu Manchu is more than a "yellow-faced man";[18] he embodies the "Yellow Movement" as their leader, a "sinister, yellow-robed figure"[19] with a "yellow face"[20] and a countenance that is repeatedly emphasized as an "intellectual countenance." Similarly, his "even, yellow teeth"[21] are exposed as part of a "singularly evil smile."[22] Dr. Fu Manchu's evil power and intellectual brilliance (in *The Bride of Fu Manchu*, a later novel from 1933, Fu Manchu claims to hold four doctorates from major Western universities) are embodied in his stereotypical yellow features. Nayland Smith, an opposing force to Fu Manchu in the earlier novels who stands in the tradition of Sherlock Holmes, announces in *The Insidious Dr. Fu Manchu* that the "phantom Yellow Peril [...] today materializes under the very eyes of the Western world."[23] Dramatized as a violent threat, which seems uncontrollable in its coupling of Eastern and Western intelligence (thereby undermining the West), the "yellow peril" manifests itself as the threat of the non-human powers, the threat of an alien force, challenging Christianity in the satanic figure of Fu Manchu.

It is important to note that many of the novels in Rohmer's series were bestsellers, indicating that Rohmer had captured the cultural imagination of his time.[24] Rohmer's racist fears were seemingly informed by the notion that, in the city of London, the Chinese were not only "morally questionable Orientals selling and smoking opium," but also a threat at the "heart of

---

[14] Sax Rohmer, "The Insidious Dr. Fu-Manchu," in *The Fu-Manchu Omnibus* (Lexington, KY: CreateSpace, 2011), 17.

[15] Ibid., 38.

[16] Ibid., 171.

[17] Ibid., 86.

[18] Ibid., 145.

[19] Ibid., 86.

[20] Ibid., 161.

[21] Ibid., 187.

[22] Ibid.

[23] Ibid., 49.

[24] "The image of Oriental hordes invading Western nations yielded a malleable literary formula that became the cornerstone of Rohmer's commercial success: the thirteen Fu-Manchu novels sold more than 20 million copies during Rohmer's lifetime" (Urmila Seshagiri, "Modernity's (Yellow) Perils: Dr. Fu-Manchu and English Race Paranoia," *Cultural Critique* 62 [2006]: 163).

the Empire [...] revealing a network of social and cultural economies."[25] However, Rohmer's way of sensationalizing the image of "Yellow Peril's [impending] impact on London"[26] was largely fanciful, for, between the turn of the century and the Second World War, the ethnic Chinese population in East London "was counted only in the hundreds," as the sociologist Virginia Berridge has estimated.[27]

In 1915, Rohmer published *The Yellow Claw* under a pseudonym. It featured a Fu Manchu-like character, but not Fu Manchu himself; nevertheless, as the title indicates, the "yellow peril" is still very much in force. But we should note that the Sinophobic message of Rohmer's novels is supported by an aesthetic dimension: the fascination with the conspiracy of a secret society, "an international mafia with supernatural powers; powers which at once uphold and destabilize reality and whose presence is material yet invisible," as Clive Bloom notes.[28] Rohmer's books were not bestsellers simply because they were racist or appealed to racist sentiments, but because they told appealing stories about a character, Fu Manchu, who, like Sherlock Holmes, is "greater than any particular work of fiction in which he appears."[29] The association of Fu Manchu "with every evil aspect of the Chinese image that existed in the early twentieth century"[30] performs his incarnation of the "yellow peril."[31] The fusion here of the aesthetic dimension with racism is precisely an index of the visceral power of the color yellow, a by-product of its multivalent figuration.

If there is one constant (besides the color yellow) that runs throughout all the instances of "yellow peril," it is the theme of *invasion*. While the subversiveness and uncontrollability of the invasion is often more effectively embodied in a singular figure (at least with respect to its literary

---

[25] Ibid., 171.

[26] Ibid.

[27] Victoria Berridge and Griffith Edwards, *Opium and the People: Opiate Use in Nineteenth-Century England* (New York: St. Martin's Press, 1981), 202.

[28] Clive Bloom, *Cult Fiction: Popular Reading and Pulp Theory* (New York: St. Martin's Press, 1996), 191.

[29] William F. Wu, *The Yellow Peril: Chinese Americans in American Fiction 1850–1940* (Hamden, CT: Archon Books, 1982), 174.

[30] Ibid.

[31] Peter Christensen stresses in his analysis of the "Political Appeal of Dr. Fu Manchu" that all the characters of the series are made of cardboard, except for Fu Manchu, who "looks back at us with his face, Satanic and Shakespearean, as the thriller anti-hero who reminds the Western democracies of the need to locate the non-Western world in the balance of power" ("The Political Appeal of Dr. Fu Manchu," in *The Devil Himself: Villainy in Detective Fiction and Film*, ed. Stacy Gillis and Philippa Gates [Westport, CT: Greenwood Press, 2002], 87).

representation), the imagery of mass invasion ("yellow hordes") is sometimes directly figured, as in Jack London's 1910 short story "The Unparalleled Invasion."

Jack London's "The Unparalleled Invasion"

London is seen as the writer who, in the words of one critic, "fixed the idea of a yellow peril in the minds of the turn-of-the-century Americans."[32] Sent by the news daily, the *San Francisco Examiner*, as a foreign correspondent to cover the Russo-Japanese War (1904–5), he was described thus by one of his fellow journalists: "Jack's dislike of the Japanese outdid mine. Though a professed socialist, he really believed in the Kaiser's yellow peril."[33] Both his belief in the coming of the socialist revolution as well as in the threat of the yellow peril are two topics that thoroughly pervade his fiction and journalistic writing.

In "The Unparalleled Invasion," London envisions the total disappearance of the "yellow populace"[34] in a genocide, enabling resettlement by other, non-Asian nationalities according to a "democratic American program."[35] The biological warfare that London envisions is directed at a modernized China, which is described as breaking away from Japan in 1922, after a war to annex Japan, Korea, and Manchuria. While growing stronger over the next decades, China eventually overwhelms Europe and the United States. The Western powers strike back in the form of total war, which culminates in the vanishing of the "yellow populace":

> But on May 1, 1976, had the reader been in the imperial city of Peking, with its then population of eleven million, he would have witnessed a curious sight. He would have seen the streets filled with the chattering yellow populace, every queued head tilted back, every slant eye turned skyward. And high up in the blue he would have beheld a tiny dot of black, which, because of its orderly evolutions, he would have identified as an airship. From this airship, as it curved its flight back and forth over the city, fell missiles—strange, harmless missiles, tubes of fragile glass that shattered into thousands of fragments on the streets and

[32] John R. Eperjesi, *The Imperialist Imaginary: Visions of Asia and the Pacific in American Culture* (Lebanon, NH: University of New England Press, 2005), 108.

[33] Ibid.

[34] Jack London, "The Unparalleled Invasion," http://www.jacklondons.net/writings/StrengthStrong/invasion.html [accessed January 27, 2012].

[35] Colleen Lye, *America's Asia: Racial Form and American Literature, 1893–1945* (Princeton, NJ: Princeton University Press, 2004), 41.

house-tops. [...] Had the reader again been in Peking, six weeks later, he would have looked in vain for the eleven million inhabitants. [...] But for the rest he would have had to seek along the highways and byways of the Empire. And not all would he have found fleeing from plague-stricken Peking, for behind them, by hundreds of thousands of unburied corpses by the wayside, he could have marked their flight. And as it was with Peking, so it was with all the cities, towns, and villages of the Empire.[36]

The "chattering yellow populace" is an anonymous mass, neither human nor inhuman, unified by one physiognomic feature ("slanted eyes") and by its yellow appearance. London's detailed description of a Chinese genocide, of the extinction of "yellow life," the "sanitation of China," and its resulting colonization, reverses the theme of a massive Asian invasion of the West. The total destruction of China is Jack London's blatantly racist social vision; it stages a regeneration of "white identity"[37]—along the conceptual lines of the *Gesamtkunstwerk*, as discussed above—under Western tutelage. In an article for the *San Francisco Examiner* in 1907, London observes: "The Yellow Peril became a tangible thing, shaped itself in the intellect, and remained to be pondered, and pondered, and be pondered yet again"[38]—thus identifying the theme that was driving his imagination during the time of the writing of "The Unparalleled Invasion."

According to Colleen Lye, London depicts Chinese and Asian civilization as

in some ways, barbarian, but they share an unusual capacity for sudden development. The examples of Japanese modernization that have "repeatedly surprised the world" present a wider epistemological challenge—one that potentially recodes a perpetually "petrified" China into a "sleeping giant" about to be awakened.[39]

The Asiatic threat to overrun the West is thus based on the idea of a militarized Japan and an industrious China forming a common front, with the Chinese masses mobilized by a miraculous Japanese power. The threat thus represents a combination of efficiency and overwhelming number:

Four hundred million indefatigable workers (deft, intelligent, and unafraid to die), aroused and juvenescent, managed and guided by

[36] London, "The Unparalleled Invasion."
[37] Lye, *America's Asia*, 36.
[38] Ibid., 45.
[39] Ibid., 15. London asked: "what if Japan awakens China—not to our dream, if you please, but to her dream?" (quoted in ibid., 16).

forty-five million additional human beings, who are splendid fighting animals, scientific and modern, constitute the menace to the Western world which has been well named the "Yellow Peril."[40]

This is one of the few instances in which London actually uses the term "yellow peril" in his journalistic writings,[41] a usage that is of a piece with "The Unparalleled Invasion." The danger described—in an almost apocalyptic tone—is that of the machine-like behavior London attributes to Asians.

"Yellow children": Soloviev's pan-Mongolism

Even before the actual defeat of Russia in the Russo-Japanese War (1904–5), the first Asiatic victory over a Western power, the prophecy of a Mongolian invasion was part of eschatological visions prevalent at the turn of the century. According to the Russian idealist poet Vladimir Soloviev (1853–1900), a close friend of Fyodor Dostoevsky, the threat of the Antichrist was imminent, introduced by a "second Tartar yoke."[42] In his poem "Panmongolism" (1894), Soloviev proposed his solution to the Asian threat in the union of the Catholic and Orthodox worlds, creating the ideal of a "universal church" with the Vatican as its prototype:

Pan-Mongolism! The name is monstrous
Yet it caresses my ear
As if filled with the portent
Of a grand divine fate.
[...]
From the Altai to Malaysian shores
The leaders of Eastern isles
Have gathered a host of regiments
By China's defeated walls.

---

[40] London, quoted in Andrew Furer, " 'Zone Conquerors' and 'White Devils,' " in *Rereading Jack London*, ed. Leonard Cassuto and Jeanne Campbell Reesman (Stanford, CA: Stanford University Press, 1998), 163.

[41] In her critical biography of Jack London, Jeanne Campbell Reesman interprets London's most racially charged journalistic writings as a deliberate form of sensationalism: "he wanted to startle the public and to situate himself as someone knowledgeable enough to warn Americans about what they did not imagine" (Jeanne Campbell Reesman, *Jack London's Racial Lives: A Critical Biography* [Athens: University of Georgia Press, 2002], 102).

[42] Marlène Laruelle, "The Orient in Russian Thought at the Turn of the Century," in *Russia between East and West: Scholarly Debates on Eurasianism,* ed. Dmitry Shlapentokh (Leiden: Brill, 2007), 26.

Countless as locusts
And as ravenous,
Shielded by an unearthly power
The tribes move north.

O Russia! Forget your former glory:
The two-headed eagle is ravaged,
And your tattered banners passed
Like toys among yellow children.

He who neglects love's legacy,
Will be overcome by trembling fear…
And the third Rome will fall to dust,
Nor will there ever be a fourth.

The threat of pan-Mongolism is imminent, for it is already the next generation ("yellow children") that is calling Russia its home. Russian banners are degraded into objects of play, suggesting the weakness of the Russian people in the face of the strength of an "unearthly power" invading from the North. Instead of dehumanizing the "yellow race" as such, Soloviev evokes "yellow children" at play, in quasi-admiration of the power of the Asian conquerors. The invocation of a "third Rome" ("And the third Rome will fall to dust"), which Soloviev envisioned as happening in Moscow (the first two "Romes" being the Roman Empire and Constantinople), is elegiac; the decline of spirituality ("He who neglects love's legacy") has led to the definitive victory of "Panmongolism" ("Nor will there ever be a fourth").

Similarly, in his article "China and Europe" (1890) and also in the later "A Short Story of the Anti-Christ" (1900), Soloviev describes the principle he sees at work in the ability of the "yellow race" to conquer the Russian Empire. It is because Russia and Europe are unfaithful to their Christian principles that they are vulnerable to a Chinese invasion, while the "great idea of Pan-Mongolism"—that is, the unification of "all the races of Eastern Asia," as Soloviev exclaims in "A Short Story of the Anti-Christ"—aims at conducting a "decisive war against foreign intruders, that is, against the Europeans."[43]

---

[43] Soloviev, "A Short Story of the Anti-Christ" (1900), http://www.goodcatholicbooks.org/antichrist.html [accessed January 12, 2013]. The concept of intrusion is also performed stylistically, for the first lines of his poem "Panmongolism" intrude in the narrative in the form of an epigraph and, as Judith Deutsch Kornblatt has argued, become the object of a "self-parody" (Kornblatt, "Soloviev on Salvation: The Story of the 'Short Story of the Antichrist,'" in *Russian Religious Thought*, ed. Judith Deutsch Kornblatt [Madison: University of Wisconsin Press, 1996], 70).

This short story, an experiment with new genres of fiction,[44] frames, in the form of a Platonic dialogue, a historical narrative presented as future history:

> Finding itself between the hammer and the anvil, the German army was compelled to accept the honorable terms of peace offered to it by the Chinese Emperor. The exultant French, fraternizing with the yellow faces, scattered over Germany and soon lost all notion of military discipline. The Emperor ordered his army to kill any allies who were no longer useful and, with Chinese punctiliousness, the order was executed with precision.[45]

Here Soloviev imagines a devastating war between Asia and Europe. The idea of the French army "fraternizing with the yellow faces" in its fight against Germany challenges not only China's values and religious beliefs, but also those of Western Europe. Soloviev's reactionary rhetoric grows out of the Slavophile movement at the end of the century, which was also opposed to Western European influence over Slavic culture. And yet, unlike his close friend Dostoevsky, Soloviev did not believe in a "Slavophile idealization of Orthodoxy";[46] rather his "religious universalism,"[47] as Anna Frajlich has called it, culminates in the unification of an Orthodox East with a Catholic Rome.

"A Short Story of the Anti-Christ" also features the appearance of a 33-year-old Superman (same age as Christ at the time of his death), who interrupts the Mongolian invasion and the historical narrative of decline. The fantastic appearance of "Emperor Superman" derives its power from a pact with Satan, obtained through his assistant Apollonius, who is a "half Asiatic and half European miracle maker"[48] and thus one of Fu Manchu's precursors:

> He combined in himself in a most striking manner knowledge of the latest conclusions and applications of Western science with the art of utilizing all that was really sound and important in traditional Eastern mysticism. The results of this combination were startling. [...] The people said of him that he could *bring down fire from heaven.*[49]

---

[44] Ibid., 71. According to Kornblatt, the genres of the short story and dialogue allow Soloviev to reflect on the notion of salvation in terms of its dependence on human and divine interaction and thus in a less prophetic and more philosophical and humorous manner (see Kornblatt, ibid., 84).

[45] Ibid.

[46] Renato Poggioli, quoted in Anna Frajlich, *The Legacy of Ancient Rome in the Russian Silver Age* (Amsterdam: Editions Rodopi, 2007), 38.

[47] Ibid.

[48] Kornblatt, "Soloviev on Salvation," 78.

[49] Soloviev, "A Short Story of the Anti-Christ" (original emphasis).

The combination of Eastern and Western elements culminates in a dystopia; for the Promethean figure of the Antichrist will eventually abuse his power, and his reign will culminate in an "earthquake of unprecedented violence."[50]

A yellow Russia: Bely's *Petersburg*

Unlike the authors we have just examined, the Russian modernist writer Andrei Bely, in his epic novel *Petersburg*, one of the greatest, if obscure, works of twentieth-century literature (it is considered to be the Russian equivalent of Joyce's *Ulysses*),[51] seeks to systematically and exhaustively subvert or deconstruct the motif of the "yellow peril."

Dmitry Shlapentokh describes *Petersburg* as the transformation of Soloviev's "Mongolian allegory into a fantastic and morbid reality."[52] Set in the revolutionary year of 1905 (*Petersburg* was written in 1911–12, serialized in 1913–14, first published in book form in 1916, then extensively revised in 1922), at the time of the Russian Navy's defeat at the hands of the Japanese, who "annihilated a large Russian squadron in a few hours, thereby creating the impression that Imperial Japan was a world power to be reckoned with,"[53] *Petersburg* envisions a "new city," in which Russians appear "internally and physically colonized by the Mongols."[54] Describing the city as being haunted by a "fatal crack in the world between the Orient and the West," Bely plays on the figure of the "yellow peril," not as an impending threat, however, but rather as a form of confusion about Russia's origins. Although Bely draws on Soloviev's ideas as expressed in his poem "Panmongolism," "the "truth" in *Petersburg* is given in no postulate, but takes form from a complex of contradictions and half-truths that are in ceaseless movement,"[55] as Robert A. Maguire and John E. Malmstad conclude in their commentary on the novel.

Nietzsche's notion of the "eternal return" had a strong influence on Bely, who was inspired by his reading of *The Birth of Tragedy* and *Thus Spoke*

[50] Ibid.
[51] Vladimir Nabokov considered *Petersburg* to be one of the four greatest novels of the twentieth century.
[52] Laruelle, "The Orient in Russian Thought," 27.
[53] Robert A. Maguire and John E. Malmstad, Notes to Andrei Bely, *Petersburg*, trans. and ed. Robert A. Maguire and John E. Malmstad (Bloomington: Indiana University Press, 1978), 325.
[54] Laruelle, "The Orient in Russian Thought," 27.
[55] Robert A. Maguire and John E. Malmstad, "*Petersburg*," in *Andrei Bely: Spirit of Symbolism*, ed. John E. Malmstad (Ithaca, NY: Cornell University Press, 1987), 144.

Zarathustra. If "movement without end along the spiral"[56] characterizes *Petersburg,* this movement is also embodied in the "yellow peril" that inscribes itself repeatedly until it becomes ubiquitous ("saffron yellow" is found all over the city). Bely's undermining of the "yellow peril" through yellow figures is linked to Nietzsche's notion of anthropomorphism as the figure of an unstable truth: "What, then, is truth? A mobile army of metaphors, metonymies, anthropomorphisms."[57]

Nietzsche's tropological conception of truth is apropos here, due to his inclusion of the "trope" of anthropomorphism, which differs from the other tropes on his list in that it does not involve substitution. As Paul de Man has remarked, what Nietzsche is really talking about is exclusion: for anthropomorphism "is not just a trope but an identification on the level of substance. It takes one entity for another and thus implies the constitution of specific entities prior to their confusion. [...] Anthropomorphism freezes the infinite chain of tropological transformations and propositions into one single assertion or essence which, as such, excludes all others."[58] An anthropomorphism is no longer a proposition, but a proper name—or rather an act of naming, the naming of an appearance, the giving of a human form. This operation brings truth to the fore, violently inscribing what remains excluded as inhuman. Anthropomorphisms are in this sense a transitional moment on the verge of inhumanity, revealing the truth about human beings. The inhuman thereby receives its attributes from the idea of the "yellow peril," as figured in the world of *Petersburg.*

The development of this danger, which Bely describes in terms of a violent contact between East and West,[59] can be recognized by the sense of taste: "Man is what he eats,"[60] remarks Dudkin, one of the secret agents in *Petersburg,* while chatting in a restaurant with the rival agent, Lippanchenko. "Lip" in Russian suggests sticky—and what sticks to each other in *Petersburg* are these two agents: haunted by each other, while at the same time sticking to and haunting other characters as well. The sticky material of the novel

---

56 Ibid.

57 Friedrich Nietzsche, "On Truth and Lie in a Nonmoral Sense," in *On Truth and Untruth: Selected Writings* (New York: HarperCollins, 2010), 29.

58 Paul de Man, "Anthropomorphism and Trope in the Lyric," in de Man, *The Rhetoric of Romanticism* (New York: Columbia University Press, 1984), 241.

59 Timothy Langen points out that Bely had originally intended to write a trilogy entitled *East or West,* with *Petersburg* representing *West:* "Yet as it happened, *Petersburg* turned out to be the conjunction—and not just an 'or' but also an 'and,' a 'but,' a 'however,' an 'also,' an 'if,' an 'unless,' an 'except,' and every other relation. The line running between East and West, like every other line in this novel, undergoes a series of elaborate contortions" (Langen, *The Stony Dance: Unity and Gesture in Andrei Bely's Petersburg* [Evanston, IL: Northwestern University Press, 2005], 154).

60 Bely, *Petersburg,* 26.

forms a sort of collage. Walls, wallpaper, newspaper, pages of books—these
are the surfaces upon which these two agents propagate the threat of the
"yellow peril," a threat Bely describes as existing inside as much as outside, at
the intersection of books and maps, and in the constant threat of the bomb,
around which the novel is constructed.[61]

Lippanchenko, the lifelong terrorist, is the embodiment of the "yellow
peril" invading Petersburg from the East—but also from the inside. "The
huge yellow spot"[62] that Dostoevsky's Underground Man finds on his
pants[63] prefigures the yellow-striped suit worn by Lippanchenko, with
his "little Mongolian eyes." Whereas the Underground Man undermines
society through his misanthropic demeanour and withdrawal from social
life, his position is ultimately passive; he disdains all meaningful action.
Lippanchenko, on the other hand, is an active terrorist: an apparent
spy for the underground, determined to overthrow the political system.
Lippanchenko's marginal and menacing status is accentuated and figured in
the anthropomorphic evocation of his fish-like appearance:

> The fat man, called Lippanchenko by the stranger, was about to set his
> dark yellow elbow on the sheet of newspaper covering the bundle. [...]
> His lips still quivered, resembling pieces of sliced salmon, not yellowish
> red, but oily and yellow. [...]
> Around them was heard: "What is Man?"
> "Man is what he eats."
> "I know."
> "Well, since you know, grab a plate and eat."[64]

Yellow serves in this passage to emphasize Lippanchenko's unseemly and
slimy appearance. There is also something sinister about his yellowness,
as with the idea that man is defined by an appropriation, that man
becomes what he eats and is eventually transformed into bodily fluids and

---

[61] Timothy Langen describes the conceptual triangle of *Petersburg* as a "St. Petersburg-Irreality-Book": "After all, the proof of St. Petersburg's existence is a matter of paper and ink. [...] In the logic of *Petersburg*, then, St. Petersburg is real to the extent that such books and maps are real—and it seems to share with them a mode of being on the border of thingness. Yet this is not a novel where things don't exist. Its entire plot is constructed around a tremendously powerful thing, a bomb, and its characters..." (Langen, *The Stony Dance*, 5).

[62] Ibid., 81.

[63] Like Dostoevsky in the *Underground Man*, Bely emphasizes Petersburg's existence as a "matter of paper and ink," as Langen remarks; except that *Petersburg* is at the same time constructed around a thing, the bomb, which is directly related to the agent Lippanchenko. See Langen, *The Stony Dance*, 5.

[64] Bely, *Petersburg*, 24–6.

excrements.[65] That is to say: the color yellow serves as a figure of metamorphosis, a pivot point between animality and humanity, and is in that sense an anthropomorphism.

"Lipchenky" was a pseudonym of the real-life terrorist and double agent for the secret police Alez Fishelvich, after his escape to Berlin in 1908. In Russian *lipovyi* is slang for "fake, counterfeit." Lippanchenko, also a double agent, has as many counterfeit features as his real world counterpart, Fishelvich. His fish-like skin is as oily as the sardine tin that holds the bomb that will explode at the end of the novel. The four walls of the sardine tin, the salmon lips, and the yellow stripes of his suit all indicate the linearity of a destructive plan. Whereas the "huge yellow spot" that irritates Dostoevsky's Underground Man indicates a self-destructive force, Lippanchenko's yellow surfaces accumulate a destructive energy that will self-destruct as they attack him. His yellow marks do not cause fever, as with the Underground Man, but make him shine: "Polish gleamed on his yellow shoes" [66]—yet another example of the ambivalence of yellow.

These oily and shiny surfaces contrast with the dusty surface that surrounds the grey figure of the senator, Apollo Apollonovich Ableukhov. Though inextricably linked, both kinds of surface form part of a linear system in which paternal figures occupy diametrically opposed positions: Lippanchenko, father of the criminal underground, and Apollo Apollonovich, father of the bureaucratic system. But this opposition serves only to connect them even more closely, as shown by their respective fates. Whereas Lippanchenko's corpse will explode into gases (which form part of the yellow dust that Ableukhov sweeps off his books), Ableukhov, at the end of his life, turns into "a little yellow old man,"[67] taking on Lippanchenko's skin color.

As we have seen in other works, becoming yellow is the danger signal inscribed in the "yellow peril" (invading Asian hordes). In *Petersburg*, it is becoming the texture of surfaces and skins and therefore of the "Book of Destinies," which Bely imagines in his essay "Circular Movement" as follows: "The aggregate of pages is muscles; and the title-page is the skin."[68] The exchange of Ableukhov's and Lippanchenko's respective positions (the two characters also contain each other's names anagrammatically via Ableukhov's patronymic Apollonovich) form, in a process of decomposition,

---

[65] Olga Matich discusses in "Poetics of Disgust: To East and Die in *Petersburg*" (in Petersburg/*Petersburg: Novel and City, 1900–1921*, ed. O. Matich [Madison: University of Wisconsin Press, 2010], 55), Bely's concept of spatialization and dissolution into a fourth dimension.

[66] Ibid.

[67] Ibid., 95.

[68] Bely quoted in Maguire and Malmstad, "*Petersburg*," 142.

the imagery of the "yellow peril": a spiral held together by the oily element of Lippanchenko and the dusty element of Apollonovich, in which the substance of their skins and surfaces is absorbed.[69]

The fact that Bely draws on a concrete event—the Japanese victory over Russia in 1905—displaces the discussion into a historical dimension; the novel *Petersburg* thereby becomes the destiny of the city Petersburg. Because Bely's references to literary and historical figures are typically caricatures, his historical citations are nearly always overdetermined, in the sense that the body parts of these figures are available for quotation.[70] One prototype of the Ableukhov character is Konstantin Pobedonostsev, the main representative of the Holy Synod and one of the most hated reactionaries and fanatic anti-Semites of his time. In a well-known caricature from 1905, Pobedonostsev is shown in the same pose in which Bely presents Apollo Apollonovich: a weak little man with enormous ears and the wings of a bat, he is sitting atop a sleeping female figure in a fish-like position, in Russian national dress. The sleeping woman conjures up both the struggle of the historical Pobedonostsev and the literary Ableukhov to check revolutionary tendencies and maintain the status quo. Their anthropomorphic associations move them along a vertical line in divergent directions: the wings of the bat, an animal of the air (Ableukhov) is juxtaposed with the fish, which is linked linguistically to Lippanchenko's name (Fishelvich). Both are intertwined in Ableukhov's daily habits: his favorite place is the water closet, and his first act, after the attempt to usurp him, is to clean the "yellow dust" from the books of his library. "Yellow dust" turns out to be not only a geographical reference, but also a temporal one, for it evokes the "red dust" of "the desert of our exhausted culture" from Nietzsche's *The Birth of Tragedy*.[71] Like the "saffron-yellow atmosphere," the "yellow dust" highlights geographical resonances in the form of an Eastern invasion that Apollo Apollonovich cannot escape. The name Apollo, which directly refers to Nietzsche's notion of the "Apollonian"—a concept of form that contrasts with the Dionysian concept of ecstasy and intoxication associated with the character of Lippanchenko—must face disintegration into dust, the disintegration of all form.

[69] Collages of the "yellow peril" are part of what Lucas Stratton also calls (with respect to the "medium of the bridge" in *Petersburg*) "networked spaces." It is in those spaces where Bely performs the clash between static forms and a swarming pulsation, "the pulsation of the elemental body" (*Petersburg/Petersburg*, 184). See Lucas Stratton, "The Button and the Barricade: Bridges in Paris and Petersburg," in ibid., 226.

[70] And these caricatures come together in a collage of what Bely calls a "dark yellow, saffron-yellow atmosphere" (Bely, *Petersburg*, 258).

[71] Friedrich Nietzsche, *The Birth of Tragedy and the Case of Wagner*, trans. Walter Kaufmann (New York: Random House, 1967), 123.

Dudkin's life in a shabby room on the top floor, which is referred to as a "habitation," is the equivalent of Zarathustra's mountain.[72] Instead of returning from the mountain, following his shadow (described in *Thus Spoke Zarathustra* as becoming thinner and thinner: "I almost resemble a shadow"),[73] Dudkin is pushed higher along the spiral, transforming himself into a shadow-like figure as he casts his shadow. Distinctions dissolve in the spiralling movement enacted by Bely when the two strangers, Dudkin and Shishnarfne, unite in Dudkin's habitation. Bely had proclaimed this principle of dissolution at the end of the first chapter, in the following announcement to the reader:

> Once his brain has playfully engendered the mysterious stranger, that stranger exists, really exists. He will not vanish from the Petersburg prospects as long as the senator with such thoughts exists, because thought exists too.
>
> So let our stranger be a real stranger! And let the two shadows of my stranger be real shadows!
>
> Those dark shadows will, oh yes, they will, follow on the heels of the stranger, just as the stranger himself is closely following the senator. The aged senator will, oh yes, he will, pursue you too, reader, in his black carriage. And henceforth you will never ever forget him![74]

Implicit in Bely's suggestive proclamation of a haunting force that will captivate the reader is a criticism of Nietzsche (also expressed in Bely's essay "Circular Movement"), to the effect that it was a mistake to have Zarathustra return from the mountain instead of moving him higher up the spiral.[75] With the dissolution of Shishnarfne, who, like Zarathustra, is Persian, Bely realizes the move higher up the spiral, without return.

After Dudkin visits Lippanchenko, he is followed up the stairs to his room by Shishnarfne, whom he had met at Lippanchenko's. In Dudkin's room Shishnarfne gradually becomes more insubstantial, eventually taking over Dudkin's voice in the form of the word "Enfranshish," which Dudkin has been hearing repeatedly. In the course of this scene, Dudkin comes to realize that Enfranshish (the phrase "en franchise" appears on a box of French insect powder, which in the Cyrillic alphabet becomes Engranshish) and Shishnarfne are inversions of each other:

---

[72] Maguire and Malmstad, "*Petersburg*," 126.

[73] Friedrich Nietzsche, *Thus Spoke Zarathustra*, ed. Robert Pippin, trans. Adrian Del Caro (Cambridge: Cambridge University Press, 2006), 221.

[74] Bely, *Petersburg*, 36.

[75] "For Bely, the shadow presents a constant temptation to return, a temptation to which Zarathustra (and Nietzsche) yielded" (Maguire and Malmstad, "*Petersburg*," 127).

And he understood: "Shishnarfne—Shish-narfne…" From his vocal
apparatus came the reply: "You summoned me… Here I am…"
Enfranshish had come for his soul.[76]

The conversion of Shishnarfne into Enfranshish moves from the dissolution
of sound to a transcription from French into Russian, in the direction of a
force that turns people into animals.

Just as the Oriental sound of Shishnarfne passes through the walls, the
Mongolian face of Lippanchenko enters at night, becoming visible on the
yellow wallpaper. This Mongolian face turns out to be the spot of a sow bug
during daytime:

> Lippanchenko's suit reminded the stranger of the color of the yellow
> wallpaper in his habitation on Vasilievsky Island, a color associated with
> insomnia. That insomnia evoked the memory of a fateful face with very
> narrow little Mongol eyes. The face had looked repeatedly at him from
> the wallpaper. When he examined this place during the day, he could
> make out only a damp spot, over which crawled a sow bug. In order
> to distract himself from memories of the tormenting hallucination, he
> grew garrulous, to his own surprise.[77]

This spectacle of a Mongolian face that appears in yellow spots on the wall is
a citation from Nikolai Gogol's short story *The Portrait*, in which a money-
lender with oriental features appears on the wall. In this fashion, the "fateful
Mongolian face" that appears at night on the yellow walls is implicated in
exchange value (with gold as the universal equivalent). And thus the citation
highlights the slippage (or alchemy) between yellow skin and gold: the
exchange of incommensurable values is exhibited inside, at night, on the
yellow walls of the garret; from dirt to gold, yellow endangers the stability
of value systems.[78]

Bely thus brings to life the inscription of the "yellow peril" in quotations
of yellow figures from Dostoevsky, Gogol, and Nietzsche. The movement
that culminates in the red flames of the Apocalypse occurs through a citation
of Pushkin's "Bronze Horseman," which, translated literally, is a "copper
horseman." The culminating point is the red metal, figuring the Apocalypse
by taking on the color of flames. Colors symbolize an alchemical process
in *Petersburg*, leading from black, to white, to yellow, to the red of the
Apocalypse at the end.

---

[76] Bely, *Petersburg*, 208.
[77] Ibid., 26.
[78] Freud's remark in his *Interpretation of Dreams* that displacements can turn a whole value
system upside down describes the mechanism at work in Dudkin.

The destruction of Petersburg is prefigured in Dudkin's "extravagant little action": the killing of Lippanchenko. In an act of will that moves further along the spiral (as Zarathustra was led by the dwarf), Dudkin is led in his action by Lippanchenko with "his little Mongolian eyes" that looked at him during the night, enslaving his will. Dudkin is not allowed to purchase a knife, so he purchases a pair of scissors instead. Their straight blades, combined with their circular handles, become an emblem of the "line/circle imagery" of *Petersburg*: "The straight line has become a circle, for madness is a circular condition."[79] Bely's alchemical and symbolic frameworks implode though yellow inscriptions; on yellow surfaces (yellow skin, yellow walls and suits, yellow dust) the clash between East and West, between the human and the non-human, is inscribed. Recurring inscriptions of yellow thus conjure up the political imagery of the "yellow peril" as an "imagetext" (to invoke W. J. T. Mitchell's term, meaning an indissociability of text and image).

After killing Lippanchenko, Dudkin rides on his corpse; his act of will has ended in madness, which Bely describes as a circular condition. The yellow houses that Bely describes are turning Petersburg "saffron yellow." But a seeming liberation from the "yellow peril" has become a performance of madness; yellow turns reddish in the metal of the Bronze (Copper) Horseman as an apocalyptic rider performs the iron law of the eternal return:

> Where are you galloping, proud steed, and where will you set down your hooves? Oh, mighty master of fate! Was it not thus that you, on the very brink of the abyss on high, reared up Russia with your iron bridle?[80]

This passage is a citation from Pushkin's "Bronze Horseman," which is itself a parody of its protagonist (Evgeny's ride on a lion).

As Dudkin rides on Lippanchenko's corpse, a sow bug crawls across his face. The reappearance of the sow bug (and its association with the yellow wall on which the insect originally appeared) recalls the image of the yellow wallpaper, the surface on which Dudkin could see the Mongolian face haunting him at night. In leading back to the haunting nightmare, the sow bug turns Dudkin himself into a circulation of the "yellow peril."

The alchemical process of yellowing does not simply move towards catastrophe, but towards an inscription of the "yellow peril" performed through a chain of citations exhibited in the characters' features and in their immediate environment. The dramatization of the environment in geometrical patterns

---

[79] Maguire and Malmstad, "Petersburg," 132.
[80] Bely, *Petersburg*, 324.

of circles, squares and cubes marks Bely's forms of abstraction, which are charged with a spiritual meaning. As the color that signals the coming of the Apocalypse, yellow is dramatized both as an abstract force and in its materiality of inscription (on oily surfaces and in dusty appearances) as a visceral embodiment of the "yellow peril." The combination of visceral and abstract forms dramatizing the "yellowing" of the city of Petersburg conjures the idea of non-human forces—the recurrent inscriptions of the "yellow peril" in Russian literature.[81]

The yellow rhapsody: Wassily Kandinsky and Sergei Eisenstein

The relationship between synthetic art and political visions of the clash between Eastern and Western civilizations is nowhere more pronounced than in the reflections of three Russian-born artists: Andrei Bely, Sergei Eisenstein, and Wassily Kandinsky. Already in 1903, Bely had published an article entitled "Sacred Colors," in which he approaches colors as reflections "of the Absolute in the material world." Referring to Soloviev's idea of "all-in-oneness," Bely describes color as a form of oneness "that was threatened by forces of opposition in the material world."[82] The color of gray is, in Bely's reflection on color, "the color of evil in the material world," and yellow is seen as "the primary stage of grayness."[83] As such, yellow is considered to be the "sinister reflection of impending chaos,"[84] linking the color (as in *Petersburg*) to the political discourse of its time.[85] However, Bely's "sacred colors," understood as forces in

---

[81] Bely thereby creates the collective form of a movement that Gilles Deleuze describes with respect to *Petersburg* as a continuum produced "between visceral organic states, political states of society and meteorological states of the world" (Deleuze, *Cinema 2: The Time-Image*, trans. Hugh Tomlinson and Robert Galeta [New York: Continuum, 2005], 292). Indeed, Bely himself imagines the continuum of movements between different states of mind and times as the "unrolling of a cinematographic film subject to the minute action of occult forces: should the film stop, we will be fixed forever in an artificial pose of terror" (Bely, cited in ibid., 121).

[82] Gerald Janecek comments that Bely's notion of *sacred colors* went "beyond the claims of correspondences and synaesthesia made for colors by the French Symbolists": "However, these colors were not simply a system of informative signals, additional meaningful signs in his arsenals of symbols. They became in Bely's manipulation, practically theurgic and creative" (Janecek, *Andrei Bely: A Critical Review* [Lexington: University Press of Kentucky, 1978], 113).

[83] Rosemary Anne DiCarlo, *Andrej Belyj's Petersburg and the Modern Aesthetic Consciousness* (Brown University, University Microfilm, 1980), 108.

[84] Bely, quoted in ibid., 108.

[85] Cioran summarizes Bely's use of yellow as a color that prophesizes catastrophe in "Sacred

constant movement and conflict with the material world, are funda-
mentally different from Kandinsky's idea of an abstraction of color
from all external relationships in absolute correspondences. Although
both Bely's and Kandinsky's "impulse to abstraction," as Olga Matich
argues, had a "larger philosophical and mystical dimension—the desire to
render subjective experience and the 'great spiritual' visually and synaes-
thetically, not naturalistically,"[86] Bely's impulse to abstraction insists
in his urban representation of modernity on a constant turn between
inside and outside worlds. In Bely's *Petersburg* it is the very stuff of
the bomb that destroys order and turns abstract patterns inside out.[87]
This yearning for the explosion is in Bely a central part of the process
of dissolution into fluids and dust, whereas in Kandinsky, the "dissolution of external naturalistic form" was meant to be replaced by an
"inner resonance [*Klang*]."[88] Matich concludes her comparison between
Bely's and Kandinsky's movement towards forms of abstraction thus:
"If Kandinsky experimented with colors and the way they inform the
dissolution of form, Bely's metamorphic images were the pigments
that dissolve the sensible world of Petersburg."[89] The color yellow in
Petersburg dissolves words and color into figural forces of the "yellow
peril," in particular its explosiveness, whereas Kandinsky performs in his
paintings and compositions, namely in the stage composition *The Yellow
Sound*, the disappearance or dissolution of the world as the emergence of
a new universe.

Kandinsky's book *Concerning the Spiritual in Art* (1911) is based
on the assumption of art's departure "from the objective world, and

Colors" and then in *Petersburg*, where it becomes the color of the "yellow menace," the
Mongolian leitmotif of devastation: "Just as surely as the yellowish brown spectrum of
colors appeared out of the murky greys in Bely's symbolic analysis of light's refraction,
both Lippanchenko and Shishnarfne, the representatives of the yellow menace, arose
out of the gray mists of the Finnish port of Helsingfors, where Aleksandr Dudkin first
encountered them as they began to preach his nihilistic, anarchical theories on culture
and history" (Cioran, "A Prism for the Absolute: The Symbolic Colors of Andrei Bely,"
Andrei Bely—A Critical Review, ed. Szerk G. Janecek [Lexington: University Press of
Kentucky, 1978], 106–7).

[86] Olga Matich, "Bely, Kandinsky, and the Avant-Garde Aesthetics," in Petersburg/
Petersburg: Novel and City, 1900–1921, 112.

[87] Langen points to the final paradox of *Petersburg*, which is characterized similarly as
"the urge to destroy" by the narrator of Dostoevsky's *Notes from the Underground*: "the
bomb, designated destroyer of order, is brought into the order of the novel and (even)
the plot, and it is this novel's most pervasive motif, its uniting force. It is, then, a symbol
of dizzying alternation of form and formlessness, order and chaos. The bomb is pattern
turned inside out—and, for Bely, this is the fate of every pattern" (Langen, *The Stony
Dance*, 109).

[88] Matich, "Bely, Kandinsky, and the Avant-Garde Aesthetics," 97.

[89] Ibid., 113.

the discovery of a new subject matter based only on the artist's 'inner needs.' "[90] According to Kandinsky, harmonies revealed in abstract art prefigure the dawning of a spiritual age out of a materialist era. Kandinsky thus ascribes to the artist, as well as to scientists and theosophists, the role of a prophet. In 1910, together with artists similarly driven by the belief in a coming spiritual era and its expression in forms of abstraction, Kandinsky founds with Franz Marc in Munich, Germany, the Blue Rider movement. This founding is consecrated by the publication of an almanac, which features Kandinsky's manifesto for synaesthetic art: the script for the stage composition *The Yellow Sound* (1912).

Drawing on Kandinsky's color theory, which is based on the opposition between yellow and blue, Kandinsky's *The Yellow Sound* culminates in a series of abrupt contrasts between colored objects, followed by absolute darkness and the sudden appearance of a "garish lemon-yellow" shining with increasing intensity: "everything suddenly turns a faded gray (all colors disappear!). Only the yellow flower shines ever brighter!"[91] In Kandinsky's "sounding cosmos," yellow is seen as the color that moves towards the spectator—an "ex-centric color," as he calls it—in opposition to the "concentric movement" characteristic of the color blue. In *Concerning the Spiritual in Art*, Kandinsky writes:

> Yellow and blue have another movement [...] an ex- and concentric movement. If two circles are drawn and painted respectively yellow and blue, brief concentration will reveal in the yellow a spreading movement out from the center, and a noticeable approach to the spectator. The blue, on the other hand, moves in upon itself, like a snail retreating into its shell, and draws away from the spectator.[92]

Built on yellow's capacity to engage the spectator, *The Yellow Sound* attempts to transport the spectator into a kind of meditative trance, in which "superior selves" can be reached. It is the artist who reveals the "inner tonalities" of color, which Kandinsky also terms the revelation of an "inner necessity" that determines all outward forms of movement.

Although initiated by a yellow "ex-centric movement" toward the spectator, it is thus the color blue in Kandinsky's color theory (strongly influenced by Rudolf Steiner's reinterpretation of Goethe's color circle)

[90] Richard Stratton, "Preface to the Dover Edition," in Wassily Kandinsky, "Concerning the Spiritual in Art," trans. Michael T. H. Sadler (New York: Dover Publications, 1977), viii.
[91] Wassily Kandinsky, "The Yellow Sound," quoted in Sergei Eisenstein, *The Film Sense*, trans. and ed. Jay Leyda (New York: Harcourt Brace & Company, 1974), 116.
[92] Wassily Kandinsky, *Concerning the Spiritual in Art* (New York: Dover Publications, 1977), 36–7.

that develops the "power of profound meaning": "(1) of retreat from the spectator, (2) of turning in upon its own center. [...] Blue is the typical heavenly color. The ultimate feeling it creates is one of rest."[93] Blue's "inner tonality" is stimulated by yellow, which is, on the contrary, described by Kandinsky as bursting forward in aggressive ways:

> Yellow, if steadily gazed at in any geometrical form, has a disturbing influence, and reveals in the color an insistent, aggressive character. The intensification of the yellow increases the painful shrillness of its note. Yellow is the typically earthly color. It can never have profound meaning. An intermixture with blue makes it a sickly color. It may be paralleled in human nature, with madness, not with melancholy, or hypochondriacal mania, but rather with violent raving lunacy.[94]

The raving and disturbing qualities Kandinsky emphasizes (certainly influenced by the symbolic meaning of yellow in his native Russia, where it is literally the color of madhouses)[95] is, however, entirely detached from any value system, from the political or ethical notions of the color that, as we saw in the Introduction, characterize Goethe's remarks on yellow.

The opposition between yellow and blue is staged at the limit of light—"light as it comes upon and over things"[96]—and transposes the "passage of light" in the last scene of *The Yellow Sound*, with the appearance of the "yellow giant" into the arrival of spirit itself. As John Sallis points out, Kandinsky's *Yellow Sound* anticipates the rise of a "new art," which Kandinsky also announces with reference to Wagner's *Gesamtkunstwerk* as "truly monumental art."[97] However, although *The Yellow Sound* illustrates the "synthesis of colored tone and its movement," figures such as Kandinsky's "intensely yellow giants" do not reproduce an already existing original, nor are the shifting forms, colors, and sounds available for the purpose of storytelling, as Leigh Clemons

---

[93] Ibid., 38.

[94] Ibid., 37–8.

[95] Madhouses are called "yellow houses" in Russian. Mikhail Bulgakov's novel *The Master and Margarita* (1931) famously explores the theme of "yellow walls" of madhouses, as well as yellow flowers as flowers of misery, thus emphasizing negative connotations of yellow in Russian culture.

[96] See John Sallis's discussion of Kandinsky's stage composition: "At the limit it is light itself that would be painted, light as it comes upon and over things. If, in addition, pure painting puts in play the special resource of the stage, then light itself can become also the means: there results a painting of light itself by light itself. Yet in the end the picture thus painted would be no longer picture; it would be transposed into something other, into spirit itself, as if it were an image returning to its original" (Sallis, *Shades—Of Painting at the Limit* [Bloomington: Indiana University Press, 1998], 62).

[97] Kandinsky writes in *Concerning the Spiritual in Art*: "And so the arts are encroaching one upon another, and from a proper use of this encroachment will rise the art that is truly monumental" (20).

summarizes Kandinsky's criticism of the Wagnerian methodology.[98] Without rejecting Wagner's "monumental art," Kandinsky came to the conclusion that "this musical giant's towering art achievement might be superseded."[99] Reinforced by Arnold Schoenberg's insistence on dissonance, Kandinsky's idea of a synthesis of the arts was much closer to the often improvisatory character of "shamanic ritual," as Peg Weiss comments:

> Clearly, Kandinsky's juxtaposition of Schoenberg's music and Arabian ecstatic dance is to be understood now within the context of his ethnographer's knowledge of primitive music, and in particular of his awareness and direct observation of the uses of music in shamanic ritual. The famous bear festival of the Voguls may also have stimulated Kandinsky's imagination as he conceived *The Yellow Sound*. [100]

It is in this context that the ecstatic outcries of the chorus and the ritualistic dances in *The Yellow Sound* establish a spiritual dimension. Within the pages of the *Blue Rider Almanac*, the "only full-page reproduction in *The Yellow Sound* text is devoted to Ceylonese dance masks," while the appearance of the "yellow giant" with outstretched arms in the finale seems to evoke a "double allusion to Christ and the son of Numi-Tōrem, Mirsusne-khum, the 'Golden Prince' and World-Watching-Man."[101]

Although never performed during Kandinsky's lifetime, *The Yellow Sound* was "written to be performed"[102]—both as a musical as well as a painterly composition; it was a "peculiar composition of a composition,"[103] in which the stage was framed through "broad black edges," like a canvas: "Five bright yellow giants appear on the now illuminated stage, 'as if hovering directly above the ground,' thus, as on the two-dimensional surface of a painting."[104] The subtitle of *The Yellow Sound: A Stage Composition*, with its musical resonance, indicates the transition into a new art of a spiritual experience that transcends everyday experience in its abstraction from the material

---

[98] See Leigh Clemons, "Staging New Dimensions: Wassily Kandinsky, *Der Blaue Reiter Almanac* and the Reconfiguration of Artistic Space," *Journal of Dramatic Theory and Criticism* 9, no. 1 (1994): 19.

[99] John Golding, *Paths to the Absolute: Mondrian, Malevich, Kandinsky, Pollock, Newman, Rothko, and Still* (Princeton, NJ: Princeton University Press, 2002), 96.

[100] Peg Weiss, *Kandinsky and Old Russia: The Artist as Ethnographer and Shaman* (New Haven, CT: Yale University Press, 1995), 109.

[101] Ibid., 110. Weiss also points out that *The Yellow Sound* was placed in the *Almanac* between "illustrations of Russian *lubki* and Egyptian shadow-play puppets side by side with reproductions of Christian symbols and artifacts" (ibid., 110).

[102] Sallis, *Shades—Of Painting at the Limit*, 52. The performance, scheduled for autumn 1914, was cancelled due to the outbreak of the war.

[103] Ibid., 60.

[104] Ibid.

world. In particular, one of Kandinsky's ten paintings entitled *Compositions*, *The Sketch for Composition II*, 1910 (Color Plate 12) shows Kandinsky's notion of pure painting in its proximity to music.[105] Peter Lasko emphasizes Kandinsky's insistence that he did not want to paint music, quoting Kandinsky stating: "I only want to paint good, necessary, living pictures."[106] In *Concerning the Spiritual in Art*, Kandinsky specifies his notion of "living pictures" as synaesthetic art, which is framed by the piano and the performance of the pianist; however, only as a way to reach a spiritual plane: "Color is the keyboard, the eyes are the harmonies, the soul is the piano with many strings. The artist is the hand that plays, touching one key or another, to cause vibrations in the soul."[107] What is synaesthetic is not the musical experience per se, but the simultaneous stimulation of the senses (color, music, touch) in the soul.

As in *The Yellow Sound*, Kandinsky posits in *The Sketch for Composition II* the opposition of light (in an Arcadian scene, bright, sunny, and predominantly yellow, on the right) and darkness (in a catastrophic scene that dramatizes clouds and lightning in dark blue, on the left). In this stormy scene (upper left part of the painting), "the city and its domed churches (all of them obscured) are collapsing around an apocalyptic figure standing with outstretched arms, a yellow figure (at least in the painted sketch), reminiscent of the bright yellow giant in the final scene of *The Yellow Sound*."[108] The collapse of dark and light passages into a yellow figure suggests "in Kandinsky's terms, the transition from the collapsing materialism to the new epoch brought by the reawakening spirit."[109] The painting is organized around such "spirit-like figures"[110] in movement, which carry out the transformation into the flux of "color without regard to perspective,"[111] as it then culminates in the Arcadian scene in the lower right, with its two reclining figures. The movement from the catastrophic site to Arcadia is thereby thematized as a flow, a subversive flow that moves from the yellow Christ-like figure in the stormy, dark scene at the upper left to the bright Arcadian scene in the lower right; the vertical line at the center of the

---

[105] Three of the ten *Compositions* were destroyed, and of *Composition II* only the sketch "gives us a good idea of what that work might have looked like" (Golding, *Paths to the Absolute*, 90).

[106] Peter Lasko, *The Expressionist Roots of Modernism* (Manchester: Manchester University Press, 2003), 111.

[107] Kandinsky, *On the Spiritual in Art*, 25.

[108] Sallis, *Shades—Of Painting at the Limit*, 104.

[109] Ibid., 105.

[110] Ibid.

[111] Kandinsky emphasizes the importance of *Composition II* with respect to his use of color: "In *Composition II* one can see the free use of color without regard to perspective" (Kandinsky, quoted in Golding, *Paths to the Absolute*, 90).

painting is thus suggestive of a bridge, over which a horseman leaps, while the "spirit-like figures" are "flowing through the arch from left to right."[112] The horse-rider motif at the center of the image announces the crusade for the leap into an inner, spiritual dimension (this image was also used on the cover of the *Blue Rider Almanac*).

In 1941, the year Eisenstein reflects in *The Film Sense* on his notion of film as synaesthetic art, Kandinsky's spiritual notion of synaesthetic art becomes Exhibit A in Eisenstein's critique of a notion of synthesis abstracted from all "external matter," warning, as mentioned in the Introduction, that we might end up on the "yellow path"[113]—a clear reference to the Nazis' practice of stigmatizing Jews with the "yellow star," reviving medieval markers of exclusion. Eisenstein's warning about the "yellow path" effectively politicizes Kandinsky's supposedly apolitical approach to art, thereby demonstrating once again how uses of yellow are intrinsically multivalent, with resonances that are difficult, if not impossible, to restrain or circumscribe.

In the section of *Film Sense* on "Color and Meaning," for example, Eisenstein examines Van Gogh's comments on "pale sulphur" (referring to his painting *Night Café*): the yellow sulphur creates, according to Van Gogh, an atmosphere in which "one can ruin one's self, run mad, or commit a crime."[114] Eisenstein also cites Walther Bondy's staging of Strindberg and the former's emphasis on the "connection of yellow with sin,"[115] as well as the "dual meaning" of yellow in Gauguin.[116] Concerning these examples, Eisenstein thus asks: "Perhaps there is something sinister in the nature of the color yellow? Does this touch something more profound than mere conventional symbolism and habitual or accidental associations?"[117] Eisenstein turns to Frederic Portal's work on "symbolic meaning" from 1857, *Des couleurs symboliques dans l'antiquité, le Moyen-Age, et les temps modernes*, in which Portal contends that yellow has "equally strong connections with 'loving union' and 'adultery,'" emphasizing the ambivalent meanings of the color, which he relates to Christianity:

> It was clearly the advent of Christianity that introduced a new feeling in regard to yellow [...] In very large measure, no doubt, this was clearly the outcome of the whole of the Christian revulsion against the classical world and the rejection of everything that stood as the symbol of joy and of pride. Red and yellow were the favorite colors of that world. The

[112] Sallis, *Shades—Of Painting at the Limit*, 104.
[113] Eisenstein, *The Film Sense*, 136.
[114] Ibid., 120.
[115] Ibid., 121.
[116] Ibid., 127.
[117] Ibid., 124.

love of red was too firmly rooted in human nature for even Christianity to overcome it altogether, but yellow was a point of less resistance and here the new religion triumphed. Yellow became the color of envy. Yellow became the color of jealousy, of envy, of treachery. Judas was painted in yellow garments and in some countries Jews were compelled to be so dressed [...] There is a special reason why Christianity should have viewed yellow with suspicion. It had been the color associated with wanton love. In the beginning this association was with legitimate love. [...] But in Greece, and to a still more marked extent in Rome, the courtesan began to take advantage of this association.[118]

Eisenstein sees the "basic phenomenon of ambivalence" characteristic of yellow as culturally constructed, as resulting from the clash between a hedonistic Greek culture and the introduction of Christian ethics. The changing nature of the color yellow becomes a screen of projection for all that was condemned by the early and medieval Christian church, such as Jews and courtesans. In what could be considered a montage of collision, Eisenstein combines the reversal of yellow in the Christian tradition (into the color of betrayal and stigma) with the celebration of yellow in the Chinese tradition, where yellow is placed at the center of the color wheel and associated with the earth and faithfulness. Within the framework of these colliding, culturally constructed notions of yellow, Eisenstein presents Kandinsky's *The Yellow Sound* as an "extreme case" of the artistic use of color, in which the fixed and absolute systems of correspondences evoke parallels with political ideologies.

"I am a yellow stinking flower": Hans Henny Jahnn's *Perrudja*

In 1929, another contemporary of Kandinsky's, the German writer and composer Hans Henny Jahnn took issue with Kandinsky's notion of a "sounding cosmos" and its absolute spiritual relationships as manifested in the Blue Rider movement. Counterposing his figure of the "yellow rider" to Kandinsky's figure of the Blue Rider in an eponymous painting (1903), Jahnn confronts in his epic, fragmentary novel *Perrudja* (1929) the pressing political realities of mass migration in the twentieth century. Strongly influenced by Joyce's *Ulysses*, *Perrudja* (a modern version of the *Odyssey*) converts and inverts the Romantic *topos* of the "search for the blue flower" into the leitmotif of "I am a yellow stinking flower," thus expressing Jahnn's

---

[118] Quoted in ibid., 126.

opposition to a spiritual notion of art.[119] "I am a stinking yellow flower" is the zero degree of a cogito that is already announcing its decay while it is only starting to bloom.

Perrudja spends his childhood in the secluded mountains of Norway, before he unexpectedly inherits large sums of money from a mysterious stranger, Mr. Grigg. Perrudja endeavors to change the world for the better; he thus builds himself a temple-like fortress and founds a youth organization, with the aim of fostering worldwide peace. But despite his peaceful intentions, Perrudja, together with Mr. Grigg, plans a final war with modern weaponry, to save humanity from its decadent civilization. Throughout the narrative, Perrudja embodies the role of an antihero, or a "not-hero," as he is also called by his wife.

Perrudja's cogito is ecstatic in that it is not enclosed in a system of oppositions of reason and unreason, but is rather an excess that suggests larger historical and even mythological structures. For Perrudja sees himself as heir to king Dareios, who gained power through his stallion. Split by his past, Perrudja is doubled. Raised by a donkey, he is closer to his horse than to any human being. As Perrudja rides on it, feeling the mare under his thighs, he senses an ineffable connection. Hence the orgiastic moments in *Perrudja*, which precipitate apocalyptic visions: the apocalypse of a "great yellow flood" echoes the political keyword of the "yellow peril," warning against an Asian invasion.

While Perrudja is turning away from life, anticipating death in his youth (hence the "yellow stinking flower"), he represents the blooming of these flowers in an Eastward orientation; but it is the East of a bygone era, existing only in the utopia of the Western historical imagination. Contemporary issues are transformed into the countermovement—not warning of, but moving towards the East—of a smell, spaced out from inside of the body: "I am a yellow flower on a big meadow. I smell. Yellow, yellow, yellow."[120] The prospect of a Golden Age is contrasted in *Perrudja* with the destiny of the coming catastrophe, an ineluctable fate. Jahnn's model for the reversal of the temporality of a fulfilled moment into catastrophic moments is, of course, Novalis's novel *Heinrich von Ofterdingen*, with its apotheosis of the blue flower—hence the yellow color of great floods ("Der Schatten der gelben Sintflut") in Jahnn's great work.[121]

---

[119] See Angelika Overath's study of the tradition of the poetics of the color blue: Angelika Overath, *Das andere Blau. Zur Poetik einer Farbe im modernen Gedicht* (Stuttgart: Metzler, 1987).

[120] Hans Henny Jahnn, *Perrudja. Werke in Einzelbänden*, ed. Uwe Schweikert (Hamburg: Hoffmann und Campe Verlag, 1985), 221.

[121] Ibid., 349.

"Follow the yellow brick road!": *The Wizard of Oz*

Of the children's novel published by L. Frank Baum in 1900 under the title *Wonderful Wizard of Oz*, made into an iconic film in 1939, Salman Rushdie wrote that it was "the anthem of all the world's migrants."[122] Prima facie this might appear to be a somewhat surprising interpretation of the children's classic, but, as we shall see, the film can indeed be viewed according to the *topos* of an escape from a negative reality and the concomitant hope for a better—and (literally) brighter—life.

I will here mostly analyze the film—which, significantly, became one of the most famous films of all time—because of its spectacular color schemes and, in particular, of its foregrounding of the color yellow. *The Wizard of Oz* (as the film was titled) follows the adventures of a teenage girl, Dorothy, into the land of Oz, after being carried away by a tornado. Fulfilling her dream of leaving Kansas for a land "over the rainbow," Dorothy's dreamworld is structured by a ubiquitous yellow brick road that begins in a tight spiral and then winds circuitously towards the enigmatic Oz. We should recall that *The Wizard of Oz* was one of the first Technicolor films (along with *Gone with the Wind*, released the same year). As with many early films that used the Technicolor technique, color was considered a kind of "special effect" rather than an index of realism. The very bright colors of Technicolor were thus perfectly suited to the creation of the dreamworld effect that defines much of the film. The opening sequence, which features Dorothy at home in Kansas, in "normal" (for the period) black and white, explicitly contrasts the "greyness" of Kansas with the colorful world of the imagination. As Rushdie argues, what the female protagonist embodies is the archetypical story of

> the human dream of leaving, a dream at least as powerful as its counter-
> vailing dream of roots. [...] In its most potent emotional moment, this
> is unarguably a film about the joys of going away, of leaving the greyness
> and entering the color, of making a new life in the "place where there
> isn't any trouble."[123]

Mediating between the two dreams (of leaving and of coming home) is the yellow brick road itself. The repeated motif of "follow the yellow brick road" (also a song in the film) inscribes yellow as the discursive as well as the visual center of the film, for the characters do indeed walk along a very bright yellow road as they travel towards Oz. This motif has been interpreted by some critics as an allegory of the gold standard (the name

---

[122] Salman Rushdie, *The Wizard of Oz* (London: BFI Publishing, 1992), 23.
[123] Ibid.

Oz itself is decoded as the short form of "ounce") and its opposition to the silver standard, as embodied in the silvery slippers (though exchanged for the ruby-red slippers in the film version, to enhance the visual contrast to the yellow brick road) that Dorothy receives from the Good Witch upon her arrival in Oz. Both visually and semantically, the "yellow bricks" conjure up the image of gold bars.[124] In her book *Goldbugs and Greenbacks*, Gretchen Ritter describes the political background of the film:

> When Dorothy goes off to find the Wizard of Oz, she is sent down the yellow brick road to the Emerald City. In the Land of Oz, it is a road the color of gold that leads to the political center. According to the Populists, Washington, D.C. was controlled by the "Money Power" and gold traders. After the Cleveland administration arranged some bond sales with the New York financial community to replenish the Treasury's gold stock during the 1890s depression, one Oklahoma editor wrote, "the United States today is completely under the control of the money power and the bondholders. Wrong doing, extraordinary oppression, and monopoly are so firmly entrenched that they will not yield, even to the plain laws of the country." [...] The significance of the yellow brick road is altered, however, when Dorothy dons her sliver slippers to travel along. Here Baum's story provides a visible representation for bimetallism by combing silver with gold.[125]

Only effective in combination with each other, silver and gold together set the yellow spiral in motion. Its spiralling movement works its magic as a unifying force, combining not only silver and gold, but also Emerald City and Kansas—the dream of leaving with the dream of returning home.

In fact, the entire novel can be read as a cartography of the 1890s, keyed by color codes: blue for the Munchkins; yellow for Winkies; red for Quadlings; green for Emerald City; and purple for the Gillikins. In the original edition of the novel, Frank Denslow's illustrations show the inhabitants of Munchkinland, as Martin Blythe points out, with "their long beards

---

[124] Ranjit S. Dighe comments: "The duality of yellow bricks and yellow gold might well have crossed Baum's mind. In John Bunyan's *The Pilgrim's Progress*, which was a likely inspiration for the general plot and several specific aspects of the *Wizard*, the streets of heaven are literally paved with gold. Moreover, the last story in Baum's earlier book, *Mother Goose in Prose* (1897)—the same story, incidentally, that introduces a gentle little farm girl named Dorothy—describes a castle made of gold and silver bricks (261). Also, Baum's short story 'The Wonderful Pump' (in *American Fairy Tales* 1901, 152) and the second Oz book (1904, 66) contain explicit references to yellow gold" (*The Historian's Wizard of Oz: Reading L. Frank Baum's Classic as a Political and Monetary Allegory*, ed. Ranjit S. Dighe [Westport, CT: Praeger, 2007], 52).

[125] Gretchen Ritter, *Goldbugs and Greenbacks: The Antimonopoly Tradition and the Politics of Finance in America* (Cambridge: Cambridge University Press, 1997), 24–5.

and shaven heads with little topknots of hair [that] resemble awful American cartoons of Chinese during the late nineteenth century leading up to and during the Boxer Uprising."[126] The wicked witch is shown dressed "in Manchu pigtails and imperial regalia."[127] In the novel, Dorothy even trespasses the Great Wall into the "Dainty China Country." A parallel scene occurs in the land of the yellow Winkies in the West, allegorizing Asian immigrants. It is in the region of the yellow Winkies where Dorothy establishes herself as a heroic liberator, freeing the colonized Winkies, who have been interpreted as allegories of Asian Americans: "that Winkies were liberated is important and progressive," comments Victor Bascara, "but the question of what to do with these putatively liberated people is left unresolved. Upon such a conception of Asian and Asian American liberation, narratives of Asian assimilation to America have been built."[128] However, Baum's narrative of assimilation and anti-imperialism is characterized by its "sympathy for the oppressed," even though, as Bascara emphasizes, "that sympathy resulted in the displacement of one colonizer for another."[129]

In effect, Baum reverses in *The Wonderful Wizard of Oz* the warning of the "yellow peril." The leitmotif of "follow the yellow brick road" can itself be read as a counter-motif to the warning of the "yellow peril." Uniting Dorothy and Toto (the emblem of the whole: *totum*) with those in trouble (the tin man, the lion, the bear) on the yellow brick road creates a counter-allegory to divisive politics.

However, to argue that Oz represents China and the Wizard the Emperor in Beijing seems to overlook the central narrative of migration that pervades the novel (and the film). A closer look at Baum's inspiration for the leitmotif of the yellow brick road suggests seeing the East as a source of inspiration for occult practices: the yellow brick road as a spiritual path that leads to a special realm, Oz, where fears and struggles can be worked through and overcome. This idea draws on Baum's fascination with Theosophy and its "allusion to an astral realm," as Evan Schwaertz argues in *Finding Oz*:

> To get to the land of Oz, one projects a phantom of oneself, magically flying to a spectacular place, just as Dorothy does. In Theosophy, one's physical body and one's Astral body are connected through a "silver cord," a mythical link inspired by a passage in the Bible that speaks from a return of a spiritual quest. "Or ever the silver cord be loosed," says the

---

[126] Martin Blythe, "Oz is China. A Political Fable of Chinese Dragons and White Tiger", http://www.sexualfables.com/OzisChina.php [accessed November 11, 2011].

[127] Ibid.

[128] Victor Bascara, *Model-Minority Imperialism* (Minnesota: University of Minnesota Press, 2006), 45.

[129] Ibid.

Book of Ecclesiastes, "Then shall the dust return to the earth as it was: and the spirit shall return unto God who gave it."[130]

The reference to Theosophy shifts the emphasis from the power of the supposedly god-like Oz to that of the brick road as a medium of transformation; for Oz itself is precisely not presented as the fulfillment of the immigrant's dream, but is rather its disillusion.

Departing in Yellow: Josef Albers and Helmut Federle

Josef Albers's abstract painting *Homage to the Square: Departing in Yellow*, 1964 (Color Plate 13), one of his over 1000 homages to the square, could be read as a screen of projection *par excellence* of the waves of migration in the twentieth century, which, as we have seen, are marked in yellow. Albers, who started his career at the Bauhaus before emigrating from Nazi Germany to the United States, observes in his treatise "Interactions of Color" that the nuance of a color, its shade, is the exposition of detail in "permanent movement."[131] In contrast to the historical notion of the nuance, which is rooted in Romantic and decadent concepts of vagueness, Albers uses the square, considered the most stable form, the form of foundations, to expose an instability.

In *Departing in Yellow*, Albers folds four squares into each other; dyed in different nuances of yellow, a sense of movement is conveyed. Albers notes that "color is permanent movement, an aggression towards and away from the spectator... a breathing and a pulsating in color."[132] To see is to have an insight into the act of seeing itself. The interaction between oil, paint, square, and subtitle creates a constant flux between objective and subjective characteristics of color, between what Albers calls the "physical fact" (the materiality of color, texture, and tonality) and the "psychic effect." In this sense, the impact of the subtitle *Departing in Yellow* is crucial, for

---

[130] Evan I. Schwaertz, *Finding Oz: How L. Frank Baum Discovered the Great American Story* (New York: Houghton Mifflin Harcourt, 2009), 109.

[131] As Ulrich Finke shows with respect to painters such as Delacroix and poets from Verlaine to Baudelaire and Mallarmé, the French notion of the *nuance* (derived from *nuer* "to shade," based on the Latin word for cloud, *nubes*) attracted both painters and poets of the nineteenth century. See Ulrich Finke, *French 19th Century Painting and Literature: With Special Reference to the Relevance of Literary Subject-Matter to French Painting* (Manchester: Manchester University Press, 1972), 340. See also Wolfgang Lange's extensive study entitled *Die Nuance: Kunstgriff und Denkfigur* (Munich: Wilhelm Fink Verlag, 2005), in which he explores the history of the term nuance and the central role this notion plays in European decadence and its reflection on style, as in the philosophy of Nietzsche and the poetics of Mallarmé and Baudelaire.

[132] Josef Albers, *Interaction of Color* (New Haven, CT: Yale University Press, 1971), 174.

it points to the persistent movement of color in Albers's square paintings: the three or four superimposed squares become three-dimensional as one shade of color seems to advance, while another shade appears to recede, due to their contrast. In *Departing in Yellow*, the contrasting movement between advancing and receding shades of yellow embodies the notion of departure. In constant migration across planes of different shades, yellow resists its reduction to any one shade.[133] Thus the *Homage* series, as one critic writes, "exists only in the here and now of the visual experience."[134] Albers's statement that "color deceives continually"[135] is exemplified in *Departing in Yellow*, which shows how Albers pursues pure and timeless fundamentals, while destabilizing the very fundamentals (primary colors, square) that he exposes.[136]

While Kazimir Malevitch's *Black Square* (1915) and *White Square on White Background* (1918) were, despite their formalism, considered political art in the Soviet Union of the time (subverting the Bolshevik claim to know the course of history through mythic notions of time), square paintings lost their political impetus on their way across the Atlantic, becoming in the second half of the twentieth century an international prototype for "pure" art that, as Susan Buck-Morss remarks ironically in a "A Short History of the Square," "could only flourish in a political democracy."[137]

Nevertheless, "artistic impurity"[138] strikes in the abstract paintings of

---

[133] Charles Riley II, *Color Codes: Modern Theories of Color in Philosophy, Painting and Architecture, Literature, Music, and Psychology* (Hanover, NH: University Press of New England, 1955), 155.

[134] Achim Borchardt-Hume, "Two Bauhaus Histories," in *Albers and Moholy-Nagy: From the Bauhaus to the New World*, ed. A. Borchardt-Hume (New Haven, CT: Yale University Press, 2006), 78.

[135] Albers, *Interaction of Color*, 1.

[136] Albers's emphasis is on an active reflection on color perception, and he is therefore critical of a reduction of color to movement, as in kinetic art. In Op-art, for example, yellow plays an important role as the closest color to light. In his "Yellow Manifesto" (1955), Victor Vasarely emphasizes the notion of movement in the act of looking itself: "Movement does not rely on composition or a specific subject, but on the apprehension of the act of looking, which by itself is considered as the only creator," http://www.op-art. co.uk/victor-vasarely/ [accessed November 2, 2012]. While Albers foregrounded a rather cerebral contemplation on the dichotomy between the physical fact of a color and its constantly changing physical effect, Vasarely shifts the emphasis towards the kinetic reaction that the color yellow triggers in the spectator.

[137] Susan Buck Morss, *Dreamworld and Catastrophe: The Passing of Mass Utopia in East and West* (Cambridge, MA: MIT Press, 2002), 89. Buck Morss concludes her chapter on "A Short History of the Square" thus: "Conceived in the revolutionary turmoil of Russia at the beginning of the century, its fate, ironically, is to have become the recognized logo of U.S. 'high culture' at the century's end" (ibid., 95).

[138] Mitchell comments on the reopening of the artistic field to "worldly concerns" as follows: "Among the accomplishments of the revolution signaled by John's Flags and Targets was the reopening of art (for better or worse) to what Edward Said would call

Helmut Federle, namely in his controversial painting *Asian Sign*, 1980 (Color Plate 14). The color scheme of yellow on grey recalls the stigma of the "yellow star" that Jews were forced to wear in Nazi Germany, but of course what strikes the viewer immediately is what appears to be the figure of the swastika. Upon closer inspection, however, we notice that the swastika is in fact inverted. According to the artist, it is a depiction of Asian sunwheels (hence the title *Asian Sign*):

> [*Asian Sign*] is an abstract work in a climatic sense; it carries all possible readings in itself and is fundamentally without morals, thus dissolving the question of a specific reading. [...] It is important, it seems to me, to see the code "Africa" or "Asia" in an artistic orientation and conceptualization.[139]

The evocation of the Nazi symbol is doubly ironic, for it also evokes the motif of the "yellow peril" that I have explored in this chapter. The symbol is perverted both by its formal inversion and by its color, yellow, which explicitly recalls the victims or marginalized group, whether the European Jewry or Asian immigrants. However, the stigmatizing color of the Jewish star is here turned back against the persecutors, insofar as it announces in the same stroke the innocence of the victims and the condemnation of the perpetrators.

Federle insists that despite the radical symbolism of his work, he is not interested in its political implications. And yet, his dramatization of yellow in its dirty condition ("pure yellow never interested me")[140] connects the color yellow inadvertently to its visual or, more precisely, its racial politics. The clash between the color of the Emperor's clothes and the color of the "yellow star," which became after the Second World War an emblem of genocide, is the clash that Federle performs in the multivalent figuration that is *Asian Sign*. Federle's exploration of the impurity of yellow itself thematizes the mechanism of staining a sacred symbol (the inverted swastika as a symbol of the sun in China, the Star of David as modern symbol of the Jewish

---

"worldly" concerns—to kitsch, mass culture, the mixture of media, political propaganda and theater—the resurgence of artistic impurity, hybridity, and heterogeneity summarizes as the 'eruption of language into the artistic field'" (*Picture Theory: Essays on Verbal and Visual Representation*, [Chicago: University of Chicago Press, 1994], 239). Federle's *Asian Sign*, which recalls the Nazi emblem, the swastika, strikes not only through its form of artistic impurity (thematizing propaganda art), but especially through the thematization of impurity through an impure yellow that dominates Federle's paintings from the 1980s on.

[139] Personal email, March 12, 2012 (my translation).

[140] In a personal email (March 12, 2012), Federle emphasized the ambivalence of yellow and yellow's multivalent figurations. What interests him in the use of an impure yellow is the impossibility of fitting it into any conventions.

community) with the stigmatic power of yellow. The racial politics that its form (swastika) and color scheme (impure yellow) invoke takes on "a life of its own," in W. J. T. Mitchell's phrase:

> If any set of images seems to have a "life of its own," it would seem to be the racial stereotype. And yet there is something paradoxical in saying this, insofar as the usual notion of the stereotype is that it is a static, inert form of representation, an unchanging, compulsively repeated schematism. [...] What the stereotype wants, then, is precisely what it lacks—life, animation, vitality. And it obtains that life by deadening its object of representation and the subject who uses it as a medium for the classification of other subjects. Both the racist and the object of racism are reduced to static, inert figures by the stereotype. Or perhaps more precisely, we should define their condition as a kind of "living death," the zombielike condition of the borderline between the animate and the inanimate.[141]

---

[141] W. J. T. Mitchell, *What Do Pictures Want?: The Lives and Loves of Images* (Chicago: University of Chicago Press, 2005), 297–8.

6

Yellow Stars and the Visual Politics of Genocide

with ten nail-moons in tow,
near to snakes, in the yellow flood,
quasistellar.

—Paul Celan

On September 1, 1941, it was decreed that all Jews in German and German-occupied areas had to wear a "yellow star" stitched to their clothing to signify their outcast status. In the literature and visual art of the second half of the twentieth century the "yellow star" emerges as a powerful and unique symbol of Jewish suffering. In films as diverse as *Schindler's List*, *Mr. Klein*, *Life is Beautiful*, and *Jacob the Liar*, the symbol is literalized through the techniques of perspective and close-up, becoming an emblem of dehumanization and oppression. The "yellow star" functions as a sign of a common fate: all who wear it are literally marked for death. In literature and painting, on the other hand, artists have often sought to avoid the literalness of the "yellow star"; in fact, some of the most powerful artistic confrontations with the Holocaust—W. G. Sebald's *Austerlitz*, Paul Celan's poetry, Thomas Pynchon's *Gravity's Rainbow*, and Frank Stella's abstract paintings—refuse to directly name it. Yellow's indirect referentiality (its negative presentation) is a sign of its dual meaning having reached an extreme point, the point at which any redemptive significance of the color is rendered moot. The color closest to light, yellow is irremediably transformed in these literary works into a color of darkness, or the negation of color itself.

The iconic uses of the "yellow star" owe a great deal to one of the first sound pictures in Europe, Fritz Lang's *M* (1931), released just two years before the Nazi rise to power. This film reflects on the power of the stigmatic sign, not with regard to the victim, but rather to the serial killer. The film attracted the attention of propaganda minister Joseph Goebbels, who invited Lang to become a filmmaker for the Nazi Party. Lang not only declined, but promptly left Germany for Hollywood. Goebbels no doubt saw in Lang's portrayal of the child murderer an exemplary way of stigmatizing the Jew (the actor who plays the criminal is Peter Lorre, a Jew). Peter Lorre's performance in the scene where the mass murderer seeks to justify his crimes (in which he explains, in an onomatopoeic spectacle, his drive to kill—"I must, must, must murder"—while dramatizing the stigma of the *M* through sound and gestures) was quoted in one of the most infamous Nazi propaganda films *The Eternal Jew* (*Der ewige Jude*, 1940, by Fritz Hippler) as a prime example of the supposedly depraved nature of Jews.

As Max Horkheimer and Theodor Adorno have suggested (in their seminal *Dialectic of Enlightenment*), the revival of anti-Semitism by the Nazi regime was not simply an aspect of the fascist movement in Germany, but its defining feature.[1] Though yellow markings had been used to stigmatize Jews in Europe since the Middle Ages, the marriage of a stigmatic yellow with the Star of David was a specifically Nazi invention. Guido Kisch concludes in his study *The Yellow Badge in History* that "the treatment of the Jews in the Middle Ages must have been studied systematically and carefully by the Nazi leaders."[2] Yellow as the traditional color of anti-Semitism is thus brought together with a heightened interest in the symbolism of the star and its black magic, which since medieval times was associated with Jews.

The Star of David (*Magen David*) became a conventional symbol of the Jewish community only in 1897, at a Zionist congress in Basel (though it was far from being universally accepted). It is in this sense a modern symbol, but it was not coded as yellow or as any specific color (it often appears in blue, in fact). Thus in the yellow patch or badge (the "yellow star") that Jews were forced to wear after 1941, the Nazis sought to pervert a symbol that the Jews had chosen for themselves, as if, in retrospect, this original choice had been an act of self-stigmatism. Michael Taussig has called this propaganda mechanism a form of "mimetic excess," in which a racial Other or imagined savagery is simulated "in order to dominate or destroy it."[3] Following this logic, then, it is because Jews invented the concept of kosher meat that "they are persecuted as swine."[4] Thus Jews are stigmatized with their "own" symbol of the star. While the imagery of "Jewish swine" goes back to medieval times, the stigma of the "yellow star" only enters the Western imaginary with the

---

[1] In their seminal essay "Elements of Anti-Semitism: Limits of Enlightenment," Adorno and Horkheimer write: "For the fascists the Jews are not a minority but the anti-race, the negative principle as such; on their extermination the world happiness depends" (Theodor W. Adorno and Max Horkheimer, *Dialectic of Enlightenment: Philosophical Fragments* [Stanford, CA: Stanford University Press, 2007], 137).

[2] Guido Kisch, *The Yellow Badge in History* (New York: Historia Judaica, 1942), 32.

[3] Michael Taussig, *Mimesis and Alterity: A Particular History of the Senses* (New York: Routledge, 1993), 80.

[4] Quoted in ibid., 68.

Holocaust. However, after being perverted by the Nazis, the Jewish star is then re-sacralized in art and popular culture in the wake of this event as the victimary sign par excellence.

In his *Star of Redemption* (1921), Franz Rosenzweig analyzed relationships between God, humanity, and the self, using the Star of David as a figure through which he schematizes his notion of revelation and redemption in the here and now.[5] As both a sign of hope as well as of doom, the ambiguous power of the Star of David is similarly explored in Paul Wegener's 1920 film *The Golem: How He Came Into the World (Der Golem, wie er in die Welt kam)*. Wegener's recreation of the Jewish folktale through symbolic sets and expressionistic lighting portrays medieval Jewish life in Prague, including the wearing of a stigmatic yellow circle, which is ubiquitous in the film. However, the "iconography of Jewishness" exceeds the "mythical foundation of the Golem story,"[6] as Noah Isenberg argues; for Wegener also highlights contemporary problems, such as the feared invasion of Jewish masses from the East into the city—a theme specific to Weimar culture. In the creation scene of the film, Rabbi Löw's wielding of a pentagram evokes associations of Jews with sorcery; the figure of the Jew is that of a "master of the power over the spectacle—over the aesthetic medium."[7] In addition, the idea of a star-gazing Rabbi ominously prefigures the Nazi conflation of the Jewish star with yellow stigmatism, namely in the systematic juxtaposition of the stigmatic yellow circle (seen in the black-and-white film in a shade of white) and the pentagram in its star-like shape (which, in the creation scene, is what brings the Golem [literally "shapeless man"] to life); the pentagram is the Golem's vital sign, his heart, as it were, ever visible on his chest. Once the pentagram is removed from the Golem, he is lifeless again, as in the last scene of the film, when the gates of the ghetto close behind the group of Jews who carry the lifeless Golem away. The film culminates in an abstract shot of an oversized Star of David, superimposed on the closed ghetto gate. The shape of the Star of David, formed out of clay, like the Golem, exposes the shaping power of the star itself, becoming a *scène en abîme* of creation-destruction evoking the "failure of the Jewish dream of assimilation";[8] for the yellow that shines and emanates from the Star of David announces the

---

[5] Franz Rosenzweig, *The Star of Redemption* (Madison: University of Wisconsin Press, 2005).

[6] Noah Isenberg, "Paul Wegener's *The Golem: How He Came onto the World* (1920)," in *Weimar Cinema: An Essential Guide to Classic Films of the Era*, ed. Noah Isenberg (New York: Columbia University Press, 2009), 45.

[7] Ibid., 41.

[8] Cathy Gelbin, "Narratives of Transgression: From Jewish Folktales to German Cinema," *Kinoeye* 3, no. 11 (2003), http://www.kinoeye.org/03/11/gelbin11.php [accessed 12/12/2012].

revival of Jewish culture even as it foreshadows its doom. Interestingly, the film poster features the Star of David colored in yellow at its center, surrounded by an eerie cityscape reminiscent of the expressionist film *The Cabinet of Dr. Caligari* (1920).

Wegener's iconic closing image of the Star of David was used twenty years later by Veit Harlan as the opening shot of his anti-Semitic propaganda film *Jew Süss* (*Jud Süß*, 1940), presenting itself thereby as a kind of sequel to *The Golem*: "Again, Rabbi Löw is seen star-gazing, this time a morally corrupt and physically deformed man in contrast to his aestheticized portrayal in Wegener's *Golem*."[9] The passive stigmatism of *The Golem* is transformed in *Jew Süss* into active stigmatism: the stellar iconography is completely unambiguous; it announces the destruction of the Jewish dream.

The stars of Rainer Maria Rilke

After the Holocaust, the appropriation of a language of stars—by the Zionist movement, the Symbolist movement, the Nazis, and in silent film through its interest in magic, mad science, and technology—is seen as a site of projection in a discourse concerning the figurability or representability of the Holocaust. Two of the most iconic writers of the twentieth century, Paul Celan and Thomas Pynchon, thematize the problem of naming the stigma by returning to the symbolist poetry of Rainer Maria Rilke, whose dark, enigmatic star symbolism offers a model of indirect reference, a unique mode of access to the greatest tragedy of modernity.

Rilke spells out relationships between words and objects to convert an outer space into an illuminated inner world. Paradoxically, Rilke's poetic exploration of inwardness, the desire he announces in the *First Duino Elegy* "to feel" (*spüren*) constellations of stars, connections between inner and outer worlds, becomes the matrix for a reflection on the possibility of a language of stars after the Holocaust. The "new stars, of Grief-Land," in Rilke's *Duino Elegies*, thus become the focal point of a radical reversal. In Rilke's poetics the "new stars" constitute auratic points of an immaterial, ethereal light, which Celan and Pynchon transform into the concrete reality of the yellow star. Their refusal to name the "yellow star," to activate its stigmatic meaning, can be interpreted in terms of a desire to explore the moment of reversal itself—or what Werner Hamacher has called, in reference to Celan's poetics,

---

[9] Ibid.

"the second of inversion."[10] These moments of reversal or inversion reveal, as we will see, apocalyptic dimensions in a world "without color" (Celan).

Rilke's replacement of an imagery of *Diesseits* (on this side) and *Jenseits* (on the other side) through the dynamic figure of falling and ascending becomes the focal point for both Celan and Pynchon. The ascending movement opens the cosmological dimension of stellar constellations, in which Rilke's *Tenth Duino Elegy* culminates:

> And higher, the stars. The new stars of the land of grief.
> Slowly the Lament names them:—Look, there:
> the *Rider*, the *Staff*, and the larger constellation
> called *Garland of Fruit*. Then, farther up towards the Pole:
> *Cradle*; *Path*; *The Burning Book*, *Puppet*, *Window*.
> But there, in the southern sky, pure as the lines
> on the palm of a blessed hand, the clear sparkling *M*,
> that stands for the Mothers......[11]

> (Und höher, die Sterne. Neue. Die Sterne des Leidlands.
> Langsam nennt sie die Klage:—Hier,
> siehe: den Reiter, den Stab, und das vollere Sternbild
> nennen sie: Fruchtkranz. Dann, weiter, dem Pol zu:
> Wiege, Weg, Das brennende Buch, Puppe, Fenster.
> Aber im südlichen Himmel, rein wie im Innern
> einer gesegneten Hand, das klar erglänzende „M",
> das die Mütter bedeutet......)[12]

The fictive star constellations of "Rider," "Staff," "Cradle," "Burning Book," "Doll," and "Window" point to the poetic space of origin embodied in the initial "M," which "stands for the Mothers." Rilke inverts the cosmological dimension of an outer space into an illuminated inner world—or, in Rilke's words, the poetic space of an "inner-worldliness" (*Weltinnenraum*). In Celan and Pynchon, we find this figure of inversion inverted again in the rising movement of a fall.

Thus in a direct response to the strophe from Rilke's *Tenth Duino Elegy*, Celan inverts the fictive constellation of stars, which in Rilke's elegy initiates

---

[10] Werner Hamacher, "The Second of Inversion: Movements of a Figure through Celan's Poetry," in *Word Traces: Readings of Paul Celan*, ed. Aris Fioretes (Baltimore: Johns Hopkins University Press, 1994), 219.

[11] Rainer Maria Rilke, "The Tenth Elegy," in Rilke, *Duino Elegies and the Sonnets to Orpheus*, trans. Stephen Mitchell (New York: Random House, 2009), 61.

[12] Rainer Maria Rilke, "Die Zehnte Elegie," in Rilke, *Werke in Drei Bänden, Erster Band: Gedicht-Zyklen* (Frankfurt am Main: Insel Verlag, 1991), 481.

the turn of a movement of ascension towards origins into a constellation of endings:

> [...] the marten stars in the abyss
> spelled, spelled, spelled
> out, out.
> ([...] der Mardersterne im Abgrund
> buch-, buch-, buch-,
> stabierte, stabierte).

The stars named "marten stars" do not lead to origins, but to a state of entropy. "Marten stars" are named after a robbing animal (the marten) of the night. Its name "Marder" echoes "Mater" for "Mother," suggesting a scenario of stolen mothers rather than of mothers giving birth. In the spectrum of "M," "Mardersterne" resembles "Mörder-Sterne" ("murderer stars"), pointing downwards into the abyss, where letters are not illuminated, but where the word "spelling" (*buch-stabieren*) is itself breaking down.[13] However, the last line "stabierte, stabierte" refers back to Rilke's fictive star "Staff" ("Stab"), turning the falling movement into a counter-movement that rises into a stabbing counter-attack. It is this pointedness of a turn in a "second of inversion" (Hamacher) that marks what Celan calls a "spectral analysis"[14] of the symbolists' "alphabet of stars,"[15] in its inevitable entanglement with the emblem of the Holocaust: the Star of David converted into the stigma of the "yellow star."[16]

---

[13] Aris Fioretos comments on Celan's response to Rilke's "M" as an "initial of life and language": "In Celan, this initial of life and language is neither genetic nor blessing anything; it stands only for repeated murder and deprivation (*Mardersterne*). Violently undercutting Rilke's *Stab* and *Buch* in writing 'buch-, buch-, buch-, / stabierte, stabierte,' Celan's poetry comes into being as the pain of language itself: a syntactically wounded stutter breaking down language into its smallest elements: *Buch-staben*" (Fioretes, "Nothing: History and Materiality in Celan," in *Word Traces*, 331).

[14] An expression Celan uses in a letter to Hugo Huppert in December 1966: "Since I am unfortunately unable to present things from all angles, I attempt to reproduce segments from the spectral analysis of things and to show them in several different aspects and permeations, with the similar, the consequent, and the opposite. [...] I am trying to show you why I contend that my so-called abstractness and actual ambiguity is a slice of reality" (quoted in Nicholas J. Meyerhofer, "The Poetics of Paul Celan," *Twentieth Century Literature* 27, no. 1 [1981]: 8).

[15] Aris Fioretes points to Mallarmé's "alphabet of stars" in *Variations sur un sujet* (see "Nothing: History and Materiality in Celan," 330).

[16] Entanglement is the theme of the strophe, which is constructed around the figure of the "knot."

Paul Celan's "Yellow Flood"

The problem of the transformation of the Star of David into a stigmatic figure is a recurrent motif in Celan's collection of poems entitled *Breath-turn* (*Atemwende*). For example, in the poem "TAKE A REST FROM YOUR WOUNDS," Celan counters the stigmatic turn with the Jewish symbol of the Tree of Life, a tree that grows upside-down. Counter-attacks on anti-Semitic attacks[17] create inversions of inversions,[18] which culminate in TAKE A REST FROM YOUR WOUNDS in a "yellow flood," evoking the color of stigma flooding the skies. However, the stigma of the "yellow star" is not named; instead, the structure of the poem is based on the Kabbalistic notion of the ten Sephirot and the 22 letters of the Hebrew alphabet (correlated with the 22 paths of the Sephirot). The 22 lines of the poem, arranged in four strophes, turn Kabbalistic notions against anti-Semitic rhetoric, and the astrological notion of the brightest constellation of stars against the abyssal notion of the star as an anti-Jewish stigma.[19]

TAKE A REST FROM YOUR WOUNDS
full of babble, and silhouetted on tracing paper.

The round one, small, the steady one:
it comes out of the corner of the eye,
rolling up close,
with nothing on.

(It
—pearl, it was so hard
because of you—,
it dipped the saltbush in the double sea).

It rolls without light, without
Color—you,

---

[17] Amir Eshel analyzes Celan's "poetic provocation" of "Jewification [*verjuden*]": "Celan's morpohological deviations—his use of words like *Haeusel* or Yiddish syntactic characteristics (*bin ich*) and German-Jewish stylistic features (*mauschel-deutsch*)—rewrites anti-Semitic discourse and thus turns it against itself" ("Paul Celan's Other: History, Poetics, and Ethics," *New German Critique* 91, Special Issue on Paul Celan [2004]: 67).

[18] In his article, "The Second of Inversion" (224), Werner Hamacher states that the formulation "inversion of inversion" hardly does justice to Celan's attempt to radicalize and ultimately abandon the figure of inversion.

[19] Fioretes coins the term "abyssal stars" (in "Nothing: History and Materiality in Celan," 331) for these stars colored in yellow that recur in Celan's poetics, as in "Tausendgüldenkraut-Sternchen" or "Sechsstern."

poke the ivory needle through
—who doesn't know,
that the striped stone that pounced on you
shattered from ringing?—,
and so—where did the earth fall away to?—
let it go on revolving forever,
with ten nail-moons in tow,
near to snakes, in the yellow flood,
quasistellar.[20]

(RUH AUS IN DEINEN WUNDEN,
durchblubbert und umpaust.

Das Runde, kleine, das Feste:
aus den Blicknischen kommts
gerollt, nahebei,
in keinerlei Tuch.

(Das hat
—Perle, so schwer
wars durch dich—,
das hat sich den Salzstrauch ertaucht,
drüben, im Zweimeer).

Ohne Licht rollts, ohne
Farbe—du
stich die Elfenbeinnadel hindurch
—wer weiß nicht,
dass der getigerte Stein, der dich ansprang,
an ihr zerklang?—,
und so—wohin fiel die Erde?—
lass es sich drehen zeitauf,
mit zehn Nagelmonden im Schlepptau,
in Schlangennähe, bei Gelbflut,
quasistellar).[21]

[20] Trans. Cal Kinnear, http://ekleksographia.ahadadabooks.com/skillman/authors/cal_kinnear.html [accessed July 14, 2011].
[21] Paul Celan, *Gesammelte Werke in fünf Bänden. Zweiter Band*, ed. Beda Allemann and Stefan Reichert (Frankfurt: Suhrkamp Verlag, 1983), 103.

Starting out with a movement of sinking from gaping wounds into an ocean of tears, we encounter a desert of salty bushes at the bottom of the ocean, into which the tears—crystallized in heavy pearls—roll. The pearl rolling into the open is a Rilkean motif.[22] Celan confronts Rilke's concept of openness with the divided space of a "double sea" (*Zweimeer*), split in two halves, like the poem itself. The sinking movement of the first half of the poem (the first three stanzas) is turned, in the second half (the longer fourth stanza), against the stream towards the sky. What is opening up between ocean and sky is the apocalyptic dimension of an abyss. Celan's allusion to the Great Flood as the "yellow flood" points to an additional ocean, as the word-play *Zwei-meer* (double sea), also meaning "two more" (*Zwei mehr*), implies, prefiguring the coming of the Great Flood, characterized as a flood of stars ("yellow flood/quasistellar"). The stigma of the yellow star is not named, but its appearance (color, shape of star) is transformed into the apocalyptic scenario of the Great Flood.

"Without light" and against the flow of time, the rolling movement leads upstream into a darkness, which not only implies the darkness of the night, but also of the black continent, Africa, as the reference to the tusks of elephants and tiger-fur suggests. However, these animals do not appear in flesh and blood, but rather as objects of decor transformed into weapons. The ivory needle made out of elephants' tusks is the "white gold" for which the race of elephants has been exploited; the pattern of tiger-fur is the "striped stone" for which the race of tigers has been exploited. The exploitation and extinction of a race due to its valued attributes evokes the Nazis' attempt to extinguish the Jewish race. Killing movements of "stabbing through," "pouncing at," and clanking sounds create a scenario of displacement and dispersion filled with a dissonance that leads nowhere, except to resignation: "and so—where did the earth fall away to?—/ let it go on revolving forever, / with ten nail-moons in tow, / near to snakes, in the yellow flood, / quasistellar." The battle lost, the poetic voice asks to let go, not with the flow, but rather against the flow, which is the flow of time "revolving forever," thus reaching into an outer-space of cosmological and even biblical time; for the reference to snakes and the flood figures the two catastrophes of the Old Testament, the Fall from Paradise and the Great Flood, as the ultimate expression of God's anger.

---

[22] Judith Ryan comments on "Pearls roll away" that "the world of this poem is one in which no element fits neatly with another; everything is slipping out of one's grasp; things are cracking apart and breaking into pieces" (*Rilke, Modernism and Poetic Tradition* [Cambridge: Cambridge University Press, 1999], 124).

These turning points are preceded by a configuration of the Kabbalistic notion of the ten Sephirot,[23] also presented as the Tree of Life,[24] since the Tree of Life grows upside-down with its roots in *En soph*, in the divine light, as mentioned in the Zohar: "The tree of life is extended from the top till the bottom and the sun illuminates it entirely."[25] The Tree of Life is one of the most emblematic figures of the *Breath-turn* cycle, not least because of Celan's inversion, which turns it into a corporeal death scene. Although the Tree of Life is often depicted as a human body and as such is thought to symbolize the first "heavenly" (or primordial) man, Adam Kadmon, the body parts that Celan mentions are "ten nail-moons" (*Nagelmonde*)—an expression used in German to describe the whitish part of fingernails, forming a crescent in the shape of a moon at the very point between nail and skin. Through the figure of the "ten nail-moons in tow," Celan opens the spectrum of the corporeal, which also possesses a religious significance.[26] The corporeality of the fingernails, a dead body part, like the aforementioned ivory tusks, points at the same time to the body parts of the first human being—hence the overall double-structure of the poem, shifting between the generality of the prototypical and the singularity of the corporeal.

The single word of the last line of the poem is "quasistellar," which, together with the preceding scene of the "yellow flood," is an image diametrically (or dialectically) opposed to the announcement at the beginning of the stanza: "It rolls without light, without color." However, the "yellow flood" appears to be mere color, a monochrome yellow spectacle, whereas quasi-stellar objects, also called quasars, are known to be the brightest objects in the galaxy.[27] The nearest color to the light—yellow—and the most luminous stars are turned

[23] Sephirot are literally translated "enumerations" and thus the number 10 ("ten nail-moons") suggests 10 Sephirot in a self-reflexive gesture.

[24] The Tree of Life also figures prominently in the poem "DIE SCHWERMUTSSCHNELLEN HINDURCH," mentioned there explicitly as the "forty skinned trees of life" (da werden die vierzig / entrindeten Lebensbäume geflößt) (Celan, *Gesammelte Werke in fünf Bänden. Zweiter Band*, 16).

[25] The French anthropologist Gilbert Durand explains: "The cosmic tree of the Upanishads stretches its roots into the sky and stretches its branches into earth. The image of the upside-down tree can be found in the sabea tradition, in the sepharoth esoterism, in Islam, in Dante as well as in certain rites of the Laps, the Australians and islanders" (Gilbert Durand, *Les structures anthropologiques de l'Imaginaire* [Paris: P.U.F., 1963], 347).

[26] Rilke already uses the imagery of the "Tree of Life" in the figure of the "Trees of tears" ("Tränenbäume"). Instead of rolling down and dissolving, they grow into the sky. In Celan, the sinking movement materializes first in salty bushes and then in the reference to fingernails.

[27] Quasars are considered to be the most luminous members of the galactic nuclei: "The increase of redshift with distance has been well established for ordinary galaxies, but the object with the largest redshift, and therefore presumably the greatest distance, are the enigmatic quasars" (Harry L. Shipman, *Black Holes, Quasars, and the Universe* [New York: Houghton Mifflin, 1980], 150).

into the darkest constellation of stars, indicating a universe where there is neither color nor light. Celan thematizes the impossibility of transforming the star into a stigma: linguistically, in the use of "as if" and "quasistellar"; and astrologically, by using the term for the brightest star, suggesting its turn into the darkest star, that is, into the stigma of the "yellow star."

In the quasi-stellar yellow flood, the yellow appears as a counter-color, counter to the light (which Celan also names "counter-light"). The expression "yellow flood" points to a recurrent motif in Celan's poetry, that of flooding yellow matter, which Adorno referred to as a "language of dead matter of stones and stars."[28] However, by turning the Jewish symbol of life (the Tree of Life) against the turn of the star into the wounding stigma, "TAKE A REST FROM YOUR WOUNDS" does not show or thematize the stigma of the "yellow star"; the turn into the stigma is rather presented in a "non-manifestation," as Jacques Derrida phrased Celan's attempt to "let time speak" (and, we could add, to let the time of the wounded speak).[29] Without naming the stigma, but by addressing its history of inversion, its color and shape, the poem allows for the activation of what Celan called in his Meridian speech the "presentness and presence" (*Gegenwart und Präsenz*)[30] of the stigma, actualizing the moment of wounding in the turn from the brightest into the darkest star. Yellow (and therefore color in general in Celan) is thus no longer seen, but rather felt in its massiveness and its materiality (flooding) as an inscription (a quasi-constellation of stars).

Rilke's "new stars" and Thomas Pynchon's *Gravity's Rainbow*

In Thomas Pynchon's 1973 novel *Gravity's Rainbow*, the attempt to actualize rather than make manifest the dynamic of the transformation into the stigma of the "yellow star" is based on Rilke's principle of fall and ascension. However, Pynchon's perspective and tone shifts towards the side of the persecutors (i.e. the Nazis) and their moral fall from the height of cultural

---

[28] "They [Celan's poems] emulate a language that lies below the helpless prattle of human beings—even below the level of organic life as such. It is the language of dead matter, of stones and stars" (Theodor W. Adorno, *Aesthetic Theory*, trans. C. Lenhardt, ed. Gretel Adorno and Rolf Tiedemann [London: Routledge and Kegan Paul, 1984], 444).

[29] Jacques Derrida, "The Majesty of the Present," *New German Critique* 91, Special Issue on Paul Celan (2004): 26.

[30] Celan, "Der Meridian," in *Gesammelte Werke. Dritter Band*, ed. Beda Allemann and Stefan Reichert (Frankfurt: Suhrkamp Verlag, 1983), 198 (also quoted in Derrida, "The Majesty of the Present," 24).

and technological achievement. The polarity inherent in yellow—the color of the sun, of the bright light, and of decay and excrements—finds expression in the explosiveness of a rocket, which begins its descent at the novel's opening.

The development of the dye industry forms the historical background of *Gravity's Rainbow*: from the first synthetic dyes in the second half of the nineteenth century to the later discovery of hundreds more dyes, which, as Katherine Hayles and Mary Eiser explain in "Coloring *Gravity's Rainbow*," ushered "in the chemical technology that branched out to such fields as photography, plastics, pharmaceuticals and explosives."[31] Pynchon discusses the dye industry's role in creating chemicals suitable for warfare. In one of his most striking examples, Pynchon points to the case of the chemical concern *IG Farben*, which shifted from the production of synthetic colors to the production of the gas used in the concentration camps. In light of these dramatic shifts, Pynchon develops the recurrent theme that all patterns and systems "originate in death-obsessed consciousness."[32] The emblem of the Star of David is presented as one of these patterns, which leads from order to chaos and entropy. In Pynchon's example, the Star of David is used as a pattern by the Jewish industrialist Pflaumenbaum (plum tree) to develop new patents for paint. When his paint factory explodes, Pynchon suggests that he caused the explosion himself to get the insurance. In this parody of the stereotype of the smart and greedy Jew, the name Pflaumenbaum also refers to the song "Der Pflaumenbaum" by the Jewish composer Hanns Eisler (1898–1962), written in exile. Pynchon not only offers a blatant parody of "Jewishness," but also of high culture—and in this context one of his main points of reference is Rilke's *Duino Elegies*.

The famous scream opening Rilke's first elegy also opens *Gravity's Rainbow*, together with a constellation of "new stars," thereby quoting Rilke's "new stars, of Grief-Land" from the tenth elegy. However, "Grief-land" will be turned into "Happyville," and Rilke's fictive star of "fruit-garland" will be parodied as an arrangement of banana trees on the roof of a high-rise building. The bananas are themselves a parody of the German rocket, which begins its fall in this opening scenario, in which the constellation of rocket and star is established as a monochrome-yellow spectacle:

> Rooftop dance in the morning. His giant banana cluster, radiant yellow, humid green. His companions below dreadrooling of a Banana Breakfast. This well-scrubbed day ought to be no worse than any—Will it? Far to the east, down in the pink sky, something has just sparked very brightly.

[31] In *Pynchon Notes* 16 (1985): 5.
[32] Ibid., 3.

A new star; something less noticeable. He leans on the parapet to watch. The brilliant point has already become a short vertical line. It must be somewhere over the North Sea... at least that far... ice fields below and a cold smear of sun. What is it? Nothing like this ever happens. [...] This is the new, and still Most Secret, German rocket bomb. [...] Pick bananas. He trudges through black compost in to the hothouse. He feels he's about to shit. The missile, sixty miles high, must be coming up on the peak of its trajectory by now... beginning its fall... now.[33]

The explosiveness of the constellation of star and rocket is embedded in the polarity of a luminous, bright yellow and the dirty-yellow of compost and excrement, between the heated atmosphere of the hothouse and a "cold smear of sun." This spectrum of polarities characteristic of the color yellow unfolds according to opposing principles of illumination (the brilliant star, the growing of "yellow chandeliers") and decay (to shit, to drool, a smear of sun, compost)—of order and chaos, brightness and darkness. The novel ends with the explosion of the German rocket bomb in black-film; the absolute darkness after the implosion of the projector's light bulb thus stands in stark contrast to the bleaching process towards whiter and whiter colors throughout the novel, which Pynchon parallels with the Nazis' politics of racial cleansing. The whitening of the world is suddenly turned into the blackness of a screen.

Pynchon juxtaposes Rilke's quest for the "pure word, the yellow and blue Enzian" with the Nazis' ideal of the blue-eyed and yellow-haired Nordic race, in an explicit reference to the Holocaust:

this Oven-game with the yellowhaired and blueeyed youth and silent doublegaenger Katje (who was *her* opposite number in Suedwest? what black girl he never saw, hidden always in the blinding sun, the hoarse and cindered passage of the trains at night, a constellation of dark stars no one, no anti-Rilke, had named ...)—but 1944 was much too late for any of it to matter. Those symmetries were all prewar luxury. Nothing's left for him to prophesy.[34]

Opposing color schemes of the black and the white continent prepare the inversion of Rilke's "new stars" into a constellation of dark stars that "no anti-Rilke, had named." Indeed, Pynchon seems to suggest that only Rilke's prophetic power could name the dark constellation. Ulrich Baer analyzes Rilke's prophetic speech according to the "tradition of moral perfectionism," following Stanley Cavell's conception of this tradition: "Making oneself

---

[33] Thomas Pynchon, *Gravity's Rainbow* (New York: Penguin Books, 1973), 6–7.
[34] Ibid., 102.

intelligible means to be willing to stammer, to probe silence, to resort to prophetic speech, or to scream and to resort to intense pathos in order to express 'the exposed human condition.'"[35] It is this "exposed human condition" to which Pynchon also seems to refer in Rilke and which could be seen as prefiguring the catastrophe. The novel ends with the explosion of the light bulb; what remains is black-film and what appears to be a star: "But it was not a star, it was falling, a bright angel of death. And in the darkening and awful expanse of screen something has kept on, a film we have not learned to see."[36] The turn away from the star into the unknown inverts Rilke's ascending movement ("higher, the stars") into an enveloping darkness, on the path that Celan called "this impossible path, this path of the impossible."[37]

This impossibility of a "language of stars" in Pynchon and Celan signals a turn towards the ambivalence of the luminous or dirty-yellow matter of stars. The dynamic of the turn from absolute darkness into luminosity or dirty-yellow matter opens the apocalyptic dimension of a "yellow flood" (Celan) or "black-film" (Pynchon), which, in its monochromatic vastness, is the contrary of the symbolists' quest for the sudden appearance of a constellation of stars in their purity and clarity. The vastness of a "yellow flood" or "black-film" suggests a "presence beyond represen-tation" (as Jean-François Lyotard states in *The Inhuman*, reinterpreting the Kantian notion of the sublime), i.e. a noumenal presence.[38] However, in his gesturing "beyond representation," Lyotard is pursuing a form of knowledge that does not seek the known but rather the revelation of the unknown. His notion of "*le différend*" denotes an unstable state, which Heidrun Friese, also pointing to Saul Friedlaender's notion of excess,[39] has described as the state "where something demands to be said and suffers from the fact that it has not yet been said or cannot be said in the admitted idioms."[40]

[35] Ulrich Baer, "The Perfection of Poetry: Rainer Maria Rilke and Paul Celan," *New German Critique* 91 (2004): 174.

[36] Pynchon, *Gravity's Rainbow*, 760.

[37] Celan, *Meridian*, 413. See Derrida, "The Majesty of the Present," 20.

[38] Jean-François Lyotard, *The Inhuman: Reflections on Time* (Stanford, CA: Stanford University Press, 1991), 152.

[39] Saul Friedlander, Introduction, *Probing the Limits of Representation: Nazism and the "Final Solution,"* ed. Saul Friedlander (Cambridge, MA: Harvard University Press, 1992), 19.

[40] Heidrun Friese, "Silence—Voice—Representation," in *Theoretical Interpretations of the Holocaust*, ed. Dan Stone (Amsterdam: Rodopi, 2001), 163.

Mendel Grossman's photographs of the Lodz ghetto

While in Celan and Pynchon the limits of representation were probed in an excess of yellow matter, photographic media are entranced by the unavoidable insistence on the emblem of the "yellow star," which only a film as radical as Claude Lanzman's *Shoah* (where the possibility of representing the Holocaust through archival footage or reenactment is denied altogether) could avoid. As soon as the past is made visible, however, the photographic medium is subject to the realism of the "star."

The presence of the "yellow star" is perhaps no more imposing or poignant than in Mendel Grossman's photographs of the Lodz ghetto, with which he attempted to record the horror he witnessed by focusing on "man in motion." Employed by the Nazis in the photographic laboratory of the department of statistics in the ghetto, Grossman was able to work with a hidden camera. While Mendel suffered the same death as most of the subjects of his photos, the negatives survived at the bottom of a well.

Without the star, his photos of the deportations appear mundane or indeterminate; instead, the star, often seen on a person's back as the focal point of the picture, makes them strike powerfully, introducing an unbearably tragic sensibility. The faces connected with the star on the back

Figure 6 Mendel Grossman, *Forced deportations of families from Lodz.* © 2012 Holocaust Education & Archive Research Team, H.E.A.R.T., www. holocaustresearchproject.org. All rights reserved.

Figure 7   Mendel Grossman, *Saying goodbye to children held at the Lodz ghetto prison before they were deported to Chelmno in September 1942.* © 2012 Holocaust Education & Archive Research Team, H.E.A.R.T., www.holocaustresearchproject.org. All rights reserved.

take their cue, as it were, from the stigma of the star. In *Forced deportations of families from Lodz*, the stoic expressions on the faces of the old man and the young man to the left, staring into the bleakest future on their journey to the death camp of Chelmno;[41] the expression of the woman to their right, trying desperately to maintain her position in the horse wagon; the feet in the foreground, literally suggestive of the ground that has just been torn from underneath on the last journey of these deportees—all these looks and body fragments merely form the background of the star, which becomes the photo's literal and metaphorical vanishing point.

The looks of the children that Grossman captured in *Saying goodbye to children held at the Lodz ghetto prison before they were deported to Chelmno in September 1942* point in different directions—to the ground, backwards, to the side; no one is looking at their mother in the eyes; she is talking through the wired fence to one of her sons, whose back carries the "yellow star" (although the photographs are in black and white, the yellowness of the star is nevertheless present; the viewer reads it into it). The mother's insistent

[41] Mendel Grossman, *With a Camera in the Ghetto*, ed. Zvi Szner and Alexander Sened (New York: Schocken Books, 1977), 27.

voice endeavors to hold the family together, even if visually it is already falling apart in the twin separation of the fence (physical separation) and the star (as a mark of death).

As the focal point of each photograph, the star manifests a shining power suggestive of the color yellow. The star tells a story, without words. It is the story told by the inscription of the "yellow star," which is not a *merely* stigmatic sign: for all who wear the "yellow star" are in fact condemned to death. Thus after the Holocaust we know that there is no stigmatization without victimization.

Jiří Weil's *Life with a Star*

The Czech author Jiří Weil, a Jew in Nazi-occupied Prague who escaped internment at Terezín by staging his own death and living underground, offered literary testimony to the fate of Czech Jews during World War II in his novel, *Life with a Star* (1949).[42] In this work, Weil subverts the imagery of the "yellow star" through an ironic misunderstanding of Nazi inscriptions and signs, showing the absurdity of what in the end cannot be understood:

I didn't particularly care for the star. It was yellow and had a word in a foreign language written in black scraggly letters. [...] I went home and stitched down the star with a needle and thread. There were six tips and a word on the star, all contorted and twisted, in a foreign language that seemed to make a face at me. I felt for my heart through my coat and marked the place with pins. It beat quite regularly. I looked into the splinter that was my mirror. The black and yellow star looked provocative; it called out for help or screamed in alarm.[43]

Weil's animation of the "yellow star" in its loudness, calling for help or screaming in alarm, indicates a fundamental change in the life of its carrier, Josef Roubicek, who develops through the stigma of the star a sense of self-spectacle. When he goes out into the streets with the star stitched to his coat in Nazi-occupied Prague, he experiences a transformation from an ordinary bank clerk to a "special person": "I was now proud that people were looking at me."[44] The bitter irony with which Weil presents the transformation of Roubicek's role in society from an ordinary man to being

---

[42] *Life with a Star* was banned in Czechoslovakia in 1951, and was translated into English only forty years later (mainly due to Philip Roth's promotion of the novel).
[43] Jiří Weil, *Life with a Star* (Evanston, IL: Northwestern University Press, 1998), 64–5.
[44] Ibid., 65.

singled out—that is, stigmatized—exposes the power of the stigma itself. Nowhere in the novel are the Nazis called *Nazis* or the Jews *Jews*; nor are the signs that Roubicek encounters legible to him. Weil's narration resists the language of the Nazis (their rules and categorizations), thus making the "yellow star," the exclusive pointer to the Nazi regime, stand out almost in a mode of abstraction.

Impossible to resist, the star's presence is felt even—or perhaps especially— in its absence. When, for example, Roubicek is working at the cemetery on a hot summer day with his shirt off, he invokes the star as he, again with bitter irony, remarks: "we couldn't sew the star onto our skin."[45] Weil's ironic observation, suggesting the image of cattle branding, renders the stigma of the star all the more palpable and insidious.

Even at night, in darkness, the "yellow star" casts its shadow; or more precisely, it casts a "yellow sheen"[46] in the streets and squares of the city. As the focal point of the novel (as in Grossman's photographs), the star determines life at any moment. The darker Roubicek's life with the star becomes, the brighter the star shines through. This is nowhere more apparent than in one of the most spectacular scenes of the novel, in which Roubicek dares, temporarily, to live without the star.

Denounced as a "swine," Roubicek is pushed out of a moving streetcar (which Jews were not allowed to use). After his fall, Roubicek resists talking to the man who helps him up off the ground; instead Roubicek points to his stigma, the star stitched into his now dirty coat: "It was dirty, but its yellow color was still shining in the dusk."[47] Even when the stigma itself is stained, Roubicek notices, ironically, the shining power of the yellow star, shining through the dirt.

The image of yellow shining through the dirt appears to mark a moment of empowerment in the midst of Roubicek's misery. Breaking Nazi rules (which require the wearing of the star in public at all times), Roubicek follows the man's advice to tear the star off his coat, thus allowing him to clean himself in one of the nearby taverns (which he would not otherwise be allowed to enter, with the stigma of the star). With the help of his pocket knife he removes the star from his coat, enters the tavern, has a drink with the man, and then takes the streetcar home, this time unmolested without the stigma of the star. Though Roubicek risks his life by not wearing the star, this fact is not mentioned in the novel. Weil's matter-of-fact style only allows Roubicek to reflect on a physical detail: that in removing the stitches (with

---

[45] Ibid., 182.
[46] Ibid., 152.
[47] Ibid., 81.

which the star was sewed on to his coat) he might have left traces of the star. Weil thus maintains his focus on the materiality of the stigma, exposing the "yellow star" as a mere piece of cloth, thereby revealing its power over Roubicek's life in all of its macabre absurdity.

Resistance and the yellow star: *Jacob the Liar*

The East German author Jurek Becker, a survivor of the Holocaust who lost his mother in the camps at the age of six, addresses, in his bestselling novel *Jacob the Liar* (*Jakob, der Lügner* 1969), what he describes as a tale of resistance.[48] In 1975, Frank Beyer made Becker's story into a film, which garnered an Academy Award nomination for Best Foreign Language Film (the only East German film ever nominated for an Academy Award).

What is on the narrative level a story about a lie—Jacob claims to possess a radio and spreads the news that the Red Army is making advances and will soon liberate the ghetto—is, on the visual level, dramatized in a color cinematography centered on the color of the Jewish star. Spreading hope among the hopeless is dramatized against the visual backdrop of the "yellow star," which is present in almost every scene (and is larger than the actual historical Nazi stigma). The "yellow star" is mentioned in the novel at least nine times as an essential part of life in the ghetto, namely at moments when the star is checked by the authorities ("the yellow star on his chest is exactly on the prescribed spot"[49]), is missing ("pedestrians not wearing yellow stars will catch Kirsch-baum's eyes,"[50] "the officer couldn't stand the sight of a Jew without yellow star"),[51] has to be transferred from one piece of cloth to another ("she would have to unpick yellow stars from her dress,"[52] "he was wearing the wrong jacket, the jacket without the yellow stars"),[53] or evokes the possibility of its transcendence—a life without the star ("no one will stop her and ask where she has left her yellow star").[54] However, the motif of the "yellow star" in the novel does not approach the ubiquity and power it possesses in the film, where it appears in almost every shot.

---

[48] Becker's novel was awarded the Heinrich-Mann Prize in 1971.
[49] Jurek Becker, *Jakob the Liar*, trans. Leila Vennewitz (New York, London: Plume, 1999), 4.
[50] Ibid., 174.
[51] Ibid., 8.
[52] Ibid., 202.
[53] Ibid., 61.
[54] Ibid., 98.

The "yellow star" announces itself from the very opening of the film as its visual theme, as when we first see Jacob from the front and then from the back, turning in a circle, showing the star from both sides. And, as we will soon realize, it is not only Jacob (together with his fellow inmates) who is constantly captured with a yellow sign on front and back; in Beyer's cinematography the yellow hue is extended into the worksites, into the yellow color of the wooden boxes the inmates lift and shuffle around, into the color of the walls and window frames of the ghetto, and, even more importantly, into the flashbacks and flash-forwards of the main characters, Jacob and the orphaned girl, Lina, whom Jacob takes in.

In this yellow continuum, Beyer actualizes the virtual power of the star as part of a Jewish world out of which it emerged and to which it might lead back. Thus instead of having the star stand out in the otherwise grey world of the ghetto (as was done in the far more conventional 1999 remake of *Jacob the Liar* by Peter Kassovitz, starring Robin Williams), Beyer's extension of the color of the star into the past, present, and future world of the film constructs a virtual dimension that points beyond the iconography of the star.[55]

Concerned with the lives of others, Jacob is (unlike Kassovitz's dramatization of the character) not a hero; rather his seeming ordinariness and humbleness, his status as one among the many stigmatized with the "yellow star," makes it possible for him to be at the center of a virtual redemption from the deadly reality the "yellow star" entails. Caught by a guard on a walk shortly before curfew time, Jacob is sent to the police station, where he waits in the hallway within earshot of the radio news reporting on the advances of the Red Army. As he listens, his jacket gets caught in the door; thus he is not only caught eavesdropping, but is also caught for a moment without his "yellow star." However, the news he has just heard on the radio is potentially the promise of a future liberated from the stigmatic symbol.

While being interrogated by a Nazi officer, whom he humbly asks for his "fair punishment," Jacob is framed by a yellow wall in the background, which enhances, together with the yellow alarm-clock (which shows that there is still half an hour left before the end of curfew time, thus emphasizing Jacob's "Jewish" rights), the meaning of yellow stigmatism. Caught between yellow signs, Jacob is nonetheless set free. The fact that he leaves the police station alive, and in possession of the news of a potential liberation, is the beginning of a narrative of hope, which is emphasized in Jacob's "illuminated" way home, as he is followed by Nazi spotlights targeting the stigma on his back.

---

[55] The fluctuation between the virtual and the actual could also be thought according to Gilles Deleuze's notion of the "time-crystal": a crystal of a Jewish star.

Jacob first shares the seemingly good news with his young friend Mischa, who is about to steal potatoes from a train wagon (an act punishable by death in the ghetto). As Jacob holds him back, he blurts out the news about the Russians' imminent arrival, and, reacting to Mischa's disbelief, invents the lie that he owns the radio from which he heard the news. The power of the lie not only saves Mischa's life, but also spreads across the entire camp, drastically reducing the suicide rate. The potential of hope and the actualization of a sort of virtual redemption on the narrative level are thereby framed visually (and silently) with the "star," which is often filmed in over-the-shoulder shots. Tirelessly and insistently, Beyer shows the power of Jacob's lies, the power of the false, unfolding through the visual armature of the "yellow star." The deadly stigma of the "yellow star" is thus subversively transformed into a sign of resistance and the beginning of hope.

However, once Jacob confesses to his best friend, the barber Kowalski, that he was never in possession of a radio, the barber hangs himself and turns Jacob (in his view) into a murderer. While Jacob removes the rope from the barber's neck, we see the window frames painted in yellow on the opposite side of the street, emphasizing the color of the stigma within the overall color scheme of the ghetto—the view of which Jacob, in a highly symbolic gesture, shuts out for a moment by closing the curtains (it is also a theatrical gesture, announcing the end of his performance). As Jacob advances toward the barber's corpse, he passes his coat (which he had removed) with the "yellow star," hanging on a hanger. Here the star is again associated with death; indeed, it will oscillate throughout the rest of the film between hope and death.

However, as soon as Jacob envisions life after the liberation without the "yellow star," his vision is deconstructed, as it were, through Lina, that is, through a child's perspective. Lina's insistence on the presence of the "yellow star," even in a future dimension, indicates not only that the star has always been part of her life, but in a broader sense that a future can only be envisioned within the framework of the "yellow star." In other words, a tale about resistance in the ghetto is possible only from within the world of the ghetto (encapsulated by the "yellow star"). The yellow hues of Jacob's past and Lina's future crystallize in the "yellow star" as it fluctuates between actual stigmatization and the virtual redemptive power Beyer attaches to it through Jacob's lies.

Annette Insdorf's remark that for the survival of the ghetto community "Jacob's lies are pernicious"[56] (implying that his lies prevented the

---

[56] Annette Insdorf, *Indelible Shadows: Film and the Holocaust* (Cambridge: Cambridge University Press, 2003), 144.

community from forming an organized resistance) thereby misses the point, in my view; for the form of resistance Beyer attempts to visualize is a form of resistance from within through the *creation* of a truth—or rather, the truth of a lie. In Beyer's adaptation (unlike Kassovitz's), Jacob's lies do not cause the deportation; the deportation happens anyway, thereby stressing the point that we are witnessing an insider's form of resistance (Jacob's attempt to save the lives of others), which Beyer visualizes through a subversion of the "yellow star" into a sign of a virtual redemption. Thematizing the "yellow star" itself, Beyer's *Jacob the Liar* is more than the dramatization of an individual "escape in the imagination," as Insdorf holds, but a far more realistic form of resistance. Large-scale organized resistance in the ghettos was rare, for obvious reasons. Yet, as Jurek Becker, the author of the novel, said in response to a question about why active resistance is absent from the novel: "The only theme in this book, so it seems to me, is resistance."[57]

Liev Schreiber's *Everything is Illuminated*

In Liev Schreiber's filmic debut, *Everything is Illuminated* (2005),[58] part comedy-drama, part adventure film, the stigma of the "yellow star" appears for only a few seconds in a couple of flashbacks. However, the actual symbol of the Star of David dominates the film as a Jewish emblem, which a young American Jew, Jonathan Safran Foer, worships in the form of a golden pendant he inherited from his grandmother. Together with the yellow amber stone that his grandfather had given him several years earlier on his deathbed (with a petrified insect inside), these golden-yellow pendants frame the search for his grandfather's past and figure its circular structure. Already the opening shot shows a yellow screen, which turns out to be a close-up of the yellow amber stone, leading us inside its petrified yellow world, which is about to come alive in a "very rigid search" for Jonathan's grandfather's birthplace, a small Ukrainian town called Trachimbrod, one among the many "shtetls" in Eastern Europe wiped out by the Nazis. Half a century after the Second World War, Jonathan hires a guide from "Odessa's Heritage Tours" (as the sign on top of the blue car announces, which is marked with a Star of David, here used as Jewish emblem for commercial

---

[57] Jurek Becker, *My Father, the Germans and I: Essays, Lectures, Interviews*, ed. Christine Becker (London: Seagull Books, 2010), 40.

[58] Schreiber's film is based on Jonathan Safran Foer's novel of the same title, published in 2002.

purposes), a most unlikely guide, in fact: an old anti-Semitic man, accompanied by his grandson, Alex, a translator, who could not be more of a contrast to the spiritually driven Jonathan, himself presented as a caricature of a pious Jew, with his thick glasses, black suit, and tie.

However, it is through the unification of polar opposites that *Everything is Illuminated* is illuminated—and comes full circle at the end of the tragicomic journey. The trio finds the only survivor of Trachimbrod, a collector like Jonathan himself, in a massive field of (yellow) sunflowers in full bloom.

While the woman named Lista describes the massacre of Trachimbrod at the scene of the crime (near the riverbank, where there is now a tombstone surrounded by a circle of stones, in memory of the 1224 Trachimbrodians who were killed), her wartime memories trigger the grandfather's flashback, which reveals him as the other survivor, and former Jew, of Trachimbrod. The flashback consists of two parts, following the organizing principle of the film as a whole, built, like the Star of David itself, out of two triangles. The first part occurs before the encounter with the collector Lista in a sunflower field. War debris at the side of the road triggers the first flashback, which ends with an explosion in a close-up of a "yellow star." Through a montage-sequence, we are confronted with a soldier's eyes looking through his gun sights in a close-up, targeting faceless but stigmatized men. All we see in the sepia colors of this first flashback are shoes, jackets, and finally a "yellow star," which then explodes into a white screen.

The second flashback completes (and illuminates) the first: after the grandfather closes his eyes while standing in front of the memorial for the slain Trachimbrodians, the face of a young man in close-up emerges out of a white screen. While the camera pulls back, the young man is soon revealed in a full-body shot as stigmatized by the "yellow star," which is now shown in bright yellow—as bright as the sunflowers in the "overture to the illumination." The flashback ends in black-film, however, only to continue in white film and yet another flashback. This time we see the young man on the ground opening his eyes; the open wound on his forehead indicates that the second survivor, next to Lista, was Alex's grandfather, for his face is still marked by the scar on his forehead. He throws a jacket marked with the "yellow star" on top of the dead bodies surrounding him, leaving the scene of the crime and his Jewish past behind. The grandfather's refusal to face the past is illuminated by the grandchildren's search for the past, which, however, after everything has been illuminated, appears even more obscure than before. The "yellow star" thus simultaneously reveals and conceals.

Exploding the star: Felix Nussbaum, Daniel Libeskind, W. G. Sebald, Frank Stella

Felix Nussbaum's *Self-Portrait with Jewish Identity Card* (Color Plate 15), painted in 1943 in exile in Brussels, is an ironic self-portrait, for its self-stigmatization questions the very genre of the self-portrait. When personal features (of the artist and his style) are rendered meaningless by the overwhelming presence of the "yellow star" on the coat and the identity card in the hand, we are left to ask what remains of "art." The inscription of "Juif—Jood" on the identity card and the stigma of the "yellow star" with a "J" at its center embodies the reality that encircles the artist from left and right. Though in some sense it recalls Gauguin's *Self-Portrait with the Yellow Christ*—in both cases yellow is stigmatizing a Jew (Christ at the Cross, the artist Nussbaum himself)—Gauguin's figurative reference to the artist as a wretched victim of society is in Nussbaum's *Self-Portrait* transformed into the image of an artist marked for death.

The work features the painter in the corner of surrounding walls, gazing at the viewer while holding up his identity card, an image in an image, illuminated, as it were, by the "yellow star" adjacent to it. The juxtaposition of card and stigma, which dominates the appearance of the haunted figure, is repeated in the color scheme above the surrounding walls. The color of the "yellow star" corresponds to a window with yellow curtains high above in the building behind the walls, while the white color of the identity card corresponds to a branch with white blossoms of an otherwise barren tree, also behind the walls. The white blossoms and the yellow curtains suggesting an illuminated window are out of reach for the stigmatized; they address the viewer directly from a world outside the walls—the world of the bystanders.

In its direct address to the viewer, *Self-Portrait with Jewish Identity Card* evokes the tradition of religious icons. However, whereas in icons the frontal image of eyes serves as a "window to the soul," in Nussbaum's painting the spectator's focus shifts immediately from the eyes to the frontal image of the stigma of the "yellow star" and the inscription "J." The two stigmata define the image of the artist; they are the windows, as it were, into his doom, which was sealed in 1944, when Nussbaum and his wife were deported from Brussels to Auschwitz, where they perished soon after.

In 1998, the *Felix Nussbaum Haus* was inaugurated in Nussbaum's hometown of Osnabrück (Germany). It was designed by the architect Daniel Libeskind in the form of an exploded star. Confronting the visitor directly (like Nussbaum's self-portrait) with the destabilizing impact of the stigma of the "yellow star," Libeskind's architecture is an architecture of interrogation, investigating "the culture and civilization that built it."[59] Best known for his design of the extension of the Jewish Museum in Berlin, which opened in 1999,[60] Libeskind entitled the plans for this design (which is closely related to the design of the *Nussbaum Haus*) "Between the Lines," commenting:

> I call it ["Between the Lines"] because it is a project about two lines of thinking. [...] One is a straight line, but broken into many fragments; the other is a torturous line, but continuing indefinitely. These two lines develop architecturally and programmatically through a limited but definite dialogue. They also fall apart, become disengaged, and are seen as separated. In this way they expose a void that runs through this museum and through architecture, a discontinuous void.[61]

The form of a twisted and jagged lightning-bold runs through the building, extending to the outside, thus creating a sense of building around a rupture, while the zigzag lines also form triangles that are reminiscent of the Star of David. Libeskind explains this nexus thus:

> At the same time, I felt that the physical trace of Berlin was not the only trace, but rather that there was an invisible matrix or anamnesis of connections in relationship. I found this connection between figures of Germans and Jews; between the particular history of Berlin, and between the Jewish history of Germany and Berlin... So I found this connection and I plotted an irrational matrix which was in the form of system of squared triangles which would yield some reference to the emblematics of a compressed and distorted star: the yellow star that was so frequently worn on this site, which today is green.[62]

The star that is the matrix of Libeskind's design both holds the broken and torturous lines together and makes them explode. The "distorted star" refers to openings of the wall behind the vitrine inside the museum; the

---

[59] James E. Young describes Libeskind's design of the Jewish Museum in Berlin, which is similar to the design of the Nussbaum Haus, as an "architectural interrogation" (James E. Young, "Daniel Libeskind's Jewish Museum in Berlin," in *Visual Culture and the Holocaust*, ed. Barbie Zelizer [New Brunswick, New Jersey: Rutgers University Press, 2001], 195).

[60] The Jewish Museum was planned as an extension of the Berlin Museum; however, ironically, Daniel Libeskind's design of the extension quickly became an icon of Jewish history. James Young comments on the historical irony: "Where city planners had hoped to return Jewish memory to the house of Berlin history, it now seems certain that Berlin history will have to find its place in the larger haunted house of Jewish memory" (ibid., 195).

[61] Libeskind, quoted in ibid., 187.

[62] Daniel Libeskind, "Between the Lines," in *Daniel Libeskind: Erweiterung des Berlin Museums mit Abteilung Jüdisches Museum*, ed. Kristin Feireiss (Berlin: Ernst & Sohn, 1992), 63.

Figure 8   *Roll of Cloth with Yellow Stars,* © Jewish Museum Berlin.

vitrine features a yellow roll of cloth, seemingly torn, like an old parchment, imprinted with a pattern of numerous Stars of David tracing the German word for Jew *Jude.* As we can see from the photo, the juxtaposition between the pattern of the "yellow star" and the form of the distorted star defines a dialectical space. *Roll of Cloth with Yellow Stars* exposes the aspect of the mass-production of the stigma that announces the mass-killings, both of which are made possible by modern technology. What Adorno and Horkheimer named the "Dialectic of Enlightenment" is most blatantly exposed in the combination of a medieval tradition (to stigmatize in yellow) and modern productivity (mass-produced roles of cloth).

The anonymity of the death machinery is captured in the vitrine that exhibits *Roll of Cloth with Yellow Stars*; it is suggestive of both the process of stigmatization and its seemingly ordinary nature;[63] for it is still a roll of yellow cloth, except that the inscription of the Star of David transforms each part of the star-pattern printed on the cloth into an extraordinary sign of exclusion and inhumanity.

W. G. Sebald's photo-novel *Austerlitz* (2001) seems almost to offer a literary commentary on Libeskind's design of the Jewish Museum. Similarly constructed around a void, the novel engages the reader in the search for the protagonist's origins, which leads to the star-shaped architecture of Theresienstadt, the concentration camp where Austerlitz's mother, as we find out towards the end of the novel, was killed. Transported as a child from Prague to Wales, Austerlitz, a retired art historian, speaks "at length about the mark of pain which, as he said he well knew, traces countless lines through history."[64] The histories he remembers, namely those of fortresses and railway systems, seem to be disconnected from his own, and yet, what connects them are the invisible parallels they draw to the star-shaped architecture of Theresienstadt and the trains of deportation. Nowhere is the "yellow star" or the Star of David mentioned, and yet the original notion of the Magen of David, a shield of protection, appears to be at the center of the protagonist's attraction to the star-shaped architecture of fortresses. While Austerlitz, the historian, buries himself in the study of architecture and railway systems, which protect him, as it were, from a direct confrontation with his life, his unknown past, Austerlitz's attraction to the architecture of the "bastions" of the past and to modernity's emblem, the railway system, is driven and guided by his unconscious search for his own past: the loss of his mother in a concentration camp, her disappearance on one of the infamous deportation trains.

> I still had an image in my head of a star-shaped bastion with walls towering above a precise geometrical plan, but what I now saw before me was a low-built concrete mass, rounded at all its outer edges and giving the gruesome impression of something hunched and misshapen: the broad back of a monster.[65]

Like Libeskind's design, what Austerlitz actually encounters is a distorted star. However, what is paradigmatic for Sebald is the potential *reversal* of a

---

[63] As Zygmunt Bauman writes: "Modern Holocaust is unique in its double sense. *It is unique among other historic cases of genocide because it is modern. And it stands unique against the quotidianity of modern society because it brings together some ordinary factors of modernity which normally are kept apart*" (Bauman, *Modernity and the Holocaust* [Ithaca, NY: Cornell University Press, 2000], 96, italics in the original).

[64] W. G. Sebald, *Austerlitz* (New York: Random House, 2001), 16.

[65] Ibid., 20.

protective structure into the structure of imprisonment. The reversal of the Star of David—a protective sign—into the negative sign of exclusion is at the heart of Sebald's focus on the shape of the star, which shapes, as it were, his protagonist's vision of the world (both consciously and unconsciously). As Amir Eshel comments: "The star-shaped Theresienstadt is the model of a world made by reason and regulated in all conceivable respects," a world that was enabled by standardized "time," by the "modern temporal consciousness reflected in railway transportation."[66] Austerlitz's dual obsession with the architecture of medieval fortresses and of modern railway systems thus exposes the Holocaust itself, with its combination of medieval persecution and modern technologies of deportation and killing. The duality itself is, however, encapsulated in the imagery of the star: while "a single golden star" on the ceiling of a Free Mason's temple emits "its rays into the dark clouds all around it,"[67] or the stars decorating an Oriental setting inside a circus tent strike through their luminosity,[68] Sebald does not fail to emphasize the reversal of a star-like appearance into its opposite. Thus when Austerlitz on a "dark December morning" remembers reading about a few drops of belladonna that young women used in order to create the effect of eyes shining with radiance (with the side-effect that the women themselves could see almost nothing), he connects the memory of reading about belladonna with his own progressive loss of eyesight, and moreover with the notion of extinction itself, so that the radiant appearance in Austerlitz's mind "had something to do with the deceptiveness of that star-like, beautiful gleam and the danger of its premature extinction."[69] The "star-like" appearance of the radiant gleam is immediately revealed as deceiving, a blind spot, as it were, that reveals and conceals the "yellow star" (its connection to the extinction of the Jewish people) throughout the photo-novel, neither naming nor depicting the stigma; instead, Sebald creates a "collective network" of stars shining through the darkness of a world where "many of the loveliest colors had already disappeared."[70]

In the early 1970s, American artist Frank Stella created a series of paintings called *Polish Village*. Inspired by an illustrated volume entitled *Wooden Synagogues*, which contained "the last images of seventy-one 'monuments of Jewish culture'" photographed during the 1920s and 1930s

---

[66] Amir Eshel, "Against the Power of Time: The Poetics of Suspension in W. G. Sebald's *Austerlitz*," *New German Critique* 88, Contemporary German Literature (2003): 86.

[67] Ibid., 42.

[68] "We saw a quantity of stars traced in luminous paint inside the top of the tent, giving the impression that we were really out of doors" (ibid., 273).

[69] Ibid., 35.

[70] Austerlitz's great-uncle Alphonso comments on the notion of "fading before our eyes," which Sebald dramatizes throughout the novel.

and destroyed in the 1940s, Stella painted forty of the "martyred buildings," sometimes in several versions, naming each work after the village of the synagogue. What is most striking about the series is the great variety and lack of resemblance between the paintings: "the only common feature is that each work had an irregular, straight-edged external shape, and was composed internally of a number of connected irregularly shaped, straight-edged monochrome sections."[71]

One of the works, entitled *Odelsk I* (Color Plate 16), appears to depict a dispersed yellow star. Mark Godfrey describes the painting thus: "between the central yellow triangle and the underlying black section, a grey strip runs along its left side, suggesting, if this is read as a shadow, that the yellow section lies further away from the wall than the black; such illusionism is entirely absent from the other works."[72] However, the illusionism that makes the yellow star appear as part of the background depends entirely on the viewer's position: seen from a different perspective, the triangle of the star appears to be closest to the viewer. While the painting itself stands out through its conjuring of the "yellow star," the "yellow star," through an optical illusion, literally stands out, in a fragmented and deconstructed form, from the three-dimensional space the painting creates, its yellow color barely discernible, a pale version of the color of the stigma. The reference to the "yellow star" insists on the "singleness-of-aspect" that Rosalind Krauss sees as the characteristic feature of the series as a whole.[73] Reestablishing the singularity of each "martyred building" in his highly crafted paintings of *Polish Villages*, Stella attempts to construct the "look of destruction"—not of a totality, but of each individual synagogue. In its paleness and fragmentary appearance, Stella's star seems to suggest with its own vanishing the vanishing of the Jewish people and their culture in Poland.

---

[71] Mark Godfrey, *Abstraction and the Holocaust* (New Haven, CT: Yale University Press, 2007), 84.
[72] Ibid., 85.
[73] Rosalind Krauss, "Stella's New Work and the Problem of Series," quoted in ibid., 91.

Conclusion

I have sought in this book to demonstrate how a particular color, yellow, came to define the cultural unconscious of an era. The works examined herein were not selected according to a principle of completeness or to correspond to a specific canon—hence the heteroclite juxtapositions of famous and little-known authors, tragedy and trivia, artists and agitators. The very fact that colors know no boundaries, cultural or material, has allowed me to explore what one might call a "cultural mood," that is, a set of shared cultural attitudes that, taken collectively, reveal often surprising, but nevertheless deep-seated, patterns and connections.

The choice of time period—"late" modernity—may perhaps appear to be somewhat nebulous or arbitrary, for it does not correspond to conventional periodization. In fact, I have endeavored to break out of the traditional notion of the "historical period," seeking instead to develop a concept of "cultural time," that is, a concept that sees time itself as culturally conditioned, as dynamic, heterogeneous, and open, as opposed to linear and circumscribed. Thus, while I have centered my attention on texts and artifacts from the 1890–1980 "period," I have also had recourse to reach beyond these dates—as in, for example, my analysis of Vermeer's *View of Delft* and Balzac's *Eugénie Grandet*, as well as in my references to Goethe's color theory and medieval practices of stigmatization—to explore the different temporal regimes implied in the various uses of yellow (e.g. the sensationalist temporality of scandal; the ecstatic temporality of Gilman and Woolf, the *longue durée* of stigma).

In this sense, my approach is reminiscent of Mikhail Bakhtin's concept of the "chronotope," which he defines as "the intrinsic connectedness of temporal and spatial relationships that are artistically expressed in literature."[1] In his essay entitled "The 'Nineteenth Century' as Chronotope," Hayden White proposed that Bakhtin's concept could be considered appropriate for historical-cultural analysis as well:

> To conceive a prior age as a chronotope [...] has a distinctively different effect upon the way we approach the study of a segment of history and the *attitudes* with which we approach it. This is so because the

---

[1] Mikhail Bakhtin, *The Dialogic Imagination: Four Essays*, trans. Caryl Emerson and J. Michael Holquist (Austin: University of Texas Press, 1981), 84.

chronotope will be apprehended as having a dimension of *depth* quite different from that of the period. Here depth is apprehended, not so much as what is *implicit* in the thought and practice of an age, as rather what is *latent*—in the sense of being dynamically repressed—in the form of the valorizations, obsessions, fantasies, and anxieties that inform and provide the systemic "secrets" of the age's actual and *manifest* practices. Unlike the notion of a "content" that is only *implicit*, and which will inevitably insist itself into the consciousness of succeeding generations as they wrestle with the "contradictions" contained therein, the "content" of an age conceived as a chronotope is identifiable with the sleights of hand by which a society and its cultural endowment seek to suppress a tacit awareness of the contradictions between what it regards as its ideals and what it knows to be its dominant practices.[2]

This is essentially what I have endeavored to do in this study, though in this context I could perhaps propose the term "chromo-tope" (chroma = color) as a variation on Bakhtin's notion. Whereas the chronotope functions as a time-marker, singling out time as the fourth dimension of space, the chromo-tope spaces out time by means of color.[3]

I have herein explored the convergence of time and the color yellow, contending that yellow motifs function as time-markers and hence as *multivalent* chromo-topes. Chromo-topes inhabit the liminal space between the political and the aesthetic, without, however, involving the question of intentional structures or explicit nexuses of power. I have therefore explored not so much "what is *implicit* in the thought and practice of an age," as "what is *latent*." The multivalent figuration of chromo-topes implies an intrinsic displacement, a meaning recognizable only after the fact, via "the valorizations, obsessions, fantasies, and anxieties that inform and provide the systemic 'secrets' of the age's actual and *manifest* practices." It is the relation between these "systemic secrets" and their manifest social practices that I have endeavored to bring to light through the color yellow.

[2] Hayden White, *The Fiction of Narrative: Essays on History, Literature, and Theory, 1957–2007*, ed. Robert Doran (Baltimore: Johns Hopkins University Press, 2010), 243 (original emphasis).

[3] However, though I have previously explored the idea of the "chromo-tope" in an essay, I elected not to employ it in this book, for I thought that it did not adequately capture the multiplicity of meanings of the color yellow in late modernity; hence my preference for the concept of "multivalent figuration." See Sabine Doran, "Chronos/Chroma: Yellow Figures in Proust's *La Prisonnière* and Bely's *Petersburg*," *The Comparatist* 28 (2004): 53–75.

Index